A Call to Teach

A CALL TO TEACH

*In Service of Waldorf Teacher Education
and Lifelong Learning*

Torin M. Finser, Ph.D.

Published by:
Waldorf Publications
351 Fairview Avenue, Unit 625
Hudson, NY 12534

© 2020 Waldorf Publications

ISBN: 978-1-943582-48-8

Contents

Acknowledgements

My thanks to work-study research assistants over several years, especially Eden Motto, Ana Coffey, and Jessie Morin. In various stages and in multiple ways, these three remarkable women have provided invaluable support for my research during this project.

I am ever so grateful to my colleagues in general, both at Antioch University New England and the Center for Anthroposophy for their support. For this project I have been especially fortunate to have several thought partners:

> Douglas Gerwin for his chapter on high school teacher education and his constant support in sharing ideas and sample portions of the text

> Leonore Russell and Carla Comey for suggestions on the chapter on eurythmy and Carla for additions to the advising chapter

> Debbie Spitulnik for her wonderful chapter on speech

> Colleen O'Connors for her conversations on the future of teacher education and her "threefold contribution" in the last chapter

> Karine Munk Finser for her constant support for my creativity and her beautiful cover painting

Most of all, I am deeply grateful to all my students over these past three decades. They have taught me more than I can express regarding the art of Waldorf teacher education. Many are represented in this book, both in the chapter Listening to our Alums, and in the essays and stories included in another chapter. We need to listen to our teachers, because they speak for the needs of our children.

I am likewise grateful for the wonderful editing done by Melissa Merkling, as well as her ever-present professionalism and organizational skills. And I want to thank Waldorf Publications, particularly Patrice Maynard, for producing this book. My hope is that the contents provide a stepping stone toward a professional development and training program for future Waldorf adult educators.

Preface

Before Covid-19, when walking through an airport as many of us did far too often in those days, I often heard a familiar announcement: "We wish to honor the men and women who serve our country in the military." And more than once I have made a silent wish that one day I would hear: "We wish to honor the women and men who serve our country working in our classrooms each day, striving to prepare citizens for a more peaceful and just society."

I am in favor of honoring those in the military (one of my sons served in the reserves for many years), but there are others in society who also deserve recognition. Far too long our teachers have been told what to do and how to do it. They have been handed mandates and standardized tests designed by people who often do not even understand basic educational principles such as child development. Rather than administering tests conceived by the privileged few in Princeton, teachers long for more freedom to use differentiated teaching, project-based learning, outdoor, sensory rich education and other commonsense practices to meet the diverse social and emotional needs of their students. At the same time, teachers have had to pick up more and more of the basic tasks that used to be carried by others, from serving breakfast in public schools in Alaska, staying late to help with tutoring in Florida, constructing outdoor classrooms over summer 2020......teachers continually give over and beyond. The abrupt transition to virtual instruction and a world of zooming added a whole new dimension to the teaching profession recently. In short, we now need a fundamental revolution in how we view and support education. The times have changed and we must too.

During 2019-2020, Waldorf education celebrated its 100th anniversary. In over 1,100 schools around the world, many found ways to honor their legacy, recognize achievement, and begin to look beyond 100. There is a growing need to turn a corner; many things have to change. In September 2019, in an article that appears in the appendix of this book, I called for a sober assessment of what is working and what is not. Some of our independent Waldorf schools have been struggling for a while, and all too many public school teachers are leaving the profession. Waldorf teachers are not (and should not) be immune to demographic and societal influences: Covid-19, police brutality, racism, various forms of addiction, trauma.... The founding of the first Waldorf school in 1919 was based on a social mandate; our times have changed but the urgency of our social needs have not.

We need to re-examine the core principles of Waldorf education. Which aspects need to be maintained and strengthened? Which practices need to be discarded to make room for the new?

To have vibrant schools, we need inspired teachers. Those who choose to enter the profession need solid preparation and continued professional development along the way. This book attempts to outline some of the basic ingredients of teacher education by looking at themes such as adult learning, Rudolf Steiner's indications for teacher education, group work, social intelligence, the art of lecturing, strengthening the memory, and more. A chapter called "Demoralized" will take us to the depths of the challenges faced by teachers today, and chapters such as "Imagination, Inspiration and Intuition" will lift us up to the archetypes that can help us find new direction.

This author is deeply indebted to Coen van Houten and his seminal work on Destiny Learning, which is featured in one extensive chapter. Many years ago, he called for a training program for adult educators, something that is more needed than ever as many present leaders in teacher training centers are approaching retirement age. Perhaps this book can assist in providing aspects of a curriculum for a "train the trainers" program as envisioned by van Houten.

In addressing many social themes and the need for professional learning communities within each school community, we hope this book will also appeal to parents, potential teachers, and friends of educational reform. We need to find new ways of working together so as to renew the Waldorf movement beyond 100 years.

Finally, this book ends with research and stories from the classroom told by a variety of teachers. We hope they inspire others to share the success of their children so that in airports, farmers' markets, coffee shops and through social media, we find new ways to share and celebrate our children and their teachers. They are creating our future!

Dedication

This verse is spoken by the Eurythmy Spring Valley faculty to begin each week, and serves as a suitable dedication to all who serve anthroposophical adult education:

For those who will to work
  with those who guide
the future of humankind:

Bring forth spirit potentials
  in yourself —
And so achieve
  the power to awaken
  dormant faculties
  in others.

Cultivate the seed points,
Foster forces of growth.
Recognize future becoming.

—Rudolf Steiner

1. Education as a Social Issue

The question of education is a question of teacher training, and as long as this fact is not recognized nothing fruitful can come into education.
Rudolf Steiner, *Education as a Social Problem*, p. 80

It is significant that just a few weeks before launching the first Waldorf teacher-education course and opening the first school, Rudolf Steiner gave lectures on how education can help with the social problems of our time. If we are looking for insights on teacher education, then reviewing comments made in the summer of 1919 may be helpful. Indeed, some of the observations made a hundred years ago are all too relevant still today.

He began by describing how the anti-social forces are now so strong that they have fragmented human beings. "Mechanization of the spirit, vegetizing of the soul, animalizing of the body—this is what we have to face without deceiving ourselves" (p. 11). He continues by saying that since the middle of the 15th century we have developed a knowledge that is specter-like and is divorced from reality. Much of the will effort used in operating machines is meaningless for further evolution. Then come the key sentences:

> We had to emphasize that the entire social question contains as its chief factor, education.... The training of teachers is the most important auxiliary question (p. 64).

He sees education as a way forward to overcome the materialistic wave of the times and once again gain access to the spirit. And this struggle is ever so present in teacher training. Much of what happens in education deadens the soul. As a result, we end up with "problem-laden personalities" (p. 65).

As we now look at the social situation through the lens of 2020 and beyond, we can see a continuation of materialism, abstract knowledge, and mechanization in thinking, but with new manifestations. Covid-19 has brought forward many of the latent issues of leadership dysfunction, lack of preparedness for health emergencies and social isolation. (See my March 2020 article in *Waldorf Today*, "COVID-19 and Our Existential Crisis," in

Appendix.) The topics may have changed, but the need for radical social change remains with us today.

One common denominator for addressing social justice and change is education. Although some may question the institution of schools themselves (Illich, Freire), few dispute the need for quality education for our children. And to enhance education, we need good teachers.

As we will examine in more detail in the chapter "Demoralized," fewer young people are entering the teaching profession these days, and more are leaving before retirement. How can we turn this around?

Although much of this book is about preparing teachers, many of the topics I have selected might seem at first glance to skirt the issue by not examining teacher education requirements, at least until the last sections. Instead, I taken my cue from observations Steiner made when discussing teacher education:

> What then do we have to strive for in order to have the right teacher training in future? The fact that a teacher knows the answers to what is asked in his examinations is a secondary matter, for he is mostly asked questions for which he could prepare himself by looking them up in a handbook. The examiners pay no attention to the general soul-attitude of the teacher, and that is what constantly has to pass from him to his students. There is a great difference between teachers as they enter a classroom. When one steps through the door the students feel a certain soul-relationship with him; when another enters they often feel no such relationship at all (p. 66).

The relationship of the teacher to his/her students means that so much depends on the inner soul condition of the teacher, the presence of mind and heart, and the degree to which the teacher is working spiritually. When permeated with an active connection to the suprasensory world, the teacher can access resources that promote growth and inner vitality. These qualities attract the interest of students and invite an active relationship between the teacher and child.

This thought leads to one of my favorite statements: "Every child should stand before the soul of the teacher as a question posed by the suprasensory world to the sense world" (p. 67). What does this mean? Again, it is all about an active, engaged relationship to the intangible, the unknown in each child. Rather than seeing the student as a definition, a grade or statistic, we are urged to see each child as a question asked by the spiritual world!

To get there, teachers of the future will need to acquire mobile thinking that encompasses wider perspectives—a larger view that goes beyond the customary boundaries of conventional educational practices. Rather than just dwelling on details, or on the curriculum plans designed by others, we need to connect ourselves again and again with the larger questions of life. "We must learn to listen to the revelation of spirit and soul in the growing child as they existed before birth" (p. 71). To behold what continues out of the spiritual into the physical before us as a child creates in the teacher an un-egotistical mood of soul.

Egoism leads to abstract theories and concepts. In contrast, "The un-egotistical point of view urges him to understand the world with love, to lay hold of it through love. This is one of the elements which must be taken up in teacher training; to look at prenatal man, and not only feel the riddle of death but also the riddle of birth" (p. 72).

Since the dawn of the Michael age in 1879, it is particularly important that humankind learn to overcome intellectuality. To do so, we need to work with the whole human being, not just our concepts and the learning so often perpetuated in schools and assessed in standardized tests. The challenge for those leading teacher education programs is that many of our future teachers have been miseducated. They have had a regular diet of abstractions, and supported now with several decades of technology, the ability to form pictures has diminished. Thus it is no longer sufficient to just teach the Waldorf curriculum in teacher education programs, for if we do, it likely will be taken in as just more conceptual baggage.

We need to completely revamp our practices in adult education (see last chapters), but one theme I wish to sound right here is that the holistic approach we take in Waldorf methods should be applied to adults as well as children. When we talk about the human head, we are focused on the most physical aspect of ourselves. With the chest organs, we live in rhythm and the life-giving forces of the etheric. With the metabolic system we invoke the astral, and with the ego we are in uncharted territory (p. 74).

So how can we apply this knowledge to Waldorf teacher education? If we just work with traditional instruction methods and lecturing, there is a danger of bringing too much of the death forces of abstract concepts. (See chapter on "Giving Lectures and Presentations.") Of course, if the presentation is filled with inspiration and delivered with enthusiasm, there is the possibility of engaging the feelings, and the thoughts can start to come alive. But in general, we need to avoid teacher-imposed concepts and, instead, work in a different way.

A successful adult education class often begins with an overview, perhaps then a verse or quote, and then immediately engages students in a question to consider in small groups. This has the effect of "warming up" the topic of the day. Then one needs to "harvest" some of the experiences they had, not in a pedantic way, but perhaps just sampling a few. Another option early in the class is to have students present from their projects or homework. What all this has in common is bringing them to a place where they can then take in mini-lecture material with full presence and attentiveness. My presentations are often only 20-30 minutes. Depending on the length of the class time allocated, it is then great to move into more open discussion and project-based work. There is so much that a group can do when they collaborate with one another. The ending of a class session is just as important as the beginning, not just when the clock runs out, but with some form. Often a short summary and looking ahead to the next session in a couple of minutes can suffice, but there needs to be conscious closure.

Adults learn through problem-solving, group work, discussion, and instructor-inspired encounter with new ideas. (See chapter on "Adult Learning.") Each class needs to have a balance so that we practice the balanced educational approaches we advocate for work with children.

Then there is the enigmatic statement made above about the ego. I have long pondered how to relate to the ego or self of an adult student. They are not children and cannot be led, and yet they are in a particular course for a reason and want to learn. How can one balance the needs of the material/ course with the freedom of another human being, a freedom that must at all times be held sacred? And when do we really get a glimpse of the ego of another person? This line of questioning will lead us through the extensive chapter on "Practicing Destiny Learning" later on.

> If (people) would not surrender to illusions but see reality, they would be aware of the fact that when they meet a person they cannot physically perceive his ego, only when they observe him in the various periods of his life. If you meet a man again after twenty years you will perceive his ego vividly in the change that has taken place in him; especially if twenty years ago you saw him as a child (p. 77).

So the answer seems to rest with the riddle of time. This directs the adult educator to an entirely new level of consideration: how do we place our lessons in the sequence of time?

Over the past decade or two, the trend in teacher education has been away from weekly, year-round study to summer-only or intensive weekend models. There are some students who meet in a cohort for a few weeks in the summer and then do not see each other again for eleven months. Online course work, Zoom sessions, and individual advising have helped fill this gap. More than ever, it is essential that adult students participate in planning their course of study, as they do with their year-long research projects at Antioch and the Center for Anthroposophy. Self-education has to become ever stronger. Thus, the summer sessions are more of a launching and renewed human encounter and less of a complete delivery package. For "teacher training has to be permeated by an attitude which strives to find the individuality in human beings. This can only come about through an enlivening of our thoughts about man as I have described it. We must really become conscious of the fact that it is not a mechanism that moves one forward, but the astral body; it pulls the physical body along" (p. 79).

Johannes Tautz and others remind us that a key component of teacher preparation has to do with the encounter with the third hierarchy. This allows for the threefold awakening of the teacher and assists in the process of self-education:

1. The teacher needs to come into contact with his/her own higher being, the angelic realm. This comes when the process of teacher education is chosen as a matter of professional destiny, *for our angel helps guide us on our destiny path.*

2. The teacher needs to awaken in cooperative work with colleagues. Thus, the social realm and collaborative projects are so important in our programs. *The archangels provide warmth and guidance in our group work.*

3. In addition, the teacher needs to awaken to the real tasks of the spirit of our age. *The archai work with us to awaken a more intimate connection to the time in which we live.* The archai want to "renew the whole world so that one day we can realize a threefold human society that is worthy of man" (Tautz, p. 39).

Thus, teacher education programs need to be designed as a continuous invitation to encounter the third hierarchy, a stream of encounter that leads to transformation through gradual awakening, and we can see how this task is so intimately related to the social health of our time. The encounter with the third hierarchy on many levels leads to a new mobility of soul experience, which makes teachers better human beings. It is a form of character education in a schooling of the spirit.

The science of the spirit must permeate everything, and…without it the great social problems of the present time cannot be solved (Steiner, p. 80).

The self-education of the teacher leads to a new educational impulse, which can renew our schools. Healthy schools can send forth a new generation of young people who can help transform our society.

2. Group Work

In a June 1924 lecture in Breslau, Rudolf Steiner said that people who are led to one another during one earth life seek to find each other in the next earth life as well. As a rule, we continually meet people on the earth who had been incarnated with us before (MacKay, p. 17).

If we take this as a working hypothesis, it can launch a consideration of group work on a deeper level. Although there are of course exceptions (Rudolf Steiner's geometry teacher being one he named), mostly we find people in groups whom we have known or even worked with before. This has implications for all aspects of group work, including a few aspects selected below:

Orientation

The early moments of a group finding itself can be crucial for success in future work. Most facilitators do some introductions, but in light of the above citation, it is interesting to observe how a group finds itself as a process of (re)discovery. The whole point is to spend some time so participants can find themselves in a new context. Even if some have already known one another, one has to celebrate, enjoy, and honor the stage of new beginning.

There are many "icebreaker" games one can play, many activities one can learn from others, but the best are often the ones a facilitator can do with joy and enthusiasm. Here are a few examples I have learned from others:

- If one enjoys collecting art cards and postcards, one can lay them out in the middle of the circle of participants and ask each person to pick an appealing one. Then when everyone is seated again, each person says something about the card and why they picked it. Often some biographical information is shared in small doses through these associations.

- Each person introduces themselves by making up a name of

something colorful in nature, such as Polly daffodil or Jerry oak, etc. Then one does a second round in which each person says why they chose that image.

• At the start of speech work, one can do introductions with colors, each person choosing one and then throwing a beanbag or tennis ball, or even better an imaginary object, to someone else across the room while saying their name and color. Then that person chooses a color and does the same. At the end, it is a game to remember everyone's colors.

• Many of these activities can be followed by a handshaking process in which two circles progress around the room in opposite directions and everyone says hello and uses their new name, i.e. Polly daffodil or Jerry oak. It is amazing how much easier it is to remember names when there is an image!

• On a more sedentary level, one can ask each participant to share their relationship to their name. Each person has 2-3 minutes, and so much of the identity of a person can be shared in a warm and personal way.

A more in-depth way of doing orientation is to do biography work. This can be done over a few hours or days, or even an entire week. But if time does not allow for the more extensive versions (and again there is much literature and coursework available), one can do a simplified version on the first day, which we often used at Antioch orientations: Each person is asked to highlight 2-3 events in their life thus far that led them to this moment, to start a new training. Sometimes less is more, and participants learn so much from each other that can then be followed up in subsequent sessions or even informally over meals. I have found that the facilitator needs to really keep tabs on the time, as each sharing tends to get longer as one goes around the circle.

One notion in adult education has to do with "harvesting." In the case of the above exercise, it is really helpful if the facilitator summarizes the introductions by drawing forth some of the common themes, such as "it seems many of you had experiences in school that influenced your decision to become a teacher," or "so many of you seem to have had a life-changing experience in the last few years that influenced your decision." The whole notion of harvesting is key to working in groups. Everything that happens in a group is a learning opportunity, but for many these pass by too quickly to be assimilated. The facilitator needs to slow things down from time to time and draw forth the learning, to hold it as one might hold an object in one's hands, to observe and remember. Without being pedantic, it is very important that adults learn to be participant observers, to look and listen while engaging in conversation. This builds a growing awareness of group process and helps groups build the muscles to self-correct when needed.

Establishing Norms

When we established our Center for Anthroposophy Building Bridges Program for practicing teachers in public and independent Waldorf schools, we knew we would need to be more mindful of establishing group awareness due to the off-site location and sessions that were monthly instead of weekly. When the physical circumstances are unknown, and participants may or may not have the same level of commitment or understanding, the group-forming process needs to be even more deliberate. So, from the beginning, we used a norming process to focus everyone on mutual responsibilities while learning together.

I usually begin by asking: In a group that is working well, meaning you and others are interacting in ways that support mutual learning, what does it look like? What needs to happen in a group for it to be successful? I then collect their responses popcorn-style, writing what they say on the board or flip chart. It is important that the facilitator write what is heard and not edit and comment along the way, other than to ask for clarification or whether the key words used on the board accurately reflect what may have been shared in more detail. We are modeling objective listening.

Then we look at the list together and see if anyone in the group needs clarification. Sometimes people ask to combine a couple of items, which can only be done if the sponsors of both items agree. This has to do with respect for the integrity and authorship of each individual. When we are all sure we know what is represented on the list in front of us, I can ask: Is there any one of these that you do not support? Sometimes that leads to further clarification, but rarely to any real issue. Most of the items are things such as good listening, respect for differences, punctuality, etc.

Then comes the crucial moment: Since there is nothing before us that any one of us cannot support as a matter of common striving (not perfection), can we affirm with a show of hands if we are in support and can adopt these group norms? If one has done one's job well as facilitator, there should be unanimity.

I then go on to say that any member of the group can ask to review our norms over the course of the year, and that from time to time I will ask the group how we are doing with them. Thus it becomes a living document.

It is wonderful to observe how a group deals with the norms as the year progresses. Sometimes I overhear a comment about how good listening was really working in a certain discussion, or a participant will ask that we all remind ourselves about punctuality when some return late after lunch. The group has ownership of process and observance, and can self-correct with ease. Sometimes there is a request to add an item, such as drinking (often yes) or eating (often no) during class. When an item needs to be added, we do a mini-version of the earlier process, asking for clarification, any concerns, and then group adoption. Sometimes they ask for my guidance, for instance concerning note-taking or knitting during a meditative exercise. But overall, it is so important that the group own their norms and self-monitor. We are building practices that we hope will transfer into faculty meetings and parent evenings.

Recently, as Zoom has been used more frequently, I have discovered that orientation and norm setting have to be done all over again. In a recent session that I visited, some participants were listening attentively, others forgot to turn off the audio (the instructor has to constantly monitor these things) and some had cats, laundry and children moving in and out of the screen. We need to attend to group norms no matter how we meet!

Speaking and Listening

In every group, there is at least an unconscious feeling that a balance is needed between speaking and listening. This has to do with sharing "air time," but also with how people relate to each other through the spoken word. Most can recall instances of someone talking too long or a few who dominate the conversation. Of course, some are naturally reluctant to speak, and introverts can contribute in a variety of ways. But, in general, a healthy group process requires awareness of the balance between speaking and listening. Again, a few pointers:

- Instructor modeling of how to balance. An instructor/facilitator is in a unique position to model speaking and listening. Far too often, teachers at all levels think that God placed them at the front of the room to pontificate. Of course students want to learn from the instructor, but I am always concerned when I hear the voice of a colleague in a nearby room droning on and on. When things are presented at great length, students can shut down, or even if they take notes it is likely much of the material will not be digested. So it is incumbent on the instructor to warm up the group with opening questions for discussion, to present in short segments that can be grasped, and to allow time for processing after the presentations. Some of our favorite techniques at Antioch are to move in and out of small-group work, to center activities around problem-solving, and to present projects that stimulate interest and balance theory. Likewise, students need to learn to balance their speaking and listening, not only in each class but overall.

- This has a lot to do with student presentations. Most often they really enjoy the chance to prepare and present to peers. Some of the best presentations are done when based on collaboration with others. There is no limit to their creativity if given the right opportunity. Some of the most dry material imaginable can come alive in a skit or dramatization, poetry reading, or visual collage. Rather than just to have students do a series of presentations on a chapter or assigned topic, it is essential that there is time to debrief afterwards. I have adopted the practice of asking the same two questions after each presentation, so that there is a sense of fairness and balance: What worked, how can we appreciate what we just experienced? Then, if s/he were to do that presentation again, what improvements could you all suggest? I try and limit the responses to 2-3 for each presentation so we avoid having some people get lots of positives and others not. I tell them in advance that they can offer 2-3 for each presentation, and that some will speak for others and we want to be as even-handed as possible.

- Over the years I have found that small-group work is a marvelous opportunity for all to contribute. It matters very much that participants have a chance to process the material, as many have found that adults learn best when problem-solving in small groups. I have experimented with the size of the groups, and even wrote an entire chapter on the geometry of groups in my book *Organizational Integrity*. Pairs can be quick and serve as a good warm-up; threes open the perspective and are good for in-depth study; fives are great for a project, etc. Nothing should be automatic in the assignment of small-group work.

- One way to enhance learning, and it only takes a moment here and there, is to offer commendations as facilitator when something works well, so we can all learn from it. I often thank the group when what I call supportive listening occurs in a class. Just as with learning a musical instrument, one can gradually "tune" one's instrument to listen to how people are listening! Noticing on the part of the instructor shows that this is important.

- When these practices are well underway, one can then ask every few sessions: How are we doing? No need for much discussion as just the question serves as a reminder to all. And I always use the term "we" as the group, including the instructor, has a mutual responsibility to make group dynamics work.

Discussion vs. Conversation

Most classes consider discussion the main modality. The typical format is for questions to be asked and everyone contributes as they wish. I would like to differentiate between this kind of class discussion and conversation. In the latter, we have the possibility for a much more refined form of interaction. The word means a coming together, and holds great potential for group as well as individual learning.

One of my favorite ways to build a sense for conversation is to do an exercise in Goethean conversation, as elaborated by Marjorie Spock in her little pamphlet of that name. She recommends several steps to follow:

1. Assign the question or topic a day or more ahead of time.

2. Set up the room ahead of time, preferably with chairs in a circle rather than having everyone behind desks. This sense of a different placement in the room really helps what follows.

3. Also ahead of time, describe the process that will be used: contributions are made, but with each successive one, there should be a layering, a building upon the past contributions. So if someone says something, the next should try if possible to reference what was said, even going back several steps to previous contributions.

4. At the appointed time, assemble the group and introduce the topic, reminding everyone that occasional periods of silence are OK. I often mention the Quaker meeting. Then I repeat the topic and step into an active listening mode.

5. The group has the conversation, and then we debrief.

I have found that the best Goethean conversations happen when the topic allows for deep thinking and evades easy answers. So for example, I have used the question: Where does evil come from and how can we heal? Or: How can a teacher best practice work-life balance?

When the group has successfully done a Goethean conversation, I usually suggest that there might be topics in their schools that could benefit from such an approach.

Holding a Question

In our information age of Googling for instant answers, many adults no longer have the patience for anything that does not satisfy at once. The same can be true in a classroom. Yet many professions require in-depth study, critical thinking, and testing of assumptions. To achieve this, we all need to re-learn how to learn.

Holding a question is one way to do this.

There are at least four levels of questioning: what, when, how, and why. The information age emphasizes "what" questions, and today is also slanted in that direction: What can be remembered for the next test, what does the teacher want, and what do I need to learn to get by? But that approach runs the risk of reducing the world to "things" and info bites. Information alone does not lead to knowledge, let alone wisdom.

The "when" question puts things on a timeline, but also applies to the classroom. When does one break into small groups? At what point on the syllabus does one bring up such and such topic? These things really matter. If a topic is placed in the right sequence, it can go so much further. Likewise, waiting overnight allows for digestion through the process of sleep. Often more comes back the next day than what was originally imparted.

"How" questions lead us to the art of learning. When one asks "how" questions, the participants have to dig deeper and begin to think critically. Here it is good if the facilitator asks for a variety of responses, thus building a composite picture of an issue or topic. This builds flexibility in image formation.

Finally, the "why" questions are the ultimate in adult learning. It is not enough to just know what, when and how, we need to know why we teach as we do. So for example, in studying history, the fall of the Berlin Wall many years ago was not just an event, a "what and how." It is fascinating to see how the wall came down, reviewing the footage and hearing the speeches. But then we get to the "why," and the conversations are still relevant: Was it the fall of communism, at least in Eastern Europe? Then why do we see the resurgence in Russia and continuance in China today? What was it that allowed the wall to fall, and how does this relate to building a wall on the U.S.-Mexican border today? These "why" questions promote deeper, more critical thinking.

So in teacher education, we have to re-learn how to ask questions and also how to hold questions that do not have ready answers. What has helped me the most is preparing research questions with my classes. Following guidelines I developed many years ago (which can be found in my book *Silence is Complicity*), I work through a process that takes several weeks of identifying "wonderings," to carrying potential questions into sleep, and then in multiple conversations. After much time has passed, the question that is "meant to be" seems to take hold, often touching on deep biographical and professional layers of the participants' lives. Many say that in the end, they did not find the question; it found them. (See sample research papers in the chapter "Listening to our Teachers" near the end of this book.)

Building Reflective Practices

In addition to frequently asking "How did we do?," healthy adult learning needs a structured way to review. This supports the Rückschau, the looking back at the end of the day that individuals might do, and it enhances the assimilation and digestion of learning. But some form needs to be given for this to happen.

One technique we use in our distant programs we call "fact, feeling and essence." It is a process I used in *Organizational Integrity,* and it has its origin in Steiner's *Theosophy.* The exercise below works best first thing in the morning as the group looks back on the previous day. It has three parts:

1. Fact. In the group, I ask for facts from the day before and participants offer them popcorn-style. A fact is something all can agree to: we sat on folding metal chairs, there was a vase with flowers in the corner, we shared our relationship to our names, etc. If there is something said that is debatable, it is not a fact.

2. Feelings. This is the opposite of facts, in that we are looking to share personal responses to the material from the previous day. It is best if these feelings are shared in complete sentences, and no one can respond. So one person might say she felt sad because… and another person may say he felt happy, and both can be true from a personal point of view!

3. <u>Essence</u>. Here we are looking for the seed, the kernel of what happened in terms of new learning or the content of a particular segment of the workshop. Here we are asking for single words or phrases, and again, each offering needs to stand on its own. The essence for one person may not be the same for another. But in most cases, there is a recognition that the word or phrase rings true.

Several things are possible in doing this exercise. In addition to looking back in a structured way, the fact–feeling–essence process is a soul journey. It is not always so easy to separate things out inwardly, to look at experiences. Adult learning is essentially self-education, so by acquiring skills to process, learning on an individual basis can be enhanced. People have a remarkable ability to extract from experience what they most need!

Second, we are introducing a clear demarcation between objective and subjective experiences. All too often in groups, schools, and life, these elements are thrown into the stew we call discussion. We need to work hard at simply looking at the facts, whether it is a cash flow statement, a child's biography, or a landscape. We need to look and look again, without jumping to opinions or conclusions. This is the basis of all phenomenology. Then when one turns to feelings, the adult learner can "own" what are truly his/her personal responses, and even make them visible for the group. This also has value, as often we mix in a little bit of fact with a whole lot of feeling, and then we wonder why it is so hard to self-administer our schools!

Finally, the "essence" stage involves the maturation, the distillation of assimilated experience, looking down from the top of the mountain. In our info age, we so often move from one sound bite or text to another and never give ourselves time to really digest experiences. The "essence" step in review is an aspect that we self-select to tuck away in the treasure trove of the soul for future work and reference. And in a school, it is so helpful when someone can say: Is this what we are really talking about? Or: It seems to me the real issue is… Some people do this naturally (the Saturn types, for instance) but we can all learn to distill the essence and offer our inner work with the group as a seed for further learning.

After a group has been doing the fact, feeling, and essence exercise for a while, it becomes second nature, and the facilitator only needs to do the prompts. It becomes a soul habit, and some say they then start doing it for themselves on a daily basis. Anything that can be processed on an individual basis means there is less to do in a group, and when one is in an organization, decisions can be made on a sounder basis.

Different Perspectives

Exercises such as the one described above can allow for the healthy inclusion of difference, in which it is OK to see things from different perspectives. So often we have to deal with reactive behaviors in which people feel compelled to counter what has been said by another person. When there is good facilitation, it is possible that many perspectives can live in a group, and that they actually enhance learning and productivity.

In all group situations, there is a constant tug-of-war going on between the needs of the individual and the needs of the group. One could also say this is a struggle between altruism and selfishness. On the world stage, we are witnessing more and more narcissistic behaviors in our leaders, and this infiltrates our school communities as well. There is more and more a sense of "what I need" and the spirit of service is weakening. So it is quite important that our group work, starting in our education programs, model a different way of working.

Working with different perspectives helps us build a culture of tolerance and mutual respect. One way is to become more conscious of our use of language. Phrases such as "I heard you say" work better than "You were angry." We so often go down instead of up in our communications.

A facilitator can welcome differences by using phrases such as: Is there another way of looking at this? Can someone share a different perspective? If these viewpoints are encouraged, it is easier for the person sharing as well as those that might more instinctively react to someone else. Differences that are not engaged can lead to conflict. When there is outright conflict in a group, the facilitator needs to bring more structure, such as sequencing the contributions, allowing for time intervals (such as a strategic break or two!), and asking for others to summarize what has been said. We often are working with a spectrum of differences, from the cold, more analytical pole that can become critical or sarcastic, to the warm, more feeling-driven pole that can become inflamed. The types of questions the facilitator uses and the way the conversation is structured can either cool down or heat up the level of interaction. And in an overly critical world, more cold is not always better… but the warm pole may best be worked with by having a break for an artistic activity, or a group project in which the will forces, the energy of individuals, can be channeled into constructive work.

I am convinced that thoughts are real and can have tremendous influence on the world. The concept of non-violence led to Gandhi and Martin Luther King Jr., the concept of environmental protection has led to recycling and much more. So if thoughts are realities, individuals in a group can do great harm or good by how they work with their thoughts. Negativity cannot be eliminated, but when it passes through one's thoughts, it is possible to confront it and then consciously erase and replace with something else. In facilitating group work, it is possible to cultivate more and more of a sense of individual responsibility. We need to be the change we seek in others.

Professional Learning Community

All of the above, indeed most of what appears in this book, is about developing professional learning communities. This is covered in more detail in the chapter titled "Demoralized," but the essence of recent studies is that when children experience that their teachers are part of a professional learning community, they are more likely to succeed in school. The group work described above is a key component of the development of a professional learning community. Adults in our programs need to experience a learning community while in training so that they have a greater chance of continuing those practices in schools and other organizations.

Karmic Connections

This chapter began with the observation that many people find themselves in the same groups they worked with in past lives. If this is true, it has many, many implications, of which just one can be mentioned here. Especially in organizations with a spiritual foundation and high ideals, we seem to attract people with unresolved karmic issues. Our Waldorf schools present an opportunity to bring our karma back into order. This is a high calling, and one which cannot be taken lightly. But it hints at a much deeper basis for group work. We are here to serve children, but often the parents and teachers who assemble around them have much work to do with each other. We need to spend more time and focus on how we relate as adults, learning to work together so that we can lighten our baggage and thus surround the children in our care with pure intent and good will.

3. Giving Lectures and Presentation
Based on Indications from Rudolf Steiner

One of the hallmarks of higher education is the lecture, presentation, or "talk" given by the professor or instructor. Far too many of these have been delivered over the years, some awakening interest, others just there to be endured. A scintillating lecture is unfortunately more the exception than the rule. So I looked up the indications on the art of lecturing given by Rudolf Steiner, himself a prolific speaker with over 600 talks given in his lifetime. It was wonderful to read his candid appraisal of what works and what does not when presenting.

He begins by observing that we cannot force people to be interested just because we are. If we are too willful, try too hard to be convincing, we will simply annoy people. He also has many examples of what not to do, such as handing out the lecture ahead of time or simply reading it from the podium. For a lecture in itself is a kind of imposition, even an attack on the audience. So we need to carefully examine what really happens during a lecture.

Steiner observes that active listening is very much connected to our ability to grasp something with our understanding. We need the cooperation of all parts of our being, our life forces, our senses, and a soul life that has not been exhausted by the astral body and our often distracted consciousness. If we listen well, then all parts of us begin to pulsate with the lecture, says Steiner in *The Art of Lecturing*, pp. 5-6.

This then leads to the important question: How can we move our listeners in the best way possible so that they meet what they are hearing with their feelings, their responses? And how can we do this without imposing our will on them? To begin with, the lecturer should speak out of inner experience of the material.

> And truly all lectures should come from the heart. Even the most abstract lecture should come from the heart. And that it can! And it is precisely this which we must discuss, how even the most abstract lecture can come from the heart.

We need to stir the soul of the listener through our heart connection to the theme and to the audience. For there is a constant play between sympathy and antipathy at work in the listener, at least on the subtle level of feelings. Just as a good teacher is able to get into the shoes of a student, so to speak, to understand behavior, so the lecturer needs to sense the audience while speaking.

One is free to do this if one has prepared thoroughly. This means "it is a matter of establishing the thinking for the lecture, completely establishing it, as long as possible before we lecture; that we have beforehand absolutely settled the thought element within ourselves.... Through this manner of experiencing our lecture in thoughts beforehand, we take from it the sting it otherwise has for the audience. We are, to a degree, bound to sweeten our lecture by having gone through the sourness of the logical development of the train of thought beforehand—but as much as possible in such a way that we do not formulate the lecture word for word" (pp. 10-11).

He stresses that it is not a matter of learning the lecture word for word, as that would lead to a machine-like delivery; it would become automatic. At the beginning of a lecture it is good to be present as a person, to connect on a human level. I have found that a personal story, or connecting with the school or members of the audience at the beginning, helps warm up the space. Steiner says this creates a "vibration of feeling" (p. 12). He says it is even OK to make oneself a bit ridiculous at the beginning, as long as it is not too obvious! The introduction helps set the tone and hold the attention of the audience during the more difficult parts later on. Above all, the first and last sentences must be absolutely clear as bookends. Then that which comes in between can be more freely rendered.

The key is that the body of the lecture is worked through meditatively in thought so that it can later be formulated freely. One needs a picture of the composition of the lecture, and one's thinking needs to be thoroughly embedded in the talk. It is not a matter of the individual words, but what lives between the words, "in the way in which the words are shaped, the sentences are shaped, and the arrangement is shaped. The more we are in a position to think about the 'how' of our lecture, the more strongly do we work into the will of the others. What people will accept depends upon what we put into the formulation, into the composition of the lecture" (p. 16). We need to behold a picture, an imagination that can be viewed in the mind's eye of the speaker. Finally, one needs enthusiasm for the subject, and an artistic delivery to stir the listeners and help them remember the content.

As he does elsewhere, Steiner urges the speaker to characterize rather than define. This means that one has to place a subject before the audience from various aspects. This is an anthroposophical way of presenting things. If we wish to serve the spiritual in humanity, we need to free language to live in images, artistic composition, and multiple characterizations. But one needs a comprehensive thought that comprises the total lecture, an overarching theme that is treated from a variety of angles. It is most helpful to use examples arising out of life experiences (and one's own inner experiences of the material) so as to better connect with the audience.

> If one is too serious it can cause acidity in the stomach of the listeners. So one needs some inner lightness, modulation, enthusiasm, and humor. These qualities aid in the process of digestion. And it is OK if the speaker is a bit nervous, even reluctant to speak. There is nothing worse than someone who enjoys hearing himself talk! (p. 83)

Finally, Steiner did many speech exercises with the first teachers with the aim of helping them bring language to life—to find a lyrical, dramatic or epic quality depending on the needs of the lesson. Thus, it is essential that those preparing to be Waldorf teachers do as much speech training as possible. Here are a few of the original exercises Steiner did with teachers:

> Fulfillment goes
> Through hope
> Goes through longing
> Through willing
>
> Willing wafts
> In weaving
> Wafts in billowing
> Weaves billowing
> Weaves binding
> In finding
> Finding winding
> Calling

See Appendix for more from *The Art of Lecturing*.

4. Information Overload

To begin with a wider historical context, here is an astute observation by Peter Pomerantsev in "The New Propaganda: Fighting the Bot Farms and Troll Armies" (*The Guardian Weekly*, Aug. 2, 2019):

> [T]he assumptions that underlay the struggles for rights and freedoms in the 20th century—between citizens armed with truth and information and regimes with their censors and secret police— have been turned upside down. We now have more information than ever before, but it hasn't brought only the benefits we expected. More information was supposed to mean more freedom to stand up to the powerful, but it's also given the powerful new ways to crush and silence dissent. More information was supposed to mean a more informed debate, but we seem less capable of deliberation than ever. More information was supposed to mean mutual understanding across borders, but it has also made possible new and more subtle forms of subversion. We live in a world in which the means of manipulation have gone forth and multiplied, a world of dark ads, psy-ops, hacks, bots, soft facts, deep fakes, fake news, Putin, trolls, Trump.

Education, also teacher education, is influenced by larger societal trends such as the one Pomerantsev is pointing out. When I did my summer preparation for 6th grade in 1979, my first and main task was to find the materials, which consisted mainly of some well-recommended books and pointers from experienced colleagues. Over the summer I took careful notes and outlined my lessons and block schedule. Today, we not only have a plethora of published material, but within seconds can download masses of information through a variety of online search tools. Teachers today are swamped with information. But how can we make sense of it all?

With information overload we risk asphyxiation. Without oxygen we die. Without the ability to sort, prioritize and digest, the teacher can succumb as well. We have been so concerned with finding information (the "what" described in another section of this book) that we are numbed, and often then end up selecting the packaged deal or the predigested sequence of lessons sold to us as a quick way out of the dilemma.

More than ever, teachers need to know how to self-organize and prioritize. This requires an inner strength as well as outer skills. Meditative work can help the teacher gain needed perspective and find a personal center point out of which choices can be made. Outer skills include: starting with core principles that inform curriculum content, identifying key goals for each lesson or block, and limiting and even reducing the material to find the essentials. Often, less is more.

Knowledge is acquired over time. So we need to take advantage of the flow and rhythm of preparation. Working a year, or at least a summer, in advance, provides an opportunity to prepare the *physical basis for teaching.* This includes not only the materials and lesson content, but preparing projects, getting supplies, equipping the classroom for the learning adventures ahead.

Then there is the monthly preparation. In a Waldorf school this often involves a whole block or unit of teaching in one subject. Working on a monthly basis is an opportunity to establish health-giving *life forces that sustain learning from day to day.* Here I often selected the support materials, such as poems, songs and projects that could be sustained over many days, and even grow in time as with the waxing and waning of the moon.

Then there is preparation that can occur one week in advance, mostly work a teacher does on the weekend before a unit of instruction. This involves *the astral, or consciousness-based teaching.* We wrap our minds around the week ahead in a way that can never happen in the summer. In the weekly preparation we can sift through the information from the point of view: Will I really use this? Can I sequence things in a way that my lessons have a flow?

Then we have in inevitable nightly preparation cycle, which involves the *teacher's ego, or self-directed ability to penetrate things in detail.* This is crucial, for if one is doing a project and does not have enough scissors or clay, the whole effort can come unraveled ever so quickly in a room of 25 lively third graders! This last level of preparation has to be done the afternoon or evening before, preferably with a sense of finishing touches rather than taking on new information or material at this late stage.

The above process is a path of knowledge that aims to conquer information overload. From yearly to monthly to weekly to nightly, the teacher is exercising freedom to sort, sift, digest, prioritize, and ask: what is the best way to do this with my particular class? Knowledge formation requires working artistically with time.

But there is yet a higher order of things: a quality not so often found today, but much valued when present in singular individuals who have graced the earth with their presence throughout history—a quality we can call wisdom. I often ask my classes at Antioch: Have you known a wise person? What was she or he like? For wisdom is a rare commodity these days.

Past civilizations were often founded or ruled by initiates or wise leaders. They can be found in sacred texts, cultural traditions, and mythology. The Waldorf curriculum is unique in that it introduces our students to a wide variety of wise teachers who have lived in cultures all over the world, thus expanding their cultural literacy as well as giving them access to the likes of Buddha, Zarathustra, Confucius, Isis and Osiris, Black Elk, Martin Luther King Jr., and a host of others.

Is wisdom endowed, or can it be earned? Perhaps both? But the portion that can be earned has to do again with the passage of time and how we transform knowledge into something that transcends both knowledge and information: a state of presence and seeing beyond the ordinary. A wise teacher is one who has worked with many students over the years and can "see through" the everyday antics and learning issues to find the essential child within. A wise teacher is able to make decisions that may counter prevailing attitudes and even go against established policy or pedagogical guidelines. A wise person is often one who stands out as a remarkable individual who has the courage to stand *for a high ideal even if it means standing against popular opinion.*

So the task in teacher education is to help prepare the way to *transform information into knowledge, and knowledge into wisdom.* To do that we need a better grasp of adult learning, and for that I turn to the notion of destiny learning and other considerations in the following chapters.

5. Trios

When doing breakout groups, in Zoom or in person, there is value to small-group conversation. People open up and share in different ways depending on the configuration of the group and who is engaged. Although one can find good reason to have groups of four or even five (see geometry of groups in *Organizational Integrity* for more), the comments below focus on the value of trios, especially in the context of teacher education.

If one has a conversation with just one other person, it has the feel of confidentiality, sometimes intimacy. Often in adult classes it helps to have a "partner conversation" to warm up a topic, or give a few minutes for a personal sharing on the topic. There are many times when a dialogue partner is most helpful. But when there are three people involved, the conversation tends to be different. No longer so personal, the addition of a third person lifts the dialogue into a new realm. There is a greater chance for sharing perspectives, questioning statements, examining a topic from different angles. A trio conversation presents unique opportunities for transformation.

Looking back on culture and literature, three has deep roots in mystery wisdom often found in story content. We need only remember Goldilocks and the Three Bears, Three Musketeers, Three Blind Mice, or Three Wise Men as a few examples. It is no accident that the number three is so prevalent in stories, as it is often this dynamic that allows for character development. One might even say that the creative tensions in three allow for human and social progress.

Why? It is based on the archetypal threefolding principle of wholeness. The human being, imperfect in many instances, hosts a deep-seated urge to become complete. In many myths, fairy tales, and legends, the protagonist or main character goes through a whole series of experiences that can transform the soul and lead to outer success. Joseph Campbell and others have described the hero's journey eloquently. Along the way, the number three often emerges as having great significance: three trials, three riddles, three chances. Three is a dynamic force in human development, and thus also teacher education.

How often do you find yourself breaking things down into three things to remember? How often do other people break things down into three things for you? (If you've read *Getting Results the Agile Way*, you'll know that I use the "Rule of Three" to simplify taking action and avoid information overload.)

> As the New York Times reports, research has suggested that three arguments may be more persuasive than two or four. Trios may or may not be more persuasive, but they can create a sense of poetry and rhythm, making our content more pleasurable to read and adding stress to a statement. Pay attention to good writing, and you see threes popping up everywhere (Meier 2010).

In regard to communication, professional speaker Ty Bennett shares how the Rule of Three is a rule that every great communicator understands. We are genetically more likely to understand and remember a message when the Rule of Three is used. If you are involved in speaking, selling, leading or teaching—then you should understand this rule and apply it to make your communication clear, concise, and memorable.

In *How to Write with Power and Authority, Even if You Feel Like a Nobody* we are reminded that beginners' writing classes often teach that repetition is bad, especially if it is accidental and pedantic. But the author adds that

> …when used with care, repetition can add stress and a pleasant sense of rhythm…. In the following fragment, for instance, the phrase "How often" is repeated twice and then the phrase "Life is too short" is repeated thrice: How often do we read content that surprises and delights? How often are we really inspired by a blog post? Life is too short for monotone voices. Life is too short for wishy-washy writing. Life is too short to regurgitate ideas without adding value (Duistermaat, July 2016).

In How to Write So Vividly that Readers Fall in Love with Your Ideas we are reminded of the famous:

> Veni. Vidi. Vici. I came. I saw. I conquered. – Julius Caesar
> The number three is the smallest number to create a pattern; and patterns please our minds. So go ahead. Use the magic of three in your content. Add a dash of flair. A sprinkle of rhythm. And a dollop of poetic beauty (Duistermaat, Aug. 2016).

Trios in Waldorf Teacher Education

Over the years, I have found trios to be invaluable as an adult teaching tool. Before a lecture or instructor presentation, one can "till the soil" of learning by posing a question or topic that is worthy of conversation. It needs to be related to the subject at hand and is best when there is no ready "solution." When the adult learners are in a trio format, they all get to speak and contribute ideas with less chance of exposure to critique or reactive comments from peers. Trios are a safe place to take risks and try out new ideas. Adults learn best when in problem-solving mode and when collaborating with others in meaningful conversation.

In order to assign a good question for trio discussion, the instructor needs to have an eye on the end goal of the class. If one is immersed in studying ancient Egyptian culture, it might be good to start off the trio discussions with a question on the role of Isis and Osiris in preparing the temples of higher learning (assuming they have done some of the assigned reading!). When a group is used to working in trios, they get going right away and even 10-15 minutes can yield many positive results.

Which leads to "harvesting," already mentioned in other contexts. Rather than treat the trios as a kind of "time out," which would be disrespectful to all that happened in the conversations, it is good to allow a few minutes to harvest some of the insights generated in the trios. Over the years I have become less willing to have a rigid "reporting out" from each group, with flip charts and all that, and have tended to favor a more fluid situation in which I ask for any "gems" or aha moments, with some groups contributing more and others less. It is also good to keep things moving and have a light touch, otherwise one gets bogged down in too much information and the focus on the assigned topic can get blurry. One- to two-sentence sharing of insights works best for me.

In addition to *preparing the ground* with trios, another opportunity presents itself partway through the lesson when everyone needs to come up for air and process things a bit. And then again, near the end of the class, there is often real value in convening trios to look at *applications*. What can you take from this class on Egyptian mystery schools into your own meditative practices? Or, do you have any new ideas on how you might teach Egypt to fifth graders?

Sometimes I even assign trios overnight, asking our learners to find a snack break or mealtime to sit together and process a question. For, in fact, we do not learn in 90-minute or 120-minute segments. If one understands the soul from an anthroposophical perspective (see pp. 80–88 in my book *Guided Self-Study),* the processing of experiences and the act of *re-member-ing* occurs as a life process that follows its own lawfulness. Adult learning and the omnipotent rule of the clock are not compatible. We have to bear this in mind when scheduling our classes and quantifying "contact hours" and such. The soul beats to its own internal drummer.

One can enhance trio work by occasionally assigning roles:

- One person can be the participant/observer/witness, looking at the conversation as a whole and observing patterns and other aspects from a higher elevation than that of just another participant.

- In our research course at Antioch University, I often assign trios in which one person presents a possible research topic under consideration and the other two serve as "coaches," asking clarifying questions, probing for understanding, commenting on language and word choice, etc. Then they switch roles.

- Of course, in some situations one may want to have the group assign a minute-taker or facilitator.

- One could also appoint a person to just ask questions and even challenge the other two to get beyond commonly held assumptions.

In courses that last several weeks, I have found that a "return to meeting" mode of working with trios can be ever so constructive. They become a kind of home base, a common point of reference, or even a work group that can take up a task and track it over many days.

Getting back to the theme of being incomplete as a human being, one could see trios as a chance to engage multiple aspects of our human-ness. Often when one person says something in conversation, another person instinctively responds with another perspective. This is human nature. But when there are three in conversation, it is more likely that the group will overcome simple polarity.

Our world today is more polarized than I have ever experienced it. Polarity is so strong in so many situations that many of us now self-censor and refrain from saying much at all in social situations. Our neighbors have stopped putting out political signs, and even among people with shared values, conversation has become full of "landmines." The effect is a mighty *silencing of conversation, which over time will have a profound effect on community health and the state of our democracy.*

A trio is a humble step in creating structure that can hold differing points of view in a safe structure. In teacher education programs, we need to model healthy adult interactions so our graduates have some tools to deal with colleagues and parents in their schools of the future.

6. Strengthening Memory through Waldorf Teacher Education

In recent years, those of us actively engaged in teacher education have noticed that our students struggle to tell a story from memory. They work hard to memorize some of the lines and then tell them as if they were reciting a quote. Looking into the matter more closely, it appears that they do not have the ability to see the pictures with the inner eye. Rather than move from scene to scene through image formation, they more often resort to memorizing lines.

There are no doubt many reasons for this apparent change, but we cannot help but notice that this challenge is greatest with younger students, those 20-30 years old. This is the first generation raised most completely with personal devices that form images for us!

Likewise, we have another general trend that is not confined to younger people: a growing state of forgetfulness. More and more people have trouble remembering things. Our mobile devices help us with Google calendars, note apps, and email searches, but it seems those assistants easily become indispensable. For example, I used to have a nose for navigating while driving, often finding my way back to a place after years of absence. Now even frequently navigated routes require my GPS. I have become less spatially literate.

If these trends are true, there may be serious implications. Not seeing images and not remembering could render us quite helpless in performing even simple day-to-day tasks. Especially for teachers, we need to design interventions and experiences that help rebuild memory if we are to function in classrooms of the future.

In this section, I would like to examine the nature of memory and image formation, and then draw out applications for Waldorf teacher education.

Memory

To begin with, we might want to redefine the notion of "bad memory" and, at least for the average person, characterize the challenge as a weak faculty of recollection. For there is a difference between the retention of experiences, their recall, and the flashing forth of a memory picture.

For example, an old person who forgets recent things quickly often has wonderful clarity with certain pictures from childhood. Recollection is an activity of the soul, it is a reconstruction, a creative act in which the invisible is made visible again.

How does this happen? Memories are stored in the soul, and it takes the human I or ego to call them forth again. The act of recollection is a deed. That which was below the threshold of consciousness and has slumbered for some time can be reawakened by our conscious intention when we are of sound body and mind. The truth of this can be verified simply by noticing one's own memory when one is sick or when one is well. That is because our life forces (the etheric body, according to Steiner) are holding the memories, and when we are ill, these life forces are weaker. We also need to be conscious to remember; one could say our consciousness (astral body) awakens the sleeping memory residing in the soul and nourished by the etheric.

The etheric works on the reconstruction of the physical body at night. It serves as a kind of architect of the human organism. These forces that constantly form and re-form the human body are also working hard in holding memory. Thus, when we are weak or ill, our memory can become thin.

Memory is also connected to the will, to our gross motor movements. Some people tap their fingers on the table when trying to remember, others memorize things by walking up and down. When one stops, the will forces are directed to memory formation and recollection. Moving and then stopping provides resistance and transferred will forces into the astral, or conscious, realm.

As already mentioned, one needs self-awareness—awareness of the Self or ego—to practice remembering. The same force which holds us together as an ego being is active in self-realization. The ego constantly identifies with past experiences and "identifies itself continually with itself, its experience of uniformity rests likewise upon this power of judging the identity of itself" (Poppelbaum, p. 11). Rudolf Steiner called the perception of the ego the first "intuition," a perceiving power of grasping that becomes a feeling of being within oneself: "The person who is observing and recollecting brings himself in touch with relationships which are beneficial to his etheric body (which in turn, has its origin in wisdom) and by means of which he can refresh himself anew" (p. 13).

To summarize, memory involves life forces (inner and outer vitality), will activity, conscious intention, movement (and rhythm), and a sense of Self as a point of centering within the periphery of memories from the past.

Implications for Waldorf Teacher Education

Those seeking to prepare themselves as teachers these days often engage in summer programs or part-time/weekend sessions during the school year. These options allow for better integration between theory and practice, as many can engage in teaching during the school year, or at least have long internships. Direct experiences with children allow for constant "testing" of pedagogical theory, and reflections on practice can illuminate understanding. Part-time programs are also practical, as many can hold down a job while in training, and schools often hire new teachers in the spring and then send them off to summer programs.

Yet, as a movement, we have also paid a price in terms of rhythms in teaching, advising, and the community development of the cohort group. It is simply much harder to work with the etheric (life forces) when a delivery model is arrhythmic. To work with this challenge, those responsible for adult education programs need to be much more intentional in all we do.

Rhythm helps us take things in holistically in a way that breathes and works with, rather than against, processes going on in the physical body and the soul of the adult learner. Healthy adult learning processes form a basis upon which the sounds that we hear are caught up, and how we hear influences what is retained in memory. Rather than just learning through lectures, the human soul needs time to process, to converse in trios and other configurations, and time to implement ideas in project-based learning.

Poppelbaum speaks of "traces of memory" that we commonly call concepts. They retain the musical, rhythmical character of the trace remembrance. One can think of "the trace remembrance as a living melody" that is intimately bound up with the etheric body and the life forces that sustain us (p. 7). Especially at night, the etheric works on rebuilding the physical body, organizing and creating harmony as in music.

> Anyone who has ever studied musical memory—a wonderful and mysterious thing, even though we all take it for granted—will find out how fundamentally different it is from the memory of something visible. This memory for music is based on a particular organization of the head metabolism; in its general character it is also related to the will, and therefore to the metabolism. Music memory and memory of visual images are located in different regions of the body; both, however, are connected to the will (Steiner, *Balance in Teaching*, p. 35).

So musical and visual memory functions are processed differently, with implications for how we teach. It is scarcely necessary to point out that most of what happens in a classroom either engages listening or seeing. The nuance is that retention is different depending on which sense is predominant, and, of course, some adult learners are better at retaining visual images and others lean more to the auditory.

Yet they have one thing in common that is vital to both: "Everything we perceive is comprehended by means of the rhythmic system; visual images are perceived by the isolated head organism; audible images are perceived by the whole limb organism. Visual images stream inward toward the organism; audible images stream from the organism upward" (Steiner, p. 35).

In that most of us have a preference one way or the other, it is especially important in Waldorf teacher education that we have activities that generate movement both ways, from the head inward as happens with visual images, and from the limbs up through the musical. If there is a general societal tendency today, I would say it is in favor of the visual. With all our devices and other stimuli, we are constantly challenged to "look, look, look," whereas our ability to hear, let alone listen, has decreased. Thus, adult programs need to pay particular attention to the musical realm, which of course also involves conversation, dialogue, and other forms of listening. All of which are supported immeasurably through speech, drama, and eurythmy.

Adult education, therefore, needs to foster all those qualities that support the generation of life forces: the arts, overnight processing of material, meditative work before sleep and upon waking, daily schedules that support rhythm, and a balance of large- and small-group work.

Some specifics in regard to support of memory:

1. Attend to openings and closings, as they are the portals through which memory can enter into consciousness. Wrapping up a class well allows for review that starts the inner processing overnight and gives focus for the elaboration in the etheric during sleep. Likewise, opening with established forms, such as "fact, feeling, essence" as described in another chapter, allows for deliberate sharing of memory pictures. These practices build habits that support the ordering of life and inner balance.

2. As indicated in the first course given to teachers, we need to attend to breathing, not only with children, but within our adult education classes. There are many ways to do this, but one simple practice that supports breathing is the "engagement thermometer," a term I have

coined to measure participation from warmth to cold. Both poles are needed: we need the blue/cold pole in order to conceptualize, to absorb information, to ask probing questions, to test assumptions, to see differences, and compare and contrast. These are all valid components of adult learning. We need the red/orange/warmth pole to engage with others, to roll up our sleeves and work with clay, paints, crayons, recorders, blackboard drawings, etc. Most conversations warm things up, in both large and small groups (though large-group conversations can leave some colder than others). One has only to look around the room to get a read of the engagement thermometer: how do they look? Are arms moving? Are there changing facial expressions? Or not: Both aspects are needed!

3. We need to build new habits of reflection, learning from experience by structuring adult capacity to recall. This is not only a matter of practice in review, but also in how we facilitate group discussions. For example, after a small-group project one can simply ask: How was that for you? What did you learn? Doing, reflecting, conversing, and reflecting.

4. Although this is often more associated with children, doing things backwards, even the review at the end of the day, can help.

5. Strengthen the etheric in any way possible, especially through the arts and working with nature and rhythm. How do we achieve balance in our daily living? (See chapter on "Personal Hygiene.")

6. Although this text is not the place to give adequate coverage to the theme, I do want to also mention a form of memory we call trauma. This is a huge field of needed work, not only in terms of children, but also the adults to step forward to prepare themselves to work with children. There is need to also look at trauma/memory in terms of racism and anti racism, or what Resmaa Menaken, in his book *My Grandmother's Hands*, calls traumatic retention.

7. Practicing Destiny Learning

At this point in the book, I would like to switch gears for a moment to share some excerpts from Coenraad van Houten's seminal work on adult learning. More than any anthroposophically inspired author I know, van Houten articulated a foundational approach to adult learning. He envisioned training centers for this work, but other than some modest efforts before his death, was not able to see the full manifestation of his overarching vision.

Because his work is so significant to the focus of this book, I am devoting to it several pages, first to his step-by-step approach to practicing destiny, and then to his sequel on destiny learning. The reader is encouraged to read the complete books, but for those with less available time, these pages of excerpts may prove helpful as a study text.

You may find the tone of van Houten's writing considerably denser than my own, and it may take you longer to read and digest every passage. I highly recommend it, however: as we move past Waldorf 100, it is essential that we take up his work to prepare a new generation of Waldorf teachers and other trainings working out of an anthroposophical understanding of the human being.

Part I:
From *Practising Destiny* by Coenraad van Houten

Life confronts us with learning situations; by mastering these we further our own personal development. These learning situations are destiny situations. We can be led to very profound self-knowledge through the way destiny unfolds. We can learn *for* life, but also *through* life. The second learning path has therefore been termed *Destiny Learning* (p. 13).

An adult educator wanting to bring the three learning paths into his professional work therefore faces two main tasks that should mesh with his work in all kinds of ways: *awakening the will to learn and developing the sense of truth* (p. 19).

Selflessly using the twelve senses

Since our feeling for the truth is founded on the firm ground of sense perceptions, the capacity to observe is the footing upon which any adult learning must stand.

Because we possess twelve senses, schooling our capacity to observe is a highly differentiated process, as well as being one that progresses through various stages. And since we have twelve senses, each of which shows a different quality, this process also schools our power of discernment. If we possessed only a single sense this would be impossible. Here are the twelve senses:

Sense of touch	Sense of smell	Sense of hearing
Sense of life	Sense of taste	Sense of language
Sense of movement	Sense of sight	Sense of thought
Sense of balance	Sense of warmth	Sense of Ego

Adult educators who practiced using their senses soon noticed that regular exercise of sensory activity rapidly increased their capacity for learning. Learning processes accompanied daily by short exercises in observation soon proved very effective. Capacities such as restraint, openness, wonder, and concentration should be practiced constantly, for learning is mediated by the senses. The better the senses function, the better will the learning be. Therefore the capacity to observe is the foundation on which adult learning should stand. (p. 22)

Schooling this capacity also provides the basis for developing one's feeling for the truth. So long as one cannot distinguish clearly between objective observation and the influence of one's own being on the perception, one's feeling for the truth will remain insecure. It will become more accurate to the same degree that such distinction succeeds (p. 23).

Independently forming judgments is the adult educator's second development and professional field. It is directly related to the selfless use of the senses. In this case, too, it is easy to tell how our ability to form judgments becomes less independent if we do not constantly school it. We form judgments all day long, but how often are these judgments in fact merely second-hand, induced, conditioned, or automatic "pre-judgments," i.e., prejudices? Where and when is a judgment formed independently as a conscious, original deed? We all know the extent to which public opinion is manipulated and how consumers are seduced to buy things they do not need. The trouble in this age of information overload and manipulation is that we are insufficiently aware either of how little independent judgment-forming activity we engage in or how strongly our thinking is determined by outside influences (p. 24).

Every choice of a word involves countless judgments. Behind every choice of words and every mode of expression lurks the question: Does what is being said give expression more to the speaker or to the matter in hand, or does it perhaps express both equally? (p. 26)

The process of aesthetic judgment-forming could also be termed the process of relationships or of relational judgments since it always expresses the relationship between a human being and something in his environment. In this sense the formation of *social judgments* is identical with that of forming aesthetic judgments. If we do not school ourselves in forming social judgments, we nevertheless continuously form such judgments semi-consciously or automatically, the result being off-balance. In consequence the encounter aspect is very often eradicated (p. 26).

Forming a *moral judgment* is the opposite of forming a cognitive one because in a moral judgment one is the central actor having to reach a moral decision in a specific life situation. The first type of judgment formation is a cognitive process, the second an encounter event, and the third a form of decision-making. One's own moral responsibility is called for. In the first type of judgment, the object reveals its essential nature; in the third, one must listen inwardly to the voice of one's own conscience. We are not used to this (pp. 26-27).

This professional field does not end with the schooling of the three types of judgment-forming. It requires in addition that independence and individualization be continuously strengthened through such schooling (pp. 28-29).

These facts become even more impressive when we consider that a whole value system lies hidden, more or less dormant, in our feelings. After all, we evaluate the whole world in accordance with our feelings. By schooling the three processes of judging we bring this evaluation more and more into consciousness and can reshape it (p. 29).

The fact that this internal abyss between individuals, groups, and nations is growing deeper is a sure sign of the need to develop new faculties for bringing about real encounters (p. 32).

Since this problem affects every level of society it should become one of the foremost professional fields in all adult learning (p. 33).

Increasing individualization is making people harder, more one-sided, and more reclusive. The remedy for all this is the endeavor to achieve genuine encounter in which an equally one-sided individual can be permitted to enter into one's own inner being, thereby breaking the spell of one's own onesidedness. This then enables new processes of development to take place. The increasing individualization which is so heavily emphasized in today's adult education can thus be raised to a higher level that can lead to a new form of encounter amongst two or more individualities who are fundamentally different but have no need to renounce their own independence in the process. For this to happen, this new form of encounter would have to be schooled as a new faculty within adult learning (p. 33).

a) A physical influence, a kick for example, triggers a bruise in our physical body. The kick is followed by evasion or a counter-kick.

b) Certain specific actions, such as stretching out one's hand, raising one's hat, or saying "Good morning," trigger reflex actions which are termed conditioned reflexes.

Much of human behavior is based on such almost automatic reflex actions. They are incorporated in the vital sphere. One example of this, which provides interesting material for study, is the way people have been conditioned to greet one another in their different cultures. This is the sphere of our habitual being.

c) At the soul level, responses are psychological. Specific basic convictions and values, but also desires and wishes, live in our soul and make us respond to external stimuli in specific ways (p. 35).

d) Momentarily switching off one's own responses calls for strong ego-forces. In this instance, it is the ego that says "No." At the levels on which the responses normally take place, this has the effect of the response being omitted. This is the place where the free, open space arises in which one can take in the other person, and with the help of this non-response, one can also accept him. The capacity to do this needs practice if it is to become strong enough for us to use it whenever it appears appropriate. When the ego-encounter faculty develops, the possibility to transform the other three levels consciously begins to emerge (p. 37).

3. The third precondition is that we must want the encounter, we must create an empty space where it can happen, and yet we must renounce any expectation that the other person must take part in the encounter. One cannot demand that the other person should take part in the encounter under conditions stipulated by oneself. Such an expectation would immediately create unfreedom and inhibition, and a kind of wall would rise up around the empty space. Lonely individuals often long

to encounter their fellow human beings, but in exactly these circumstances such encounters cannot take place because the longing prevents them. A pseudo-encounter is then often the result (p. 37).

Echoes from past incarnations accompany our sense impressions and color the way we look at the other person. The danger is that one tends to mistake this feeling for a reality in the present moment, failing to recognize it as a memory rising up from former lives. This gives rise to a fourth precondition for encounter.

4. The fourth precondition is that one must learn to be fully present and awake within that self-created empty inner space. One needs a strengthened awareness but also a power of discernment toward everything that goes on. Our own presence of mind enables the other person to encounter us (p. 38).

The Process of Encounter

Once two individuals begin to draw closer together they experience a growing insecurity. They become very vulnerable, having presented themselves without any protection and dropped all their lifelong behavioral defenses. Two things can now happen. Either this feeling of insecurity develops into an experience of the abyss that generates fear, or the two of them escape into a blissful experience of togetherness (p. 38).

To remain within the process of encounter, one must continuously bring one's ego into a rhythmical alternation between establishing oneself and opening oneself to the other. The danger of losing oneself in the encounter can be overcome by a rhythmical alternation between recollecting oneself and being with the other: experience the other, experience yourself, experience the other, experience yourself. This rhythmical process can lead to a culmination in which the actual encounter takes place. Which is an almost timeless occurrence that breaks through like an experience of lighting up which builds a bridge from one individual to another. An essential experience in this is: "There is always a threshold between me as an individual and the world around me." True encounter involves crossing this threshold momentarily (p. 39).

In almost all initiation paths, physical exercise to overcome bodily resistance led to the development of high spiritual faculties. This in itself shows the process of encounter to be one of the highest forms of learning for human beings, only nowadays encounter involves not an external fight but an inner struggle to overcome oneself, with the aim of taking into one's being something that is foreign to oneself. The faculty of encountering can become a fruitful source for many other fields of work and developing capacities.

The conscious schooling of encounter in many forms is something we urgently need, so it should be given a place in every kind of adult learning (p. 41).

Knowledge about the world (Vocational Learning), and knowledge about oneself (Destiny Learning), and knowledge of the spirit (Spiritual Research Learning) go together because it is all three in combination that address the whole human being with all his capabilities, with his connection to the world, to the spirit, and to himself (p. 45).

Young people who have begun practicing even only the basic elements of spiritual research are able to cope with their vocational training quite differently from those who have not made this beginning (p. 45).

The three learning paths have a healing effect when they are combined in adult learning. Vocational Learning without self-knowledge or spiritual research can lead to "blinkered professionalism." Destiny Learning that is pursued without "learning to learn as an adult" or the objectivity of Research Learning can lead to delusions about oneself. On the other hand, Destiny Learning can have a healing effect on the other two learning paths because self-knowledge can signal and overcome one-sidedness, fixations, illusions, obsessions, or any other aberrations that can accompany the other two.

Combining the three learning paths is, moreover, essential for one's further path in life. A good vocational training or university course completed between the ages of 20 and 30 can initially provide support in one's professional life, but it can easily cause an individual to get stuck in a professional deformation in the second half of life. The second learning path is particularly helpful here, since it uncovers and transforms one's one-sidedness, rigidity, and illusions. Over and above this, the basic attitude of research helps one adapt one's professional practice to new circumstances and renew it creatively in other ways.

For the adult educator this means that inwardly he must be able to integrate the three paths and base his professional work on that union (p. 46).

Encounter creates spiritually an "open space," and this open space can be entered and filled from the outside by the independent human spirit that develops when the three learning paths are followed (p. 47).

Every encounter, whether it is a success or not, creates destiny. The path of Destiny Learning brings about the recognition of destiny, whereupon it can be worked on and transformed. Combining these two elements, recognition of destiny and shaping destiny, then makes it possible to bring healing and creative order into destiny as a whole (p. 47).

All learning is based on struggle with resistances. We live in a physical body in a physical world; these provide the resistance through which our consciousness can develop. By trying to deal with our physical reality, we encounter a huge variety of resistances. Our mental, emotional, and bodily activities wrestle with these outer and inner resistances. In contrast with this, when we simply accept and repeat learning material offered by others, and when we copy methods according to instructions, this is more like a kind of conditioning that misses the point of genuine adult learning.

This still does not explain why our conscious struggle against resistances can be transformed into the formation of spiritual faculties that come to expression as gifts, talents, abilities, genius even. The process of transformation takes place during the night, beyond our daytime consciousness. We sleep, yet the learning process continues, but now without the resistances of the daytime (p. 49).

The adult learner can be helped to notice his own progress and realize how it has been achieved, thus enabling him constantly to improve his own progress independently. Independence will grow to the same extent that observing and assessing one's own learning grows. Then daytime learning becomes a conscious schooling path.

Methods such as evaluations, previews, and reviewing one's day backwards may be used. All these can be further developed and refined. Another aid to observation is the individual learning diary. A large step forward becomes possible when one has found a way of evaluating daytime learning in a manner that transforms it into sustenance for nighttime learning, since this gives an extra boost to the next day's learning process (p. 50).

In evaluating the day, it is helpful to imagine a sunset mood that generates a feeling of peacefulness in us. The sun has shone upon everything we did, said, and thought during the day. So in the picture we imagine, the sun appears as a kind of cosmic conscience evaluating our daytime activities and the contribution we have made—even when the weather is bad. At the same time, the sun can also awaken gratitude in us for all that has been given us during the day, for what we have experienced and learned, and how we coped. This basic mood of conscience and gratitude creates the soil on which nighttime learning can grow (p. 53).

Daytime learning is primarily determined by sense impressions, whereas during the night the process is a moral one. That is why the manner in which the evening evaluation of the day is carried out creates the bridge (p. 54).

One good way of beginning the evaluation is to harvest the yield of nighttime learning each morning. Ask yourself questions like: "How am I feeling now that I have woken up? What have I brought with me from the night? How do today's thoughts, feelings, and wishes for action differ from those I had yesterday?" If, for example, the participants in a seminar tell each other their nighttime learning experiences each day, there will quite soon be an increase in their awareness of nighttime learning, and the whole learning process will be speeded up (p. 56).

In their very shape, in the way they follow one after the other, the seven learning processes combine to form another process which proceeds initially from the outside inwards before turning outwards again after it has become individualized. In Steps I and II (observing and relating), cognitive judgment-forming is more to the fore, while Steps III, IV, and V (digesting, individualizing, and exercising) make more use of aesthetic, situational judgment-forming, and Steps V, VI, and VII (exercising, growing, and creative application) incline more toward the moral element in judgment-forming (p. 59).

A sevenfold learning path that existed in antiquity was seen to be linked to the seven planets, each of which possessed its own treasure-house of wisdom. In the late Middle Ages this path flourished in a new form at the School of Chartres, where it was taught in the form of the seven liberal arts inspired by the seven divine virgins revealed to the teachers at Chartres. These seven liberal arts enabled one to build a spiritual chariot in which one could journey to heaven. Those who had succeeded in building this chariot were then permitted to instruct others. Although the Chartres School ceased to exist, it nevertheless remained for many the archetypal manifestation of true adult learning (p. 60).

Learning [today] no longer arises out of the revelations from above mediated by divine virgins; it comes about when life processes are awakened in the human being. We create our own sevenfold path by transforming these life processes, and this takes place in three ways: along the path of worldly knowledge (Vocational Learning), along the path of self-knowledge (Destiny Learning), and along the path of spiritual knowledge (Spiritual Research Learning). It is as though the great School of Chartres were to arise again, but now built up from within in seven learning processes that tread a threefold path (p. 61).

Part II:
From *Practising Destiny* by Coenraad van Houten

Destiny comprises on the one hand the pleasant and unpleasant events that affect us in life, and on the other the instinctive manner in which we respond to them in our own, almost compulsive individual way. There appears to be an inevitability about destiny, as though it emanated from some unknown power. It is a reality in our lives, a reality we experience as inscrutable. However, this way of experiencing destiny changes the moment we begin to regard it as a learning situation we are being offered, a chance to learn how we can change ourselves and thus take a hand in shaping our future. When we treat destiny as a learning situation it becomes a reality in which we can live consciously.

We have a destiny, we live in our destiny, and we weave our destiny ourselves. Destiny is the reality in which we live, but, since we do not live consciously within this reality, it remains hidden from view. This is borne out when we consider our biography, for it appears to us as a picture (p. 65).

Learning from destiny entails recognizing the "whys and wherefores" so as to live increasingly in reality and manage life ever more fruitfully and meaningfully (p. 65).

It is the concept of reincarnation that helps us get to the root of why destiny (karma) is as it is, and, in addition, we also need some knowledge of the processes that take place in the life we lead between death and a new birth (p. 66).

Many people have had experiences connected with reincarnation, and awareness of karma is on the increase (p. 66).

In our destiny we encounter ourselves, for our destiny lives in the human beings and circumstances that now surround us. Many of the people we now meet have lived with us before; they too have learned and changed, having worked on their former actions in the life between death and rebirth.

People who meet each other in their present life come up against the consequences of former actions, but now they are equipped with new capabilities, new possibilities, and changed karmic opportunities. While a destiny event or a meeting with someone can thus often be regarded as the consequence of something in a past life, we must also realize that every destiny event, every successful or unsuccessful relationship, is also the cause of future consequences (p. 67).

The core aspect of any learning process involves transforming one's destiny out of an awareness of reincarnation and karma, for it is through this that one plants new seeds for the future. Every one of us can change from merely bearing our destiny to transforming it, and again from transforming our destiny to recreating it (p. 67).

Reincarnation is the gift of development; the laws of karma are the strategy of development (p. 67).

Destiny Learning begins with a destiny event that has actually happened and can therefore be observed; this is our only firm point of reference (p. 71).

Life provides us with material in the form of events; and more material is supplied by our way of dealing with those events. By objectively observing both of these we can arrive at an initial form of self-knowledge (p. 71).

Learning Step I: Observing a destiny event

The event may be a meeting with someone, a happening in our family or at work, an unexpected discovery, an accident, a surprise, or anything else. It occurs at the crossing point of two or more chains of events, but we may not be fully aware of what all these mean. All we know about is what we have observed with our senses and what inner feelings and emotions it called forth. We are not able to observe in the same way how the event affected any of the other people involved in it, nor what their feelings were. This shows that every destiny event, especially when others are involved as well, represents a crossing point in a web of destiny of which we are vaguely aware but cannot yet see clearly (p. 72).

"A higher intelligence must have been involved in bringing about an event at this particular moment, in this location, involving these particular people, at this very moment in my biography when I am wrestling with this particular life question or when I find myself in this particular psychological state." We realize that serious contemplation of this seemingly superficial event is beginning to make it speak to us. It becomes a destiny event that speaks to us in a language we must learn to understand because it is telling us something about ourselves. With this our new self-knowledge begins.

Initially it is better to choose quite simple, concrete events that are easily described (p. 73).

DESCRIBING THE EVENT

Describe as accurately as possible every sensory observation you made during the event. For example:

a) What was the exact sequence? How were the scenes arranged? Where were different people standing or moving about? Were any objects involved? Who spoke loudly and in what tone of voice? What clothes were people wearing, what colors or shades were there, what was the weather like? And so on.

b) What happened shortly before and after the event?

c) What did you think and feel during the event? Describe your inner observations in connection with the outer sequence of happenings as accurately as possible.

d) What impulses were aroused?

e) Now bring your outer and inner observations together in such a way that a characteristic gesture, attitude, or way of behaving emerges.

This last task is often the most difficult because we are trying to express a qualitative process by means of a picture (p. 74).

Those working though destiny events in the manner here described will have to ask themselves how such events can come to be orchestrated in a way that makes them happen at precisely this location, at this particular time, and with these particular participants and circumstances. No ordinary understanding would be able to arrange things in a way that enables us to experience exactly what we must experience in order to proceed in our lives. Only a higher being would be capable of doing this, so we now begin to have presentiment of how powers of destiny shape our lives (p. 76).

Learning Step II

We investigate our biography in detail and try to find events in which our behavior was similar to our behavior in the events we chose to describe. External circumstances and inner aspects may be entirely different, but qualitatively the gesture shows similar characteristics. Throughout life we are bombarded with impressions, most of which we forget immediately or indeed do not even notice in the first place. But some impressions remain with us (p. 77).

It is helpful to seek out impressions of this kind to discover what the right symptoms are. Three or four such symptoms as examples often suffice to help us recognize our destiny event as something living. This "living something" is revealed as a symptom, a characterization, of our being. It is a characteristic of our being. This means we have taken an important step forward in recognizing the reality of our destiny (p. 77).

The links between the separate symptoms can be regarded as a thread of continuity running through the whole of one's biography. Having discovered such a thread, it is important to realize that it can metamorphose during the course of one's life, especially when it turns out to be one of our life's themes (p. 78).

Destiny weaves in time; it is the golden thread running through our development (p. 79).

OVERCOMING THE MAIN BLOCKAGES AND HINDRANCES

We hinted in our introduction at various dangers that can arise in this Learning Step. The following characteristics will be needed in order to deal with them:

a) The ability to see one's biography as a picture language rather than merely an accumulation of unconnected facts;

b) The ability to observe symptomatically and not only phenomenologically or analytically;

c) The ability to differentiate qualitatively between biographical elements, instead of generalizing everything and ascribing it all to some common denominator;

d) When thinking of a name for the being who has emerged, one must think synthetically (p. 81).

Learning Step III: Finding the causes and discovering the learning task they contain (p. 82)

Our destiny nourishes us only if we digest it properly; if we do not, it creates psychological hindrances. The inevitable consequence of an unfinished destiny task, for example, is being unable to let go: we are carrying undigested destiny around with us. The ability to forget results from working through and digesting destiny in a healthy way. Soul hygiene involves being remorselessly honest in the face of destiny. We need such honesty if we are to lead our life consciously in a way that enables us to develop. Adult learners who want to take charge of their own development must be capable of seeing both why their destiny is as it is and what learning task is hidden in it for the future (p. 82).

This step is, in essence, looking though what has been perceived in the first two steps to what lies behind it. You begin to cross a threshold to touch the "force field" of karma (p. 83).

Our ordinary daytime consciousness is unaware of destiny, as the causes of our deeper feelings must be sought in the period before our birth, and those of our impulses of will in former lives. This is the reason why our legs carry us toward the very destiny situations that belong to us (p. 83).

Our biography is a picture of our destiny, but to find the forces that have created this picture, we have to look back into past lives. Powers of karma are hidden in the depths of our being; they work as intuitions in our will and also in what comes to meet us from outside. Our biography is an imaginative picture of this. So Step III begins with the question: Why? (p. 84)

The second question to be asked in Learning Step III concerns the reason for a destiny event: What is the learning task involved? (p. 84)

Life itself offers us possibilities to develop and learn if we recognize these for what they are, by learning to accept and answer them (p. 85).

1. What geographical conditions are hinted at by the characteristics we have discovered about the "karmic being" we are researching? (p. 88)

Which of the elements of earth, water, air, or fire was predominant? What kinds of etheric qualities set the scene? (This is particularly relevant in Asia: for instance the "light ether" in Russia, the "chemical ether" in China, the "life ether" in India, etc.) (p. 88)

2. What lifestyle do the characteristics of the "karmic being" hint at? (p. 88)

3. Which specific forms of initiation are mirrored in the present characteristics of the "karmic being"? Mystery centers differed greatly in East, West, North, and South—as is still the case today (p. 89).

We do not know all that much today about the kind of societies people lived in long ago, but the forces that formed those societies live on in us today (p. 89).

When people unconsciously bring the rules of an order they have belonged to into a present-day community, this alone can lead to serious conflict and mutual recrimination. The orders of knighthood—King Arthur's Round Table, the Knights of the Grail, the Teutonic Order, the Templars—each had different ideals and aims. Recognizing them liberates us from old bondages and opens up an understanding for social forms that are relevant today (pp. 89-90).

Indian tribes of North and South America, or the past forms of orders, religions, and sects in Asia, e.g., Japan, China, Tibetan monasteries, India, Pakistan, or the Near East: any one of these might have formed our own karmic heritage. Having expanded our horizon in this way, we should not be surprised to find amongst our colleagues a former Dervish, a Benedictine monk or nun, an Indian Brahman, or an African medicine man (p. 90).

The most intractable learning blockage of all has already been mentioned. It is our everyday intellect that interprets everything in terms of cause and effect (p. 91).

To overcome this blockage we need "heart-thinking," or the "logic of karma"(p. 91).

By projecting today's morality onto our behavior in a former life, we can generate devastating disturbances in the objective process of Destiny Learning, because we fail to take into account that with their different attitudes of soul, different religious laws, different duties and power structures, the cultures of other ages cannot be compared with the cultural conditions prevailing in our own time. Human sacrifice, or perhaps burning heretics at the stake, were duties imposed by religion that could not always be evaded—or indeed perhaps we belonged among those heretics. Or perhaps we were involved in tribal warfare in Africa at a time when the enemy had to be exterminated if our own tribe was to survive. Even in fairly recent incarnations there will have been remarkable mixtures of necessity and atrocity. In our life between death and the next birth, beings of the hierarchies show us and let us experience the true cause of our deeds, thereby awakening in us the impulse to compensate for past deeds in the coming life. If we measure the karmic truth against present-day yardsticks we are likely to burden it with heavy feelings of guilt. By doing this, we either cover it up or paralyze our will and fail to tackle the actual transformative task of Destiny Learning. Unconscious self-punishment for old karma that we do not clearly understand is an all-too-frequent phenomenon (pp. 91-92).

Two kinds of karmic blockage

The first type is connected with illusions we have about ourselves, a self-image to which we cling (p. 92).

We fail to realize that the only thing revealed to us is our own self-love. Our vanity appears to be a beneficial being of light, while our artistic gifts bear the mark of genius. Often there are also moral illusions: "I have forgiven everyone so I have no problems with my fellow human beings." Love of self and love of Christ are frequently confused. This euphoria about ourselves, this ego trip, has of course as many faces as there are self-illusions (p. 93).

The second type of "karmic being" is expressed not by a floating consciousness but by a hardening element in one's soul, making it difficult to let go of certain concepts, ideas, feelings, and ways of behaving which remain as though stuck inside us. We languish in a self-made prison, unable to escape and suffering as a result. Fear of karmic reality lives in this being, often reinforced by feelings of guilt.

The one type of being causes us to flee into other worlds to escape the demands of our destiny, while the other shackles us to the earthly world by means of the fear we feel concerning the demands of destiny. Both types can block Destiny Learning, but they do so in very disparate ways. Self-love leads to illusions about oneself, while fear generates a hardening within oneself (p. 93).

In the first type we experience bliss; in the second type we become isolated (p. 93).

One very damaging blockage that is usually unconscious is an inner opposition to any concrete knowledge about destiny (p. 95).

The "four-days-three-nights" karma exercise can also be a great help in finding causes in earlier lives for today's destiny in Learning Step III (p. 98).

Learning Step IV

Did not I ever choose
All my destinies myself?
Whatever happens: I will it.
    Novalis (p. 98)

Accepting one's destiny

Learning Step IV poses a riddle in the formulation "Accepting one's destiny." What is it we are supposed to accept? During the course of the first three Learning Steps, we have discovered one single aspect of our destiny, and no more. This aspect was depicted as a living being, a hitherto hidden part of our own human being (p. 99).

It is of course perfectly possible to encounter this being—and more than once—in circumstances other than those discussed on the learning path described in this book. This part of our being has been given many names: the shadow, the double, the sub-personality, "my other being," "my second being," and so on. In the present context, we are treating this being as an effect of former destiny appearing in us in this life as a second, hitherto unknown person. Since this being can be experienced in a profusion of different guises, any name we give it must be seen as a diminution of reality. We shall therefore term it our "karmic being" without wanting to fix it in any way (p. 99).

By accepting it we individualize it, thus recognizing it as part of ourselves, as something that belongs to us. But perhaps "to accept" is too narrow an expression for what is really meant here. It would be more accurate to talk of "approving" or "affirming" the karmic being, or of "confirming" one's destiny.... Our higher being, our real ego, which has worked on shaping our karma during the period between death and the next birth, experiences nightly what we have been doing with regard to our karma during the previous day. By asking those three questions regularly we connect with this higher ego of ours, and this can enhance our karmic learning path (p. 110).

Our "higher ego" supports us as we pursue the path of learning on which we want to transform our weaknesses into new capabilities. In doing this it connects with our everyday ego, growing through it and extending its consciousness of our individuality.

By accepting and concurring with destiny we enable our everyday ego to join forces with our higher ego. Our everyday ego then becomes capable of receiving the prenatal will intentions of our higher being. This strengthens our everyday will. Nothing gives our will more strength than an earnest acceptance of our destiny. Awakening the will is here an existential act (p. 100).

It is so easy to say we want to accept our destiny and transform it. But we soon forget the tremendous variety of ways in which our own destiny is linked to that of the people we meet in life. We have to accept not only the shadow being we have ourselves created but also the many justified, partially justified, and unjustified actions other people have committed in relation to us. Only when we take all this upon ourselves do we genuinely break with the terrible causality of "an eye for an eye, a tooth for a tooth." In the past, blood feuds and vendettas stood in the way of transforming old destiny into new (p. 101).

So long as we regard life as a once-and-for-all event we remain dependent on God's grace for our salvation and redemption. The concept of reincarnation changes this in that karma and reincarnation bestow on our development the element of continuity, which allows for the possibility of continual transformation until our aim is reached. Destiny itself then becomes God's grace, with reincarnation being the great gift which makes our continuing existence and our continuous development possible (p. 105).

Another means of getting to know our "karmic being" better is to understand its deeds and actions. This requires a good deal of concentration and presence of mind. We live with the question: "*When* do you put in an appearance? What occasions or what conditions rouse you to action? What sense impressions or inner images make me aware of you?" We have to catch the moment when the being appears on the scene, and when we have learned how to do this we go on to the next question: "*What* is the manner of your appearance?" After a while we begin to know our "karmic being" better and better (p. 107).

Our life of ideas, our feelings, our intentions and behavior bear the stamp of today's culture, education, and experience. Yet our "karmic being," which is the result of past lives, is also here with us and every bit as effective. Only when we have truly accepted our "karmic being" shall we be able to detect the effect is has on others.

One aspect of getting to know it is to observe attentively the effect it has on the way other people behave toward us (p. 108).

Once our "karmic being" has become quite familiar to us, we find ourselves getting rather friendly with it. Former fears and illusions, inflexibilities, and euphorias caused by it gradually disappear and it becomes a part of our own being, accompanying us always. A transformation can then begin to take place in which it can become a real friend and counselor, for our "karmic being" knows the means by which it must be redeemed (p. 108).

Four questions are important, in particular, and it is a good idea to ask them each evening like a kind of karmic daily review:

1. When, where and how did I encounter my "karmic being" today?

2. How did it conduct itself during those encounters, and how did it affect those around me?

3. What did I do for it and with it?

4. How should I act for it tomorrow? (p. 110)

Our angel bears this higher ego within its own being. Its task is to ensure that our karma runs correctly during the daytime. It often needs to adapt the shape of the following day to fit what we have learned during the previous day, because it is during the night that it prepares the events of the coming day. Thus it accompanies our process of Destiny Learning very closely, and we become aware of the gradual change in how outer and inner karmic forces work for us and in us. Thus our angel and our higher ego become our allies in the daytime and nighttime Destiny Learning, and they support the transformation of our "karmic being" (p. 111).

Practicing involves coming to grips with resistances. In Destiny Learning it is our "karmic being" that provides the necessary resistance. We maintain it by practicing correctly with it, so that we can transform it into a part of our own being, which will then appear as a new capability (p. 111).

Karmic exercises also help us to develop a new way of "perceiving": destiny-seeing or destiny-hearing. Initially we learn to apply this to the past, but then we can also use it for present life situations. In the end it becomes a perception of our karmic web (p. 112).

As we practice, we first of all notice how something sounds for us in the way a person speaks, not so much in what is said but how it is expressed. This is because the way we speak is an expression of our karma, and this can gradually come to be perceived through Inspiration. That karmic pictures also appear is not a contradiction, since these pictures are usually triggered by what we hear (p. 112).

As we continue to practice the significance of our karmic connections with our fellow human beings becomes more apparent to us, so that we can discern what their karmic questions to us might be (p. 112).

Here we are concerned only with normal learning blockages that get in the way of our destiny exercises. But we soon discover that our "doubles," which consist of undigested old karma, can be very similar to addictions in themselves, only not so strong. Among these are all of our fixed ideas and concepts, the many feelings that are always the same on similar occasions, and every instinctive action (p. 116).

Undigested old karma is an obstacle not only for one's own development but also for the way one relates with other people (p. 120).

Eastern religions have always regarded karma merely as a balancing out of former failures. Once we see it as a process of learning and development on a human scale we discover that those very failings, even the worst, can serve to help us develop specific new faculties which could otherwise not arise. Karma is the great opportunity for us to develop ourselves. In Step III this was hinted at as the learning task; in Step V it was something to practice in everyday life. In Step VI, slowly but surely, the sense of destiny arises as the means with which one can steer future actions. We increasingly discover many different kinds of behavior that are fruitful in this respect (p. 120).

Activities to support the development of the destiny sense

a) The independent adult learning path is necessary preparation for the learning path of self-knowledge described here in which selfless observation has special significance.

b) Aesthetic judgment-forming can be an especially useful support for developing the sense of destiny. This is because we practice it in all kinds of different and changing situations. Judgment-forming is then enhanced and refined until it becomes capable of observing destiny forces.

c) Any exercise that gives us experiences of metamorphosis both in nature and in the soul is especially important.

d) A thorough study of the laws of reincarnation and karma will show us how we can experience and perceive them in reality (p. 122).

We gain greater proficiency in understanding the karmic web of a destiny situation. This in itself changes our experience of that situation, so that a space opens up in which alternative ways of behaving become possible. It becomes essential to ask *how* we should act with our destiny and create future destiny (p. 123).

The first source of help is the realization that in the process of evolution the functioning of karma and reincarnation have their purpose in that the human being shall be able to make mistakes (the "Fall"), learn from these and thus gradually attain freedom of action out of this (p. 124).

The second source of help offers insight not only into the past but also into the future. Evolution can be seen as a path toward freedom. Undigested old karma always shows up as a shackle, an unfreedom, while working through karma brings liberation and openness, as well as new abilities, for the future. It is also very important for the future that we should discover karma to represent a web encompassing the whole of humanity, so that we are all karmically linked with one another (p. 124).

Let us act in a way that enables others to untie the knots of destiny that bind them to us; let us act not only correctly but fruitfully for the future; let us act in a way that serves the aims of evolution (p. 124).

A third source is the knowledge that to bring order into destiny is to place it meaningfully in the cosmic order (p. 125).

Someone acting through knowledge heals by bringing order into his destiny (p. 125).

The fourth source is a new awareness that has to do with our conscience (p. 125).

People actually know very well what they should do, but this awareness is buried underneath their intellectual arguments and body-bound emotions. They do not want to hear the voice of conscience rising up from their subconscious and telling them to do what appears to be illogical or unbearable. Destiny Learning brings the voice of conscience, when we "already know," up to the surface where we can act in accordance with it. Nighttime learning is once again a great help in this respect because it is during the night that karmic reality speaks to us (p. 125).

This new language came to expression in a verse Rudolf Steiner sent on his sixty-third birthday to his close friend and coworker Ita Wegman. We quote it here in conclusion:

Hearts will sense the meaning	*Es deuten die Herzen das*
of karma	*karma*
When hearts learn	*Wenn die Herzen lernen*
To read the word	*Lesen das Wort*
Which shapes	*Das in Menschenleben*
Human life	*Gestaltet*
When hearts learn	*Wenn die Herzen reden*
To speak the word	*Lernen das Wort*
Which develops	*Das im Menschenwesen*
The human being.	*Gestaltet*

(p. 133)

8. Advising

The success of an adult education program rests most squarely on the quality of advising. From the initial inquiry to the years of postgraduate communication, the one-to-one conversations are crucial to assisting an individual on their pathway. One could say that with advising, one is truly practicing destiny.

As seen in the chapter on Adult Learning, andragogy (pronounced an-dr*uh*-goh-jee) is not the same as pedagogy. With young children we work with their native powers of imitation, and over time the teacher becomes a source of authority, first as class teacher and then ever more so through the subject material in the high school. In contrast, in working with adults, the last thing we want them to do is imitate or accept everything we say on authority. Adults learn through problem-solving, conversation (trios and other forms), sharing of experiences, and listening to presentations (instructor and peer) that hopefully inspire. Reflection on practice (internships) and a balance of theory and practice are also essential to adult learning. Along the way, adults need guides, mentors, coaches, and even some educational counseling, all of which can be summarized in the one word: "advising."

Why? Adults have an ego, a sense of self, an identity that should at all times be respected and honored. Even those who struggle mightily have a drop of the "divine" in them. Each person is an enigma, an unknown, and all we can do in our programs is hope to catch glimpses of who that other person might be. Shy reverence is needed in all advising, a deep-seated respect for the mystery of the other human being.

We can assist by asking questions, offering observations, practicing empathy, and suggesting alternative solutions, but in the end the other person has to make the needed personal and professional decisions. All change that has any chance of taking root has to come from within the adult—has to become a resolve. Self-directed learning is what is needed, and advising can provide support and even help stimulate the change process. But the actual change can only be enacted by the individual for his- or herself.

The joy for those who are privileged to work in this way is to bear witness to transformation. When one is a guide and coach, one gets to journey along, empathetically experience the ups and downs, and join in when there is success to celebrate. We are able to partake in so much human drama and human striving, and the learning becomes mutual. We grow when we journey destiny pathways.

The advising journey begins with the first contact, the inquiry, and continues through many stages:

The Inquiry

The first moment of connection often occurs with a website inquiry, an email, or even a phone call. Often the person has a question, a need for more information, or advice on the suitability of a particular program. The "presenting question" is often not the real question, and over time one learns to assist in uncovering the real questions that lie under the surface of consciousness. It is essential that we listen for the real issue or question that has propelled the person to reach out.

A few tips learned along the way:

- Make sure you know what the question really is and don't provide an answer based on the last few inquiries you have handled.

- Do not give too much information, as that can obscure the clarity that the person is seeking.

- Test for understanding: "Is this helpful? Is this what you were looking for?" and if needed, go back to the beginning and start your response all over again.

- Listen for context, especially any biographical tips that are thrown in, so one can help with the human situation and not just stay abstract.

- Outline next steps so there is a clear pathway forward.

- Leave the person free at all times, knowing you may never hear from them again, or the inquiry might be the beginning of a life-long association!

Application

The step of applying to a program is a decisive moment. One is lucky if one third of the inquiries end up as applicants, for the decisions to fill out the online paperwork, write an essay, collect references, and transcripts are will deeds. This is a sign of strong intent, and the level of engagement has stepped up.

It is of course important to review all the written material before the interview, and each organization will have different expectations. But since most places do interviews, here are a few tips:

- Opening and closing are important. I generally open with an overview of what we will do in the interview/conversation and end with a summary and next steps.

- Most interviews involve four strands that can be taken up in a variety of ways:

  A. Biography—What led you to this moment in time and your wish to apply?

  B. Qualifications for the program in question—There are many ways to ask, but it is often helpful to pose questions that require the applicant to "think on their feet," a hypothetical classroom situation, or a possible parent situation: "If stopped in the hallway of your school by a parent, how would you answer the question, 'What are the temperaments?'"

  C. Practical aspects—Here one has a chance to problem-solve together around logistics, support structures in place or that may be needed, finances, schedules, travel. This can reveal how concrete and practical it will be to attend and whether it is the right time.

  D. Questions from the applicant—Hopefully the above conversation has developed some rapport, so at this point any fears, concerns, or hindrances can be named and discussed.

There are some that feel applicants need to pass specific hurdles *before* the application process begins, a kind of pre-screening, questionnaire, etc. Although these tools can be helpful in a very basic way, the more I work with destiny issues, the greater my willingness to suspend judgment until I have read the full application and done the interview. Some of the best Waldorf teachers serving schools and children did not "present" that well in the initial screening! We need to have open minds and entertain the notion that we may occasionally be surprised. Above all, each person does have an angel and they will receive help in deciding which program is best for them at this point in an evolving biography.

Intake Advising

Ideally one would do a week-long biography workshop with all entering students. Few teacher education programs can afford that amount of time and expenses that would have to be carried by the students, yet I often wonder if we would not save in time, resources, and advising issues if we did a more thorough intake. At the minimum, there needs to be an orientation session before classes begin, in which there is some student sharing, an overview of the program, and the early steps of forming a professional learning community.

For those enrolled in summer sequence or low-residency programs, the orientation or intake advising needs to be repeated in mini form each summer. Students need to find themselves again as a group before classes start.

Advising During the Course of the Program

There is so much that could be said here, but perhaps the most important thing is staying in contact. It is so easy to go with "no news is good news" and forget to reach out if an advisee has been out of touch. At times I have had a chart on my desktop with advisee names and would write in a date after each contact, whether phone call, email, text etc. It is amazing to look back at a semester afterwards and realize that sometimes a few students took much airtime, and others were way out on the periphery! I feel that there should be regular contact with all of them, even if it is just a "check-in" with the basic question of "How are you doing?" This is especially important with the growing cadre of distant learners.

Tips for Advising and Supervising Interns

Antioch has long had 12 to 15-week internships, and a variety of colleagues have served as supervisors: overseeing and often visiting to observe an intern while student teaching. Our students also have a "cooperating" teacher, who is host to the intern, sharing the classroom and children, and providing daily and weekly feedback. The supervising teacher provides connection with the teacher-training institute and other courses offered, and the cooperating teacher sees to the integration of the intern into the particular school and provides daily support. At the end of the semester, both do evaluations, and so does the intern. Thus the program has the benefit of three equally valid assessments, which helps with eventual school recommendations and much individual learning.

I asked our current Waldorf Internship Coordinator at Antioch University New England to pass on a few tips for the purposes of this chapter. Carla Beebe Comey offered these suggestions, which also have great value for mentorship in general:

- **Begin with trust and confidence built upon a foundation of mutual respect.** The intern needs to know you honor them as a person beyond their role as a budding teacher, whether they are currently successful or not. This doesn't mean false positivity, and may even lead to the hard question, "Is this the right profession for you?"

- **Offer observations rather than judgments.** By referring to specific observations, we can support the intern in observing their own teaching, encourage them to celebrate their successes, and give them confidence to explore new approaches when challenges arise.

- **Look for what the intern does best.** By focusing upon moments of success and nurturing them, the intern can begin to identify how to expand the capacities they already possess. And as learners ourselves, we supervisors and advisors may even learn something new!

- **Support different approaches.** As supervisors and advisors, we presumably have had many successful teaching experiences, but our approach may not be the intern's best way forward. Help them find their way.

- **Support the intern in approaching their challenges as growing edges.** We all have areas of growth and, if we embrace a growth mindset, we know it is a good thing to learn new things and expand our capacities. Help them identify a growing edge to focus upon and encourage them to continue this practice throughout their career. We are never finished growing as teachers!

Beyond the handling of advising around internship placement, courses, registration, etc, there is a larger narrative involved in the "advising arc" during the entire time a student is enrolled in an adult education program. "The" program advisor needs to be in touch all the time, even if different parts of the program are handled by others. One way to look at this overarching role is to consider the implicit question: Can we write a story together?

What might this mean? Of course, it is about the continuity of conversation, in which a topic, such as struggles with one of the arts, is carried forward over time. But usually the story quickly leans into biographical aspects, for when a person is engaged in a transformative process it is hard to change without looking at past influences. The program advisor needs to "connect the dots" between courses, negotiate issues that come up with other faculty, and serve as an advocate for the student when needed.

Often the advisor has an opinion going into the work, only to have to change it as new dimensions unfold. Along the way the key is to find the right questions and the wisdom to ask them at the right time.

An imagination for the advisor is thus the Parzival story, and the growing realization that we take on new karma as we work more intensely with the questions that rest under the surface of consciousness. (See citations in the "Practicing Destiny Learning" chapter.) One could say that our students collectively become our Grail, the fount of mystery wisdom we serve.

In Goethe's fairy tale, "The Green Snake and the Beautiful Lily," he refers to conversation as "more precious than gold." In an advising context, conversations become an opportunity to practice destiny, to join together in unfolding the deeper mysteries of the human encounter.

In order to ask the right questions, one has to let go, not only of preconceived notions but also of a bit of oneself. Less of "me" and more of "you" is needed. Partly this involves knowing what one does *not know*. Rosicrucian wisdom contains the advice: to trust that when I need to know, I will know. In the meantime, the experience of Nothingness is good soul preparation for advising.

None of us can claim objectivity, but we can strive in that direction through intense inner work. One part is looking at our image of the other person, recognizing that there are assumptions we hold, and then letting them go. The next time the advisor/advisee meet, can one start again with beginner eyes? Forming a picture of the other and then releasing it is a practice needed for all adult education.

There is also the notion from some Native American traditions of "crying for a vision," of seeing insight, a new perspective, or a healing symbol. Over time, in the practice of mentoring, one can occasionally find a symbol or inner picture of the other person that can move the soul, that might even become a healing motif. The work of advising and mentoring is then on sacred ground.

For we also have the assurance from Rudolf Steiner that we must trust in the ever-present help of the spiritual worlds. There is a vast ocean of support, if we can just make ourselves a worthy vessel.

9. Waking, Dreaming, and Sleeping in Waldorf Teacher Education

Working with these three states of consciousness is central to the transformative process of teacher education.

We all experience waking, dreaming, and sleeping, although the latter two may at times be shortchanged in our hurried lives today. Most of the "prompts" we receive daily, whether texts, emails or Google calendar alerts, tend to say: Wake up, pay attention now! The demands of daily living lead us to multitasking, which in reality is not doing things at the same time but switching the focus of attention back and forth in rapid succession. We need to develop a new understanding of the different states of consciousness involved in waking, dreaming, and sleeping and the opportunities they open up.

Waking

Most who today enter a teacher-education program have been steeped in a culture of wakefulness, especially the millennials who have been raised on technology since childhood. This is a fact, and those involved in preparing future teachers need to take this affinity into account at the outset.

Our daily waking consciousness is mostly transactional. We do many tasks—such as driving, shopping, answering emails—that are each one-time events in the day with minimal lasting value for the soul life. These tasks encourage us to live on a certain plane, a state of "getting by in the moment." One small step beyond this plane is to simply build into the day some period of reflection, of quiet time for meditation. After just a few minutes one can be lifted out of the daily grind into a new state of awareness. Mindfulness practices are widely accepted today, and they really work! (I highly recommend the paper on the effects of silence in the chapter "Listening to our Teachers," and the chapter entitled "Personal Hygiene for Teachers.")

So a concrete step in teacher education is to simply provide opportunities for the assembled adults to reflect on their learning of that day, week, or month. This means learning to review. (As mentioned elsewhere in this book, in our Building Bridges Program we use a process called "fact, feeling, essence," but there are many possible techniques). As we go through this chapter I will summarize in bold some of the specific practices that are recommended for adult education:

1. **Build into the day and the program opportunities for regular reflection that can become a habit of soul. The reflective practitioner is more likely to self-educate and learn from experience.**

Consciousness is like any other resource; it can be cultivated or expended. When we live too much in a transactional state of consciousness, we fritter away our inner resources and can feel tired at the end of the day without, perhaps, having accomplished much more than "getting by." But unlike buying something in a store (mostly transactional unless one strikes up a conversation!), consciousness has unlimited value, and cannot be bought or sold. We can work with consciousness and actually create greater abundance.

Our waking soul state has different modalities: thinking, feeling and willing. We are mostly awake in our thinking, but our feelings also inform us every moment of the day, and our deeds often speak back to us. We constantly learn more about ourselves through our thoughts, feelings and deeds. We see ourselves reflected back. One could say this is an education of the *I am*.

2. **Teacher education is essentially a process of self-education, which can be assisted by "coaches/instructors" who understand adult learning processes. The central task for each adult student is to awaken to the "I am," that kernel of the Self that can initiate personal transformation.**

Just as humans populate the earth, spiritual beings (or hierarchies) populate the spiritual world. In the practice of anthroposophy as a path of knowing, one can evoke the interest and participation of Angels, Archangels and Archai (the third hierarchy) when we truly think, feel, and will. These beings participate and assist us when we let them.

So we do things in our programs: curriculum studies, painting, recorder playing, philosophy, movement, etc. But from the point of view of the above paragraphs, the goal of these "subjects" is not to master them, but to wake up to the "I am" using the subjects and activities as a vehicle for greater engagement. The adult student can reflect: I learned to see myself anew through the lens of color, of movement, of class conversation. I am a new person each time I engage in these activities, and in becoming a new person, I can stand before children in the future as a model of transformation and learning! This realization becomes a force of the soul; it stirs the inner recesses of consciousness, and this inner activity later becomes real nourishment for the children.

Dreaming

At first glance, the last thing one might wish for is a class of adult learners who are daydreaming, or even worse, sleeping! But this is in the usual context and does not consider the insights made possible by spiritual science. For these terms can signify much more: they are different modalities of consciousness that can be put to good use in a transformational learning process.

Have you ever been to a museum and found someone standing motionless in front of a great work of art? One does not want to get in the way, for when totally entranced in contemplating art, the person is in a quasi-dream state. You stand in front of a great painting and it grabs you. What was at first just interest becomes absorption. After some minutes you start to feel yourself in the scene, whether beholding the fiery sunset of Turner's ships at sea or the placid blues of Monet's water lilies. A great work of art is an invitation to dream into the creator's images.

And to do that, our imagination has to meet that of the artist. Dreaming is a kind of seeing, but on a different level. Particularly in the art of Waldorf teaching, one needs to develop imaginative capacities to "be there" in the history or geography lesson. The teacher's imaginative capacities can help transport the children, as we all know is the case with a good storyteller.

The Aborigines used to say, "Everything begins as a dream." And Mother Teresa said, "Life is a dream." One is able to live life more fully if one dares to dream once in a while.

If the waking state is all about finding the "I am," the dreaming consciousness is part of finding a way to affirm **I live.** Some of the greatest achievements of human beings began with "I have a dream...." A new nation, civil rights, environmentalism: great leaders help lift us and give us opportunity to dream of a better world.

3. **In teacher education we use the arts, speech, storytelling, painting, and much more to develop the faculty of imagination.**

And again, we are not alone. The spiritual worlds seek to help us, to give us courage to see with fresh eyes, to look into our dreams. In anthroposophy this activity of spiritual seeing is described as the second hierarchy, the Kyriotetes, Dynamis, and Exusiai. The names are not as important as the notion of receiving help through our imagination and our ability to dream, to develop a new kind of seeing.

Students need opportunities to dream and not just memorize new content. Our dreams help us change our lives.

Sleeping

Again, on the surface one might wonder what in the world sleeping has to do with adult education classes. Yet there are deep mysteries involved in the sleep process that, if engaged, can aid the process of self-transformation essential for future anthroposophical adult educators.

Imagine a summer day infused with heat, followed by an approaching thunderstorm: the rolling in of heavy cumulonimbus clouds, the gusts of wind, and then the brilliant lightning flashes followed by claps of thunder. Such a storm can shake us to our deepest foundations. One feels the power of nature that has a will of its own far greater than any one of us.

There is a kind of "testing" of endurance, even survival, that occurs with such powerful acts of nature, as is known to all who have lived through tornadoes, hurricanes, and forest fires.

The will of nature calls for the will in each human at times, to stir us, move us, get us through life. In anthroposophical study, these elemental forces are connected to the first hierarchy of primal beings (Thrones, Cherubim, Seraphim). These are ancient forces that go back to primeval times. The Greeks had an echo of this wisdom in their mythology when they spoke of the Titans, the creators of the world.

It may be hard to believe, but when we are fortunate enough to fall into a deep sleep, we are immersed in that creative ocean of will. Overnight we practice a kind of hearing, a listening to the spiritual world. We are rejuvenated thanks to the obliteration of day consciousness and immersion in slumber. If successful, we can wake up with new determination and will to do things in the day ahead.

In Waldorf teacher education, we seek to engage aspiring teachers in will activities: making main lesson books, moving forms in eurythmy, clay modeling, and much more. In these projects our thinking is less helpful than we might believe; in fact, over-thinking something can actually destroy the project. One has to learn to trust in the movement, the emerging form of the clay or the colors on the wet paper. We can dream a bit, but most of the will forces we expend in project-based learning come from the deep recesses of our sleeping self.

Likewise, the overnight process of real sleep is essential for the processing and transforming of the work done during the day. (See more in my book *School Renewal.*) But this leads us to another core principle of adult education:

Adults need project-based learning in order to access the deep wisdom in nature, the materials used in the classroom, and the genius of creativity.

Just as in waking we seek to awaken self-education to the understanding of the "I am" and in dreaming we give permission for experiencing the "I live," so in sleeping consciousness we work with the creative forces of the **"I will."** When stimulated to work on these three levels, the aspiring teacher can not only serve the children/students better, but also become a more complete human being.

The above considerations are merely a modest beginning to the topic of how differing states of consciousness can play into adult education. So let us take one additional example: class discussion. How can one use awareness of consciousness to facilitate good adult learning in a discussion group? Here are a few tips:

- A discussion, which often is a series of individuals speaking their insights or questions, works strongly with self-expression, or the becoming "I am."

- In contrast, a Goethean conversation in which participants have to carefully build and layer their comments upon those that went before, calls for more of living into the present, the "I live."

- Setting the conversation topic a day or more ahead of time allows students access to the overnight process of sleep and the work of the first hierarchy to develop the "I will."

These are but a few simple examples. The key is that we work not just from our preferred way of teaching but that we try different modalities, since each of the above might access different spiritual forces and invite participation of students by helping them access a variety of spiritual sources for new learning.

Here are some thoughts on states of consciousness from my father, a former student and teacher at New York City's Rudolf Steiner School.

This morning I awoke to a startling thought. You know how we sometimes have frightening dreams, horrible experiences we call nightmares? It might be a terrible fire we can't seem to escape, or a tunnel with little oxygen we cannot get out of. It could be small ants or germs intent on devouring us. It could even be a ferocious plant that chases us while we seem to have feet of clay. No matter what the form, it leaves us powerless, at the mercy of something opposed to us and intending us harm.

The only way to save ourselves from a horrible nightmare is to wake up. If we can somehow elevate ourselves out of the dream condition and enter the consciousness of our daily life, we are redeemed as if by magic.

Suppose our daily life, the consciousness we have when we imagine ourselves to be so intelligent and purposeful, were also something like the nightmare. Maybe it is not quite so terrible and maybe it has wonderful moments of joy in it, but still a kind of conscious nightmare played out among forces way beyond our control! I sometimes am amazed at how rapidly our circumstances change these days. Some days I find myself besieged by worries and threats and then, gratefully, a feeling that everything is after all just fine. There are upsets, arguments, hurtful events, damaging attacks, sadness enough to match the high moments of happiness and joy. Is our current form of living a kind of very real nightmare from which we might need to awaken?

Is there another stage of humanness to which we can open our eyes still further to enter a reality even more real than the one we are currently experiencing? After all, there must have been a time in the distant past when we only had the consciousness of a stone. We must have progressed eventually to achieve the sleeping consciousness of a plant and then the dreamlike awareness of the animal, before achieving what we think of as the supreme awareness of being human. Are we at the end of the road, or is there more to the path that we have not yet imagined?

The thought that started my day is that the real antidote to all the various nightmarish aspects of our current lifetimes may very well be to wake up to a higher self, a consciousness that renders what we are now going through a useful stage, a springboard to a higher and better being.

—Siegfried Finser

10. Social Intelligence and the Emerging Teacher

Teaching is one of the most social enterprises on earth. Surrounded by students all day, most teachers also spend hours in staff meetings, parent conferences and phone or email communications. Yet not every one of us is an extrovert!

Over the years I have observed that a teacher's "social intelligence" can be crucial to success, and the lack of it can undermine even the most educated person. Some seem to have built-in social graces, while others often stumble even with everyday interactions (the nature/nurture issue). So this chapter aims to explore social intelligence in general and then apply it to the teaching profession.

To begin with, what is social intelligence? Using the research provided by Karl Albrecht in his book *Social Intelligence, the New Science of Success*, we can say that social intelligence consists of both insight and behavior: "We can think of social intelligence, or 'SI,' as *the ability to get along well with others and to get them to cooperate with you*" (p. 3).

Building on Emotional Intelligence

Zen philosophy advises: "The biggest obstacle to learning something new is the belief that you already know it" (p. 4). This applies to experienced teachers and those fresh out of graduate school; both prior experiences and newly discovered theory can get in the way of looking at situations with fresh eyes.

Teachers are faced with hundreds of situations each day that cannot be scripted or planned. Rather than just hoping for one "right answer," the choices a teacher has to make are often multidimensional, with curricular, social and behavioral implications...often all wrapped up in one moment in time. A good teacher has to be creative in a particular situation and use a healthy dose of intuition. She has to deal with ambiguity and a host of convergent factors in each situation. There is a high level of subjectivity involved.

Daniel Goleman's seminal work on emotional intelligence, or EI, identified five dimensions of competence:

1. Self-awareness
2. Self-regulation
3. Motivation
4. Empathy
5. Relationships (p. 10)

To what extent does any given teacher have to call on one or more of the above intelligences? To continue with Albrecht:

All of us have blind spots, lenses, and filters permanently installed between our sensory channels and our brains. Our unique blind spots block out those parts of reality that we have chosen not to deal with, these personal lenses magnify those aspects of reality we preoccupy ourselves with. And our filters selectively exclude or rearrange various aspects of reality to suit our existing brain patterns. These blind spots, lenses, and filters operate dynamically—they shift from moment to moment, from situation to situation, programmed by our values, beliefs, desires, expectations, fears, and evaluations (p. 15).

So our blind spots go a long way toward how we frame a situation and thus comprehend what is needed in a social context. Situational awareness is crucial, which for a teacher can mean moment-to-moment decision-making, as well as understanding the culture and larger environmental factors in a particular school.

Albrecht goes on to outline the five characteristics or competencies involved in social intelligence:

1. *Situational Awareness.* We can think of this dimension as a kind of "social radar," or the ability to read situations and to interpret the behaviors of people in those situations, in terms of their possible intentions, emotional states, and proclivity to interact.

2. *Presence.* Often referred to as "bearing," presence incorporates a range of verbal and nonverbal patterns, one's appearance, posture, voice quality, subtle movements—a whole collection of signals others process into an evaluative impression of a person.

3. *Authenticity.* The social radars of other people pick up various signals from our behavior that lead them to judge us as honest, open, ethical, trustworthy, and well-intentioned—or inauthentic.

4. *Clarity.* Our ability to explain ourselves, illuminate ideas, pass data clearly and accurately, and articulate our views and proposed courses of action, enables us to get others to cooperate with us.

5. *Empathy.* Going somewhat beyond the conventional connotation

of empathy as having a feeling *for* someone else, or "sympathizing" with them, we define empathy as a shared feeling *between* two people. In this connotation we will consider empathy a state of *connectedness* with another person, which creates the basis for positive interaction and cooperation." (pp. 29-30)

To summarize, SPACE, the five qualities above, give a person situational radar. Can we practice empathy for those who are not like us, going beyond the surface to sense feelings and intentions? Can a person/teacher "read" a situation correctly in the moment, not just after the fact? We have all experienced people who do not have situational awareness—for example, someone talking on their cell phone in the movies or at a restaurant. Lack of SI can be recalled when remembering Joey Tribbiani on "Friends" or Cosmo Kramer on "Seinfeld." A lot has to do with knowing when to speak and when to refrain from commenting. One has to be able to grasp the context of a situation and then act appropriately.

Here are some of the types of context needed for SI:

1. *The Proxemic Context:* the dynamics of the physical space within which people are interacting, the ways they structure that space, and the effects of space on their behavior.
2. *The Behavioral Context:* the patterns of action, emotion, motivation, and intention that show up in the interactions among the people who are engaged within the situation.
3. *The Semantic Context:* the patterns of language used in the discourse, which signal—overtly and covertly—the nature of the relationships, differences in status and social class, the governing social codes, and the degree of understanding created—or prevented—by language habits (p. 40).

Usually a particular teacher tends to favor one context over another, whether proxemic, behavioral, or semantic. We interpret phenomena differently. That is why it is so important for teachers to work in a professional learning community that encourages multiple perspectives and interpretations. Just as one has to walk around a house to see it fully, teachers need each other to see context. The kindergarten teacher might have a mental image from years ago that adds just the right dimension to a seventh grader's behavior. Someone working with students in gardening will see a side of them that is not necessarily present in geometry.

When a teacher then tries to share insights with the parents of that student, there is yet another demand on situational awareness: the professional or cultural identity of that particular family. Parents can bring biographical and other identifiers to the conference, and will thus interpret what the teacher shares through their own lenses. Firefighters see the world differently from pilots or carpenters. The very cohesion that unites parents in their culture, community, or profession can stand in contrast to the language and mental constructs of the teacher. We all have to be particularly aware when this framing occurs as a result of gender identification, race, or economic class. We want to welcome all children into our schools, and to do so we need multiple layers of social intelligence.

So how can we build skills to develop the various dimensions of situational awareness? Here are a few exercises Albrecht suggests:

- Sit in an airport, at a mall, or some other public place and watch people go by. Try to figure out the kinds of relationships you see between couples, families, and groups. How do they signal their relationships and their affiliation? Do they convey affection and affirmation, or do they seem cold or even antagonistic?

- Study the proxemic contexts you find yourself in. How does the physical arrangement of space and structure influence the way people behave? Who sits where in the business meeting? How does the arrangement of someone's office communicate status or authority?

- Practice identifying the various linguistic frames you encounter in a day. How do people at various levels of social status signal their membership through their language, slang, figures of speech, use or avoidance of profanity, and specialized vocabularies?

- Study the nonverbal signals people use to define and reinforce their relationships. How does the boss convey authority or approachability? How do people signal deference toward others in authority or of higher status?

- Watch a TV show or a movie with the sound turned off. Pay attention to the way the actors move, how they arrange themselves in relation to one another, and how they communicate their roles without sound. Do the nonverbal behaviors contribute to and reinforce the integrity of the scene, or do they seem artificial or contrived? (pp. 66-67)

When a teacher stands in front of a class, or a group of parents for that matter, one can sense pretty quickly if that person has "presence" or not. Often what comes through first is a sense of warmth, or disposition. But there are many levels in which presence is conveyed:

> It's the way you affect individuals or groups of people through your physical appearance, your mood and demeanor, your body language, and how you occupy space in a room. Are you approachable? Do you convey a sense of confidence, professionalism, kindness, and friendliness or do you communicate shyness, insecurity, animosity, or indifference? We all need to pay special attention to the sense of presence we communicate, especially if we want to be accepted and taken seriously (p. 69).

Sometimes schools that embrace an "alternative" to mainstream public education attract both parents and teachers who are non-conformists. This can contribute to vibrant exchanges of ideas, new programs, and spirited discussions, all for the good when done in service of the school and the needs of our children. However, sometimes parents with more traditional aspirations (college acceptances, career orientation, etc.) and those who themselves work in professional services that embrace a more conservative style of dress and conduct can be put off by teachers that come across as unkempt or disorganized. We have to be sure we are inclusive, which means ALL cultures, professions, parental aspirations, etc. There have been times when I have had to talk about "presence" with a graduate student (and there are opportunities after presentations in class when feedback is expected).

Then there is a step up from a friendly presence to charm, or even charisma, characterized by Albrecht as "being that rare combination of grace under pressure, energy, passion for your purpose, and a kind of a life essence that seems to attract energy and attention wherever you go."

> Maybe the essence of real charisma—the earned kind—is what goes on inside. Those who perceive someone as affirmative, admirable, and compellingly attractive may be reacting to the outward and visible signs of that person's inner commitment to life. One gets the sense that great spiritual leaders—Gandhi, Mother Teresa, the Dalai Lama—would go where they go and do what they do regardless of whether others chose to follow them. Paradoxically, maybe others follow them not because they lead, but because they know who they are and where they're going (p. 74).

For teacher education, of course, we cannot expect that every student who walks through the door will be a future Mother Teresa, but are some of the qualities described above absolutely necessary to survival as a teacher these days? Those who are "affirmative, admirable, and compellingly attractive" in terms of presence among others will certainly have a leg up in public situations, but do we then rule out those who are more reclusive, shy and awkward? The idealist in me wants to believe that anyone can become a teacher, and coaching, self-development, and inner commitment can overcome any hindrances. Yet this idealism is mitigated by the reality of parents who often don't hand out second or third chances when social intelligence is seriously lacking.

This then leads to the importance of self-awareness and Steiner's "basic exercises" and other tools available through work with anthroposophy. One of my dear colleagues has been leading groups of students in our Explorations programs by coaching them on one basic exercise per month. Imagine an entire group in a school community doing a month on positivity, then equanimity, then open-mindedness! They each had a conversation partner to share experiences, but otherwise were left completely free in terms of daily practices. Reports from the school have been extraordinary in terms of community impact, but one cannot begin to measure the effects on a personal level for these teachers and parents.

Albrecht frames this work in terms of emotional intelligence and living in the moment:

> It's also a question of balance, being able to parse your emotional commitment for those situations in which a human connection is called for, and not overreacting or losing perspective. This requires being emotionally self-aware and centered....
>
> Consider the way in which a Zen-like equanimity—a mode of thinking about the present experience—can give you better choices, either in dealing with others or with important situations (pp. 82-83).

He then goes on to describe practical exercises to help build a greater sense of presence in which it can begin to speak for itself (*res ipsa loquitur*):

> Things you can do to increase your skills in the dimension of Presence include:
>
> - Don't try to "present" like a movie star (or anyone else); find your most natural way of telling who you are by the way you stand, walk, talk, dress, and interact. Find and express your own "voice." Try to imagine what the experience of meeting you for the first time would be like for another person. How do you want it to be?
>
> - Write a brief description of yourself, as another person might describe you after having met you. What would you like people to say about you? Start working on specific aspects of that ideal description to make sure they're real.

- Leave a long message on your voicemail system and play it back a few days later. Get an idea of how you sound to a stranger. Make a note of any aspects of the way you speak that you would like to change.

- Record a conversation with friends, either in audio or video format. Make it long enough that everybody forgets they're being recorded. Study yourself and the other participants and note any habits or behaviors that contribute to or inhibit empathy, clarity of communicating ideas, and authenticity.

- Ask one or more close friends, preferably individually, to share with you the impressions they got when meeting you for the first time. This might also be a way to gently invite them to share with you any aspects of your interaction they feel could be improved (pp. 85-86).

Another significant aspect of SI work centers around building a greater sense of authenticity. Albrecht suggests we keep track of situations in which others tried to induce us to act in ways that went against our personal values. He suggests we monitor our reactions and the inner dialogue that ensues. When have we been able to live up to our personal code of conduct, and when have we compromised that by avoiding disagreement or direct conversation? He even suggests writing a personal mission statement that articulates personal priorities and the things that make life most meaningful (p. 105).

He also encourages use of the active voice as much as possible, something he calls the E-Prime:

> E-Prime forces you to write in the active voice; in fact, it eliminates "passive voice" verb forms automatically. To review: passive voice language tends to hide or subordinate the "actor" in the sentence: "The office *was searched* and the file *was found* by Mary." In E-Prime writing tends to make for shorter sentences. Count the words in the first, passive-voice example (11) versus the second, active-voice sentence (8). Writing in the active voice, or E-Prime, forces you to choose your verbs (and their order) more carefully (p. 132).

Along with this, we need to increase our skills in expressing ourselves with clarity to help hold the attention of our listeners, looking at the flow of ideas, sequencing, use of facts and figures, metaphors, word pictures, and of course, humor.

And then there is empathy:

This dimension invites you to look at how truly aware and considerate you are of others' feelings. Are you able to tune in to other people as unique individuals? Do you show that you're willing and able to accept them as they are, for what they are? The usual connotation of being empathetic means to identify with another person and appreciate or share his or her feeling. However, in the context of social intelligence, there is an additional level of depth—the sense of *connectedness*—which inspires people to cooperate. In this discussion, empathy is defined as a state of positive feeling *between* two people, commonly referred to as a condition of rapport.

To achieve empathy with another person means to get him or her to share a feeling of connectedness with you, which leads the person to move *with and toward* you rather than *away and against* you (pp. 137-138).

There are specific exercises one can practice to build empathetic skills:

- Study a person who seems unable to connect with others easily; make a list of specific behaviors you observe that seem to alienate others. Make a list of behaviors he or she could adopt that could enable him or her to connect more skillfully.

- Study a person who seems to connect with others easily; make a list of specific behaviors you observe that seem to attract others and invite them to connect on a personal level.

- Imagine that you meet Mr. or Ms. Stoneface at a social function. Write down five things you can say or do to "loosen him/her up," that is, to invite the person to share more freely and to express more energy in the way he or she interacts (without clumsily instructing the person to "Smile!").

- The next time you witness—or participate in—an argument or dispute between two or more people, make a list afterward of the toxic, empathy-destroying things any of the participants said or did that might have aggravated the situation, or might have made it more difficult to resolve.

- If you have a close friend or a "SOSO" ("spouse or significant other"), offer to make a deal with that person to use the four-minute rule every time you meet for the next week. Spend the first one to four minutes talking only about one another, and not doing any of the day's "business" until you've re-established your personal bond (p. 156).

In building empathy, we need to be particularly alert to toxic behaviors and killing other people's ideas with phrases such as:

- It won't work here.

- We tried it before.

- It costs too much.

- The board will not approve this.

You can often get people to listen and respond more open-mindedly if you use the following kinds of *idea-selling* statements in your conversations:

- May I ask a question?

- Before we make our final decision, let's review our options.

- I suggest we not eliminate any options at this point.

- Are we ready to decide? Have we considered all the key factors?

- Let's discuss the way we're approaching this problem.

- I'd like to back up a step and clear up a certain point (p. 141).

In short, there is the Platinum Rule: "Do unto others as others prefer to be done unto." This leads Albrecht to L.E.A.P.S, which stands for Listen, Empathize, Ask, Paraphrase, and Summarize (p. 152).

To better work with the creative tensions on the path to SI, Albrecht includes two helpful charts to work with. They might make good companions in almost any meeting as one listens and learns about social intelligence in the workplace!

Adjective Pairs Exercise

Toxic						Nourishing
Argumentative	1	2	3	4	5	Diplomatic
Boring	1	2	3	4	5	Interesting
Bossy	1	2	3	4	5	Cooperative
Cold	1	2	3	4	5	Warm
Critical	1	2	3	4	5	Affirming
Inarticulate	1	2	3	4	5	Articulate
Inconsiderate	1	2	3	4	5	Considerate
Long-winded	1	2	3	4	5	Concise
Manipulative	1	2	3	4	5	Honest

Moody	1	2	3	4	5	Even-Tempered
Opinionated	1	2	3	4	5	Open-minded
Rude	1	2	3	4	5	Courteous
Self-important	1	2	3	4	5	Humble
Short-tempered	1	2	3	4	5	Tolerant
Timid	1	2	3	4	5	Outgoing

(p. 168)

How do you prefer to interact?

By organizing these two dimensions, *social energy* on one axis and *results focus* on the other axis, we have four primary combinations, or *interaction styles*, represented by the four "window panes" in the grid diagram shown [below] (p. 170).

INTERACTION STYLES

For the teaching profession, which relies so heavily on social skills, I would like to propose that workshops and faculty conversations entertain skill development in SI and all that has been presented in this chapter. We cannot just focus on content in our teacher-education programs; delivery is crucial, and that involves presence in the classroom and with parents. These skills are capable of development, even when faced with daunting challenges.

I would like to conclude this chapter with an inspirational quote from Helen Keller, a person who, despite huge sensory challenges, was able to exemplify social intelligence:

> I who am blind can give one hint to those who see—one admonition to those who would make full use of the gift of sight: Use your eyes as if tomorrow you would be stricken blind. And the same method can be applied to the other senses. Hear the music of voices, the song of a bird, the mighty strains of an orchestra, as if you would be

stricken deaf tomorrow. Touch each object you want to touch as if tomorrow your tactile sense would fail. Smell the perfume of flowers, taste with relish each morsel, as if tomorrow you could never smell and taste again.—Helen Keller (p. 159)

Social intelligence can become a new sensory organ of perception! See Appendix for additional information.

11. Rudolf Steiner's Indications for Waldorf Teacher Education

There were no teacher training programs in Steiner's lifetime. He did it himself, as we know from the *Foundations of Human Experience, Practical Advice,* and *Discussions* lectures, but in 1924 he gave a very short course in Bern known to us as *The Roots of Education,* in which he gave a few hints in the third lecture. He mentioned that clay modeling, music, and speech were essential because they gave teachers the possibility of sensing a child's higher members, the emerging etheric, astral, and ego. "If you have acquired this insight into human nature you will discover a great deal that will help you in your teaching.... Your observations of the child will inspire you with ideas and methods for your teaching and this inner inspiration and enthusiasm will pass over into your practical work" (*Roots,* p. 59).

So the emphasis is on "acquiring insight into human nature" that leads to "ideas for methods" for teaching that will allow for inspiration and enthusiasm. Certainly we all know how an inspiration or new idea can fire us up for the task, and thus the central point of teacher education is to provide the anthroposophical tools for a meditatively acquired knowledge of the human being so that teachers *of themselves are able to find the means and methods needed* to respond to a classroom full of very particular children. This "ground tone," one might call it, cannot, must not be forgotten in the rush to simply give future teachers more and more material, curriculum coursework and methods. As described in more detail in the "Adult Learning" chapter, simply using a pedagogical, instructor-centered approach to teacher education will not work. We need *to provide the conditions that support the discovery process* in which future teachers have the tools to find their own methods and new curriculum materials.

One of the original teachers at the first Waldorf school was Caroline von Heydebrand. She had planned to travel to London to help Steiner with a teacher training course being planned for the "new school." Unfortunately she died a short time before the course was to happen, and Maria Roschl took Heydebrand's plan as it had been approved by Rudolf Steiner.

As Ron Jarman and Brien Masters state, it is in some ways the original concept of teacher education, as it contains remarks by Steiner passed on to Heydebrand (*Child and Man* article, p. 37).

> If one gives one unit to each of the three general topics [see below], two units to each set of practical arts in each column and one unit to each of the other four units in each of the three columns, one gets a total of $3 + 3 (2 + 4) = 21$ units. If each unit is then given 7 hours, one arrives at 147 contact hours. This, together with an equal time given to in-service [apprenticeship-type] training would make a good minimum for a year's training (Jarman, p. 38).

It is interesting that these early thinkers went right down into concrete units and balancing the various spheres of activity, while giving indications that are also deeply esoteric when one lives with them for a while. What follows is the original version (including wording and format) of Heydebrand's outline for a teacher-education curriculum, which we understand received Rudolf Steiner's blessing:

GENERAL WORK:

- Study of the human organism as confluence of the Arts (given by arts teachers, doctors and science teachers)
- Study of *How to Attain Knowledge of the Higher Worlds* as a guidance book on self-education.
- Learning the art of looking at artistic productions.

THREEFOLD CURRICULUM FOR STUDENTS:

The Sculptural ("Plastic") Element (etheric body—Imagination)
- Modeling, Painting, Carving, Drawing, etc.
- The element of imagination in the English language and literature (to make the student see and create inner "visions")
- The sculptural forces in the kingdoms of nature, especially in Geology and Botany
- The sculptural forces in Geometry (Synthetic Geometry)
- The power of imagination in fairy tales, sagas, legends and mythology

The Musical Element (astral body—Inspiration)
- Music, Harmonics, Tone Eurythmy
- The musical element in the kingdoms of nature, especially in Zoology; also in Chemistry

- The musical element in Arithmetic
- Rhythms in the evolution of the growing human being (7-year periods)
- Study group on teaching and education

The Speech Element (ego—Intuition)
- Speech formation, Speech Eurythmy
- The dramatic element in History (method of teaching History)
- The evolution of individuality in mankind (biographies)
- Comparative study on the spirit of different languages
- Health and illness (what the educator has to know about medicine)

There is so much here that is enigmatic, to say the least! If one can get beyond the stylistic issues due to the time in which these things were composed, how can one find value in the above indications?

First some commentary on the opening section on "General Work":

1. The call to work with *Knowledge of the Higher Worlds* and self-development seems straightforward, and most programs today have courses on research, self-development and anthroposophy. But the other statement is more challenging:

2. Study of the human organism as confluence of the Arts (given by arts teachers, doctors, and science teachers)

Does this mean coursework in Physiology, taught by teachers, doctors and science educators? I remember Francis Edmunds doing marvelous things with Anatomy in a way that all of anthroposophy seemed to come alive. One needs to be a true generalist for this kind of instruction. And doctors are not too visible in our teacher-education programs.

Perhaps the indication points more to *The Foundations of Human Experience* (formerly *Study of Man*). Those seminal lectures are full of Physiology, and when taught by an educator who also has ways of working with the arts, and with an occasional doctor guest presentation, we might be approaching this aspect of what is called "general work."

In the section above on the threefold curriculum for students in teacher-education programs, there is much that can be extracted by looking at each section in relation to the third lecture in *The Roots of Education*. We will take each section separately:

The Sculptural Element (etheric body—Imagination)

First, he draws a distinction between the physical body and the life body (etheric) as experienced in the activity of modeling with clay:

THE ETHERIC BODY AND THE ART OF SCULPTING

> First, we should learn to sculpt and work with clay, as a sculptor
> works, modeling forms from within outward, creating forms out of
> their own inner principles, and guided by the unfolding of our own
> human nature.... Now let's look at the physical body; it is heavy
> with mass and subject to the laws of gravity. The etheric body is
> not subject to gravity—on the contrary, it is always trying to get
> away. Its tendency is to disperse and scatter into far cosmic spaces
> (Roots, p. 38).

Then Steiner relates the etheric body to the periphery, in this case the
stars, and the experience of space:

> The different groups of stars are drawing out the etheric body in
> varying degrees; there is a much stronger attraction from one group
> of stars than from another, thus the etheric body is not drawn out
> equally on all sides but to varying degrees in the different directions
> of space (p. 39).

We find this dynamic when we examine the forms found in the human
skeleton, contrasting the tubular and the rounded bones:

> We must try to model these varying forms in clay, and we will find
> that, in one particular form, cosmic forces act to produce length;
> in another the form is rounded off more quickly. Examples of the
> latter are the round bones, and the former are the more tubular
> bones.... Like sculptors therefore, we must develop a feeling for the
> world—the kind of feeling that, in ancient humankind, was present
> as a kind of instinctive consciousness.... One must be able to turn
> to the great "cosmic sculptor," who forms the human being from a
> feeling for space, which a person can also acquire (p. 40).

And then we get to the point of it all, the "study of the human organism
as confluence of the Arts" mentioned under "General Work" earlier. We
develop an image of the human being by working with soft clay, and this
new knowledge of our special orientation helps teachers work with the
laws of the etheric, which of course also occur with painting, drawing,
image formation in storytelling and literature, and, I would argue, also
in many aspects of meditative work. But the arts are especially helpful in
developing a teacher's orientation in space:

> If we could only allow this feeling for space to take over, the true

image of the human being would arise. Out of an active inner feeling, you will see the sculptural form of the human being emerge. If we develop a feeling for handling soft clay, we have the proper conditions for understanding the etheric body, just as the activity of human intellect connected with the brain provides the appropriate conditions for understanding the physical body.

We must first create a new method of acquiring knowledge—a kind of sculptural perception together with an inner sculptural activity. Without this, knowledge stops short at the physical body, since we can know the etheric body only through images, not through ideas. We can really understand these etheric images only when we are able to reshape them ourselves in some way, in imitation of the cosmic shaping (p. 41).

These are mighty thoughts! Without them, we educate others only from the perspective of the physical, the brain, and outcomes-based learning. With "sculptural perception" we can begin to work "etheric images" that can reshape us, transform us into new human beings. For the artistic work we do in clay modeling imitates the greater cosmic shaping of the universe!

The Musical Element (astral body—Inspiration)

Next, Steiner moves to the second aspect of teacher education described in the Heydebrand document:

THE ASTRAL BODY IN RELATION TO MUSIC

Just as the etheric body acts through cosmic shaping, the astral body acts through cosmic music, or cosmic melodies. The only earthly thing about the astral body is the beat, or musical measure. Rhythm and melody come directly from the cosmos, and the astral body consists of rhythm and melody (p. 42).

So if we want to work with the whole human being to effect the maximum transformation of the growing teacher, one has to not only take into account the laws of the etheric, but also the astral. And we can do this in all that has a musical quality:

For example, you will find that when the interval of a third is played, it can be felt and experienced within our inner nature. You may have a major and minor third, and this division of the scale can arouse considerable variations in the feeling life of a person; this interval is still something inward in us. When we come to the fifth interval, we experience it at the surface, on our boundary; in hearing the fifth, it is as though we were only just inside ourselves. We feel in the sixth we are passing beyond ourselves; and as we enter the sixth and the seventh, we experience them as external, whereas the third is completely internal. This is the work of the astral body—the musician in every human being—which echoes the music of the cosmos (p. 43).

Again, Steiner relates this to physiology:

If you take the part of the human being that goes from the shoulder blades to the arms, that is the work of the tonic, the keynote, living in the human being. In the upper arm, we find the interval of the second. (You can experience all this in eurythmy.) And in the lower arm the third—major and minor. When you come to the third, you find two bones in the lower arm, and so on, right down into the fingers (p. 43).

Please note the words in parentheses in this paragraph: "You can experience all this in eurythmy." This not only underlines the importance of eurythmy in our teacher-education programs, but also shows again that by "musical element" Steiner does not just mean teaching a lot of music (although that is also a good thing in itself). What is meant in this second section of the Heydebrand document is the musicality, the astral consciousness that runs in many subjects, such as Arithmetic, Zoology, Chemistry…indeed all that is taught out of an understanding of the "rhythms in the evolution of the growing human being" or seven-year periods. It is hard not to include all subject areas when considered in this light. But the point is that the Waldorf teacher strives to work in such a way that the musical element is engaged, that we work with *intervals in learning* (main lesson blocks, for example) and that we work rhythmically. The teacher thus needs to become both a sculptor and a musician in this generic sense.

The Speech Element (ego—Intuition)

Then we come to the third aspect of Heydebrand, again elaborated in the third lecture of *Roots of Education*:

I-being and the Genius of Language

> Now we come to the I-being. Just as the astral body is investigated through music, the true nature of the I-being can be studied through the word.... If you understand language in this inward way, then you will see how the I-organization works (pp. 45-46)

So just as we can make the case for the teacher as sculptor or musician, we now see the third essential element of speech. Perhaps no other aspect is used more frequently in our schools than human speech. We talk all day long. But *how do we speak with the students? And what stands behind what we say?*

As indicated in the above citation, if we understand language in this deeper way, we begin to comprehend the I-organization, the holy sanctuary of the inmost human being. Thus, in a way, working with speech is deeply personal and can penetrate to the very core of another human being. Speech teachers in our programs are often challenged as no others as they tread on this sacred ground. We need to articulate more clearly than ever why we do speech, and then work with the group with a unique combination of enthusiasm for the content and shy reverence for the personal space of the other human being.

Education in medical and teacher training colleges should be advanced as indicated, so that the students' training may arouse in them an inner feeling for space, an inner relationship to music, and an inner understanding of language (p. 46).

Children in Waldorf schools are so lucky to have teachers who tell stories, who enjoy conversation, and who put on dramatic productions. None of this can be done adequately with online instruction (see more on online instruction in the "Future Pathways" chapter.) In fact, the sculptural, musical, and speech pillars of Waldorf teacher education all go to the essence of education, the fundamental goal of all we do in schools: fostering the human encounter. As long as this planet is populated with people, we will need to find ways to work together. Our teachers are pioneers in the social art of empathy, respect, and hope in a future worthy of our children and grandchildren.

Finally, I would like to honor three colleagues in teacher education who have exemplified the three aspects of the work described in this chapter. All three have served teacher education for decades, have been my valued colleagues in the Antioch and Center for Anthroposophy programs, and have "walked the talk" in all their classes. One would only have to take a course from each of the three individuals below to know, intuitively and in practice, all that was spoken above in regard to the sculptural, musical, and speech elements in Waldorf teacher education:

Arthur Auer—clay modeling
Carol Kelly—music
Craig Giddens—speech.

12. Kindling Imagination, Inspiration, and Intuition in the Waldorf Teacher Educator
A Continuation of the Three Aspects of Teacher Education Covered in the Last Chapter

In striving to be successful, most teachers try to bring vivid, imaginative stories; inspiring new techniques in teaching math and science; and an intuitive knowing of when to intervene in a student issue. How to get there is, of course, another matter. It is part of the teacher preparation process to find pathways that lead to imagination, inspiration, and intuition.

To this end, it is helpful to work in new ways with thinking, feeling, and willing. These three soul faculties, core to the lessons we teach children, are also crucial to teacher-education programs. For in working with these faculties, one has an opportunity to engage what Rudolf Steiner called the third hierarchy: the angeloi, archangeloi, and archai. "They reveal themselves as the spiritual powers active in the soul and are accessible to higher forms of consciousness" (Tautz, p. 7). But, unlike most things in life desired by humans, these powers cannot be "acquired" on the sensory plane of existence. Although close to humans, they hold back, do not intervene of themselves, but hover expectantly on the boundaries of our daily activities. This non–interference allows an individual to become conscious of his or her own being (p. 10).

This is a remarkable fact, if one really thinks about it. In order to give humans space, to allow for freedom of initiative, the hierarchies "hold back" and wait for the call. In past times, they spoke directly to human beings, especially initiates and spiritual leaders in cultures around the globe. These leaders could then teach and guide human beings in matters large and small. But today we are surrounded by silence...unless we reach out and ask for help:

> The stars once spoke to man.
> It is world destiny that they are silent now.
> To be aware of this silence
> Can become pain for earthly man.

But in the deepening silence
There grows and ripens
What man speaks to the stars.
To be aware of this speaking
Can become strength for spirit man.

　　—Rudolf Steiner, Christmas 1923 (*Verses and Meditations*)

One of the best ways to engage the third hierarchy is during sleep. Especially if prepared with a bedtime review and silent meditation, the aspiring teacher can encounter each spiritual hierarchy during the various phases of sleep. (More on this can be found in *School Renewal* and other anthroposophical sources.) But the key to this engagement with the angeloi is that we acquire new sources of imagination, through meeting the archangeloi new feelings of inspiration, and through the archai new abilities to fire up our will forces. Thinking can become imaginative, feelings are inspired, and the will becomes stronger.

An aspiring teacher needs to be able to vividly see the figure of Gandhi walking through rural India to make salt by the sea. This is not about mere telling (or memorizing the lines), but *a living into the picture* of his white robe, his bare feet, his facial expressions, seeing his gestures. The good teacher becomes Gandhi, at least for a few moments in the classroom. The children are then transported to the scene; they become participants in the drama of history. This is the use of imagination at its best.

An aspiring teacher needs to look for sources of inspiration beyond what is available in a Google search. Yes, one needs to do research, as that activity in itself stimulates inner processes, but it is not enough. How does one invite inspirations so that the science class the next day is not just "taught" but riveting? Here, one has to work in a way that spontaneity is welcome, that the unexpected thought can arise. This can happen while brushing teeth or taking out the garbage. Inspirations mostly arrive unannounced if one cultivates a kind of listening. Then one can teach magnetism by inviting just the right two students to assist at the experiment table, ask a question that holds everyone's attention, and then work with the materials to awaken curiosity. A good science class is factually correct and delivered with a flair born from inspiration.

An aspiring teacher needs to cultivate a soul life that allows for new perception, not just of sensory matters, but of the inner voice. A good teacher intuitively calls a parent, perhaps without any concrete objective, but knowing conversation is needed. So often the parent might say, "I was just about to call you! Such and such is going on in our daughter's life and we thought you should know..." This ability to take intuitive action comes from deep in the human psyche, from the soul forces of will. All too often today we rationalize away these impulses with an outer task: "I need to pick up groceries for dinner first." Of course it is important that teachers be able to feed their families, but we cannot always let the outer tasks rule us. Sometimes we need to listen to the voice of conscience, and to intuition. And again, some silence in our lives can help.

These are mighty goals for the striving Waldorf teacher, but even some progress along these pathways can make all the difference. It starts in the teacher-education process, perhaps at first simply entertaining the thoughts expressed above. Then one has to find opportunities to practice, again and again. A long internship or practicum can give multiple opportunities to work with these realities in new ways (and many encounters in sleep). It is so important that one make space for this work, and not just attend meetings and collect materials.

Speaking of meetings, it was only after writing the chapter on Rudolf Steiner's indications for teacher education that I remembered the College Imagination given at the time of the first teacher preparation weeks in August 1919:

> Behind each single member of the evolving College of Teachers we see his **Angel** standing. He lays both his hands upon the head of the earthly man entrusted to him. And with this bearing and this gesture he enables **strength** to stream forth. This strength endows the work to be done with the **Imaginations** that are needed. The Angel stands behind each single one to awaken creative Imaginations full of strength.

> If we raise our gaze, we see a group of **Archangels** sweeping along above the heads of the evolving body of teachers. As they circle around and return, they carry from one individual to the other what is coming to birth through the spiritual meeting of each individual with his Angel. They then bring back to the single member the strength which has been enhanced through uniting with all the others.

> Within this circling, which works like a spiritual sculpting, a chalice is formed above the heads of those who are united in a common striving. This chalice is composed of a very special substance: it is fashioned out of **courage.**

> At the same time, the circling Archangels who unite the teachers,

allow creative forces of **Inspiration** to stream into their moving and shaping. They open up the springs, whence the Inspirations we need for our work well forth.

If our gaze is raised to penetrate still further, it reaches up into the sphere of the **Archai.** These do not present themselves as a totality, but from out of their sphere—the sphere of light—they allow a drop to fall into the chalice of courage. We can become aware that this drop of light is given to us by **the Good Spirit of our Time,** who stands behind the founder and the founding of this new school. In this gift of light, creative forces of **Intuition** are at work in order to awaken the Intuitions needed for our new educational tasks.

In this way, the Third Hierarchy—bringing gifts of strength, courage and light—takes part in what has now been founded. These Beings have the will to unite themselves with our earthly deeds, working though Imagination, Inspiration, and Intuition (as recollected by Herbert Hahn, Jan. 11 1967).

These mighty pictures were given to the evolving group of teachers entrusted with establishing the first Waldorf school. Today, we need imagination, inspiration, and intuition more than ever if we are to continue with the work beyond 100 years.

And, one might add, the difference between a good teacher and a great teacher may be determined by the level of encounter with the third hierarchy. New imaginative capacities can give us "enlightenment" in the true sense of the word. New inspirations give us the courage to teach, because we are now enthusiastic. And intuitive capacities empower us to do what we know must be done at the right time and for the class in front of us in the moment. Looking at the teaching profession today, we can truly wish for en-lightenment, en-couragement and em-powerment. Our children, our schools, and our society today need such teachers more than ever.

13. Developing the Art of Imagination:
Why Creative Speech Formation is an Essential Part of Teacher Training
by Debra Z. Spitulnik

Every morning our classes begin with a morning verse that Steiner gave to the teachers. No matter what age we teach, we then incorporate into our classes some form of verses, poetry, movement, music, review, new material, story, instructions. We speak all the time, either individually or in chorus. Creative Speech formation makes us better teachers: clear in our instructions, enlivened in our storytelling, soulful in our poetry and objective in our experiences. We can listen more deeply and understand why a student doesn't understand. We can experience their spirit and soul in words because we have done it for ourselves.

Only when working out of Creative Speech formation in our teaching is our ego sense fully engaged. A Creative Speech class addresses every aspect of what one needs in order to be an excellent Waldorf teacher—curriculum, classroom management, self-development and artistic skills—which is why teacher training centers provide classes in Creative Speech.

To deepen our understanding of how to effectively teach Creative Speech to teachers, I began a Pedagogical Speech Study with 15 participating teachers in the fall of 2019. In March 2020, everything changed and the schools closed due to the pandemic-induced quarantine. What now, as schools scrambled to provide classes in a way never thought possible in Waldorf education? How could we do this knowing how important direct interaction and engagement are to the child—and to the teacher? Where do we find the strengths in this endeavor? Pedagogical speech is one of those strengths, as teachers must bring curriculum in an enlivening way, even (or especially) when teaching remotely. This sudden, radical change in the educational environment brought an entirely new way of studying and learning about the importance of Creative Speech in training teachers.

To those who understand the sense of speech
The world reveals itself as image.
(Steiner, *The Genius of Language*)

It is our job as teachers to imbue our speech with imagination, to allow our students to hear and learn with their whole being. Children don't hear words, they feel and experience images. When we touch their soul, integrating the intellect with feeling, they learn. We never want our students to say, as this first grader did: *"When I listen to an audiobook or a story being told, it is so boring because there are no pictures—just words words words."*

As educators we use words incessantly, hardly taking a breath. This can literally take our breath away, and with it any power to create and form images. How can "the world reveal itself as image" through the sense of speech, and how can this be useful in the classroom?

In Creative Speech, the student learns to sculpt sounds and words to create a picture. For example, the word "dust" can be experienced by moving through each sound to create "dust" as an image so real that the speaker and listener can see, feel, touch, live it. Steiner was very clear that this must be done to enliven sounds, words, sentences, whole texts. If the teacher speaks through enlivened speech, whether giving directions, telling a story, speaking in a faculty meeting or with parents, the audience will understand and listen in a newly active, engaged way.

Another important aspect of this process is creating *objective* images. When images are held too closely or sympathetically—held inside by the speaker rather than projected outward—the listener cannot experience the image properly. The speaker must project the images to the listener as though they were shown on a screen in 3D. Without this outward projection, the spoken words and images become tied to a person rather than the spiritual, etheric reality. When the speaker is too inward-focused, listeners are not free to create their own relationship to the spoken word. When the words are filled with an inner gesture and inner experience, yet still spoken objectively, listeners are free to create their own relationship with the text, and students learn, becoming part of the learning process.

Learning this skill is particularly hard for adults. All we experience in the age of individual consciousness is that "I am important and the center of the world," or "You are an individual and important." However, communicating the objective picture that we can experience between or beyond us is much more difficult. Because adults use abstract thinking as their primary learning mode, it is not an easy or intuitive jump to experience that objectivity; just to try it can be confusing. However, once adult learners "hear" it in a classmate's speech and experience the difference, they are excited and work to do it themselves.

> Speech has enhanced my storytelling, especially the images that I bring to my students. At first I was more conscious of my speech, trying so much that it felt worse, but as I keep working with speech I have experienced the depth and breadth of a story in an objective way and am able to give that to the children. (PSSP—Pedagogical Speech Study participant)

Speech formation enhances storytelling, a major component of Waldorf education, so a pillar of Waldorf teacher training must be strengthening and enlivening the way we tell a story. When we tell a story that we have *experienced*, not just heard, our listeners experience it too. When we tell a story we have read through our intellect alone, it becomes cold, sharp and linear. The students may like it, but they are not fully engaged and neither is the teacher. Modern research confirms that human beings' experiences are not just about what they themselves do, but also what they hear and see others doing (Patzlaff, 2019). They make it their own. The study shows that young children do not remember the difference between what they have done and what they see or hear others doing. According to Patzlaff, the activity of doing a task and the inner gesture of speaking that task, i.e. "Chop, chop, choppity-chop," helps the child understand language. The movement, gesture, and word take place in the child's sense organs and are recapitulated in their own language or movement.

> To those who understand the sense of speech
> The world unfolds its true being.
> (Steiner, *The Genius of Language*)

> I am not conscious of when I am "doing speech," but it is clear to me when I am not, and when the students are not. (PSSP)

When listening to another's speech, the other's true being is revealed: their thoughts, feelings and actions are exposed. This is why speaking in public has been cited as one of the most frightening activities, and why adults find Creative Speech classes challenging. By requiring the speaker to look within himself to find the image and project it outward, something of his personal experiences and feelings is exposed. But when adult learners are willing and able to be vulnerable with this learning, their ego becomes engaged and their capacity as a listener is enhanced. We now listen not just for the words, but for the gesture, images and experience behind them, and we can understand one another. This builds community, empathy, trust and respect; and it can also be very frightening, for reasons discussed below.

In the classroom we are constantly assessing our students in various ways. By listening to different aspects of their speech, we can get a glimpse of their struggles and strengths. Can they articulate properly? What sounds do they or don't they hear? Can they communicate through images and does their spoken language make sense? If teachers do not develop these capacities fully through their own Creative Speech work, what we hear may be merely abstract, ignoring a key component of the students' being.

> To those that live in the Spirit depths of speech
> The world bestows Wisdom's strength.
>   (Steiner, *The Genius of Language*)

> When I am not breathing properly, my words get stuck or jumbled and the students get breathless. My teaching of the material then is unclear, and the students misbehave or get breathless themselves. My ego is not engaged, and then I have even less control of the classroom and the material. (PSSP)

The human spirit lives in speech, which points in the direction of the future while teaching of the past and living in the present. Breath is the spirit of life, and with the breath of our speech we can create the atmosphere of our classroom's spirit. In his first lectures to teachers, Rudolf Steiner explained that our main task is to teach children to breathe (Steiner, *Foundations of Human Experience*). If we teachers are not using our breath with the healthy rhythms of our heartbeats and lungs, we will not be able to discern the proper breathing rhythm of a lesson, with its aspects of expansion and contraction. With Creative Speech training the teacher learns to use the breath artistically, experiencing the expansion, contraction and rhythm of texts in a way that enhances their speaking.

Before our recent experiences with recording lessons and providing videos for our students due to the quarantine, we rarely had the opportunity to listen to ourselves. This has now changed, giving us greater opportunity to observe how we can improve the breath and images in our speech.

> When I listen to the recording, I can hear when I do not articulate properly or when I haven't breathed into the word to create a moment or an experience—an image. (PSSP)

Throughout my work in training teachers and in our ongoing study, I have seen the lack of breath in participants' speech, especially when I observe their teaching. Creative Speech formation teaches us how to regulate our breath to a healthy rhythm without constantly being conscious of it. When we learn to speak the way Steiner indicates, we sculpt the sounds carefully, holding the image of the word as we begin to articulate its sounds. As the formed sounds move on the stream of breath, our image of the word moves along as well, and the words combined with the inner gesture and image touch the listener's soul.

The difference between vowels and consonants is not intuitive, but lies at the foundation of Creative Speech. Vowels have a musical quality; consonants are expressions of the outer world and have a sculptural quality. We can form pictures and shapes with consonants, which relate to the elements: earth, air, water, fire. We cannot form pictures with vowels, but no true word can be spoken without them. They are in some ways the heart of a word, the magical quality that brings it breath and life. If someone lives too much in vowel sounds, the sympathy in their speech is often extreme and uncomfortable. Too much breath or too much reliance on vowels can make the speaker seem ungrounded and not genuine. Conversely, if someone speaks more strongly through consonants, their presentations can be experienced as harsh. It is important in andragogy to balance these forces in the teacher so the child's soul is not imposed on by our speech.

> All vowels express inner soul stirrings that live in the sympathy we have toward things. Consonants are related to things and sounds outside ourselves. Consonants live in antipathy—they sound from the object without. In speech we have a genuine synthesis, a true uniting of the human being (Steiner, *Practical Advice to Teachers*).

> In transposing gestures into sounds, we learn by means of the consonants to imitate inwardly outer processes; and in the vowel we give form to inner experiences of the soul. In speech the inner and the outer unite. Human nature, itself homogeneous, understands how to bring this about (Steiner, *Human Values in Education*, pp. 61-62).

To those who can lovingly dwell on speech
It will grant its own creative might.
Thus, I will turn my heart, my mind
Toward the spirit and soul of Words,
And in my love for them
For the first time, I will
Feel My Self complete.
(Steiner, *The Genius of Language*)

By focusing on and improving my speech, it helps me to keep the curriculum living and imaginative, enabling me to reach the students and affect their ability to learn. (PSSP)

A teacher's voice impacts the quality of a student's articulation, modulation, breath, and, above all, engagement. Steiner emphasized the importance of surrounding children with elevated speech during the day for healthy development. "…[D]on't forget that children have to speak in class; good speaking is part of the instruction given at school" (*Speech and Drama*, p. 30). In today's overstimulating world, where children are bombarded with electronic hum, the quality of the teacher's speech is more important than ever before. Perhaps the antidote to the degradation of students' linguistic experience and development is innovating new techniques as we deepen Steiner's indications for Creative Speech.

Young children imitate the teacher's speech and find this fun; they like to play with sounds and words. If they don't know something, they are excited and curious to learn. Adult learners are the opposite. Adults' egos are already formed; their ability to move into a more intimate and precarious realm is hampered by their biographies and life experiences. Everyone has their history that guides them to become a Waldorf teacher, and that history is evident in their speech. Creative Speech comes directly from the astral body modified by the ego or "I" (Steiner, *Speech and Drama*), therefore it reveals adults' deep feelings, their etheric and astral bodies, their ego strength. Animals make sounds that convey needs; in human beings, this ability is raised and transformed by the ego. When adults begin to transform their speech, becoming conscious of form, inner movement, strength or weakness, they feel vulnerable. This presents a challenge to teacher-training students because while they are learning the Waldorf approach to pedagogy, child development, and curriculum, they are required to address some internal challenges they may not have addressed fully in their past. Clearing away those cobwebs creates space.

In addition, the adult student is expected to memorize words and sentences. Because memory and rhythm live in the etheric realm, its strength or weakness also becomes apparent during a Creative Speech class. Sometimes the student awakens to this in a conscious manner for the first time; often it is difficult. When the adult learner rises to the challenge, the result is a more well-rounded and gifted teacher. This is challenging and exciting, for the adult then has the opportunity to take up different aspects of their being and transform them, both for themselves and for the students they will teach. We are asking the adult learner to transform their already incarnated ego and give that away to another being while keeping it for themselves.

Great self-development can happen through speech, and frequently it does. But when the adult has no idea what to expect and thinks she is taking a speech class simply to learn how to tell a story or recite poetry, it can be a shock. Our task as teachers of Creative Speech to adults is to imbue ourselves with love, warmth, and knowledge for our subject and humanity, while still leaving the student free to discover the joys and struggles of finding their own authentic voice. The only way to truly find that as a teacher is to penetrate our astral and etheric bodies with our ego, to enlighten and lift ourselves out of the daily physical world to our higher self. Only then can we take up our task as teachers to help facilitate the ego incarnation of our students.

> In speech, the ego works as a puppeteer might, controlling the three other sheaths of the human being. When the ego is present, the astral is contained in a healthy way, managed. Speech strengthens the ego by awakening the individuality and sense of self. The more we participate in speech formation, the more the ego is called on to bring out this individuality. The spark of spirit that strikes the ego intensifies. Speech formation demands that the ego manipulate and move the etheric, astral and physical bodies. In this way the ego is strengthened and brought into the body (D. Spitulnik, 1995).

14. Connecting with Archetypes:
Why Eurythmy is an Essential Part of Teacher Training

My first experiences with eurythmy occurred when I was four years old. A small group of children in Spring Valley, NY was given the opportunity to enjoy some stories, verses, and songs in movement with Lisa Monges. She taught us in her large living room (the space that is now the Fellowship Community for the elderly) and I remember the unusual experience of being in a larger group, wearing red overalls and funny slippers, and meeting new children through movement. As a dreamy Waldorf student in the years that followed, I had eurythmy twice a week throughout the grades and into high school, even doing some additional individualized therapeutic work to help with back problems one year. I remember in particular the experience in 7th grade when we were asked to write poems and then the eurythmy teacher did them with us in class. Much to my surprise, my poem was better in movement!

Eurythmy classes continued in a European Waldorf high school, but often my peers and I took more joy in tormenting the instructor than anything else. I cringe when I look back on how we hid her watch, scarf, and other items, driving her to distraction (that particular teacher had some personality traits that made our antics ever so tempting). Then there was a break from eurythmy during college, and it was with mixed feelings that I encountered eurythmy again in my Waldorf teacher training in Garden City, NY. Much to my surprise, here everyone loved our Friday afternoon eurythmy classes! This was in large part because our teacher charmed us with her joy and light-hearted approach. We did some amazing work, and the relationship with that particular eurythmist has since lasted a lifetime.

As faculty members at the Great Barrington Rudolf Steiner School, we often did eurythmy before our business meetings. Our discussions were much more successful when preceded by movement. Then, in my first decade at Antioch University supporting Waldorf teacher education, I started a Collaborative Leadership Program which we took to schools around the country. Two gifted eurythmist colleagues took turns leading a particular aspect called "Eurythmy in the Workplace," a social form of eurythmy that helps teachers, parents, administrators and board members develop group skills, communication, leadership, and much more. We did a series of three institutes in a half-dozen schools during the 1990s. In 2014 we continued this work, now under the auspices of Antioch's Center for School Renewal, in a program for Waldorf school administrators and leaders.

Over the years, eurythmy has been a vital component of our Waldorf teacher-education program at Antioch New England and the Center for Anthroposophy. In fact, both the founder and the second director at Antioch were themselves eurythmists. Many, many students in our elementary and high school teacher-education programs have become better teachers because of our inspired eurythmy instructors. Just recently, we did an alumni survey, and eurythmy ranked way up there as one of the most successful aspects of our teacher-education program over 40 years.

During Renewal 2019, Eurythmy Spring Valley came to our summer site in Wilton to share a marvelous program on the Pine Hill stage. It was exquisite, one of the best I have ever seen. But my joy was ever greater as I started to feel how the audience around me was moved. Laughter, sadness, tragedy through storytelling, poetry, music…all transpired before us in living color with veils and amazing lighting. At the end, as with one accord, the entire audience rose to give them a long standing ovation. In a way that seldom happens any more in this cynical world, the audience was transported through the beauty of the art.

Of course, I am not a eurythmist (although both my mother and sister-in-law were), but I have had an experience as a teacher educator over three decades that I wish to share here: When I teach my courses, mostly research, administration, and evolving consciousness, my classes are much more successful when my students do eurythmy and the other arts *before they come to my class*. It is hard to describe why. When they walk into my room without having had an artistic experience ahead of time, they are still good people seeking to learn, but the cognitive work only goes so far. Discussions can easily stay intellectual and abstract, and I have to work hard to "warm them up" and lift them into imaginative, participatory spiritual work. But when they do eurythmy for an hour or so first, they are ready! They come in smiling with a healthy glow, they take up the work holistically, they seem integrated and truly open to new ideas. Learning after artistic experience is exponential rather than just summative.

Why does this happen? From the perspective of this one layperson, I offer an observation: We each have a higher self that strives to move us forward in life. Our deepest intentions as an individual on this earth hover as potential within us, waiting to be realized. If we can connect with archetypes that are true, if we can recognize the ever-present reality of the spiritual world—and it can happen through music, painting, poetry, story-telling, and many other ways even by those who are not overtly spirit seek-ers—there is an opportunity to let the spirit self work ever more actively with our more earthly oriented Self or "I." In the experience of eurythmy, this growing incarnation of the self-aware "I" can work more actively with our consciousness and begin a transformative process. There are many spiritual paths that work with the transformation of consciousness. But what happens in eurythmy, at least in my experience, is that through con-sciously willed movement, the experience does not just remain in the one sphere, but delves into the vast ocean of life forces and right down into the physical. In short, *the whole human being in all dimensions is engaged when doing eurythmy!* The deepest soul experiences become visible through speech and tone.

If teacher education is all about transformation, becoming the per-son our children need us to be, then I cannot think of any better way to accelerate the process than working with the arts, eurythmy, speech, music, painting, Spacial Dynamics, drama.

For decades now, many educators have been subjected to standardized testing, pre-packaged curriculum plans, learning outcomes, and more and more online instruction. Many have told me that *they know these methods are not in the best interests of their children*, but they feel they have to conform as "employees" in a hierarchical system that often fails to listen to teachers. Now, out of necessity due to Covid-19, almost all children are at home doing lessons online week after week. Of course, as in times of war and famine and other catastrophes, one has to do certain things out of necessity. But I predict we will have a new challenge to deal with after this is all over: *online sensory deficit disorder.* Yet that goes beyond the scope of this book.

As for Waldorf teacher education, there are of course areas where Zoom and other tools can help. Valuable content and some methods work can be done reasonably well. If one has established a good working relationship with students, one can even do *individual practice* with virtual prompts (I recently did the Hallelujah in a webinar led by a eurythmist). It was, at least for me, a mere echo of past experiences. When I ignored the screen I was able to do the exercise for self-hygiene, but I so missed the nourishment and joy of sensing others in the space around me. Just as stay-at-home families can have fun playing Monopoly and yet cannot bring those bills to the store to buy groceries, so one cannot pretend something is what it is not. We may watch movies featuring walks in the mountains, but it is not the multisensory experience of actually walking the Appalachian Trail. In this time of "alternative facts," it is important that we are truthful: truthful to ourselves and our students. Let us distinguish between reality and semblance, and let us not use the same name for both.

Also, as a scholar and writer, it is deeply ingrained in my being that the work of others needs to be fully acknowledged with accurate citations. It is a matter of integrity. The practice of eurythmy is also a matter of authenticity and professional standards. It is not to be overlooked that the training to become a eurythmist requires 4-7 years' work. If we do not hold to authenticity, the substance we offer (in any profession) becomes dissipated and may no longer have much value.

Our world needs fully integrated teachers who are able to work with multiple intelligences and teach holistically. Eurythmy develops social/emotional intelligence, helps us engage all the senses, helps with aesthetic judgment formation, lifts feelings through visible music and speech, and helps us become integrated, healthy human beings. These are the things teachers (and all humans) need more than ever. I urge all my readers to summon the courage at this moment in time to stand up for the arts as never before, and to stand for all that is beautiful, good, and true.

15. Practicing Between and Beyond:
Tri-une Thinking and the Training of High-School Teachers

by Douglas Gerwin

FIRE

What makes a fire burn
is space between the logs,
a breathing space.
Too much of a good thing,
too many logs
packed in too tight
can douse the flames
almost as surely
as a pail of water would.

So building fires
requires attention to the spaces in
between,
as much as to the wood.

When we are able to build
open spaces
in the same way
we have learned
to pile on the logs,
then we can come to see how
it is fuel, and absence of the fuel,
together, that make fire possible.

We only need to lay a log
lightly from time to time.
A fire
grows
simply because the space is there,
with openings
in which the flame
that knows just how it wants to
burn
can find its way.*

—Judy Sorum Brown

---

* Judy Sorum Brown, *The Sea Accepts All Rivers and Other Poems* (Miles River Press, 2000), p.34.

The graduation of the high school Class of 2020 marked a watershed in American independent and state-run education. Across the country, very few, if any, seniors participated with "Pomp and Circumstance" in a face-to-face commencement, since restrictions on public assemblies resulting from a worldwide outbreak of the coronavirus prevented schools from staging this annual ritual. Some graduates received their high-school diploma in the mail after a virtual ceremony online; others were promised a "real" celebration once the coronavirus pandemic had receded. However, except for a few courageous souls who had gone back to earn their high school diploma as adults, these graduates all shared a common trait: none of them was born into the less security-conscious world that their teachers knew when they were growing up themselves as children and young adults.

The reason? As of 2020 every child enrolled in an American educational institution—from early childhood programs through high school—began life on earth after the U.S. was shaken and reshaped by an attack of 14 terrorists using four hijacked commercial jets on the morning of September 11, 2001. We have yet to see the full measure of the consequences wrought on young souls by this assault, the only major foreign attack on civilian home targets this country has experienced in close on two centuries. Yet we can already say this much: children born in America since that date, though they may have come "trailing clouds of glory," are growing up in a culture much more conscious of security, much more concerned about germs and allergies, and much more restrictive in what teachers—parents, too—are allowed to risk with the youngsters in their care.

Feeling Safe in a New Age of Nervousness

When it comes to characterizing social trends, statements of cause and effect are guesses at best, tendentious expressions of prejudice at worst. In fact, the very concept of "cause" does not really belong in discourse about changes in the development of the human soul. Causal statements of "if/then" are really no more than relational statements of "when-then" clothed in statistics, leaving the reader to sort out what is the "egg" and what the "chicken," both of which can serve each other mutually as effect or cause.

That said, there is no disputing that teachers on the frontlines of the high-school classroom who tell us that their students are ever more anxious and "stressed out" these days, less able to sit still, more likely to make use of hand sanitizers, less likely to get a driving license or go out on a date, and more prone to attempt—and in growing numbers commit—suicide. In my own experience with high school students, I encounter fewer and fewer cases of truculent teenagers who say, "I won't!" and many more cases of trepid students who say, "I can't." We have entered a new age of heightened mental and emotional—even to some extent physical—paralysis.

Rudolf Steiner predicted this human condition more than a century ago. In a popular lecture known in English as "Overcoming Nervousness," Steiner characterized a trend of increased anxiety and fear that was already taking hold during his time. "Everywhere," he told a German audience in January of 1912, some two years before the outbreak of World War I, "something like nervousness is present." He went on:

> All this will, in the near future, grow worse and worse for people. If people remain as they are, then a good outlook for the future cannot by any means be offered. For there are harmful influences that affect our current life in a quite extraordinary way and that carry over from one person to the other like an epidemic. Therefore people become a bit diseased in this direction: not only the ones who have the illness, but also others, who are perhaps only weak but otherwise healthy, get it by a kind of infection.*

Today, even more all-encompassing than the pandemic attributed to a new strain of the coronavirus that brought social and economic commerce to an abrupt halt in the spring of 2020, we live in an atmosphere of nameless anxiety that accelerates in our students—as in ourselves—an arresting petrification of soul.

In this same lecture, delivered fully seven years before the opening of the first Waldorf school in Stuttgart, Steiner castigates educators who induce a condition of pedagogical terror in their students by making them cram for what today we would call "high-stakes testing." However, never one to leave his audience in a state of despair or hopelessness, Steiner spends the rest of this lecture outlining no fewer than ten practical exercises on how we as adults can come to grips with what is by now a worldwide psychological ailment.

In this context, we need to ask: Given that teenagers are growing up in

---

* Rudolf Steiner, "Overcoming Nervousness," lecture given in Munich on Jan. 11, 1912 and published in *Anthroposophy in Everyday Life* (Hudson, NY: Anthroposophic Press, 1995). The original title of this lecture, found in Volume 143 of Steiner's collected works, is "Nervosität und Ichheit" ["Nervousness and I-hood"], which hints at how the adult human being can best overcome this condition.

an age of societal anxiety—a condition exacerbated by the use of smart phones and the internet, which have been shown to arouse stress even at a neurological and hormonal level—how are they to be educated? And how best to prepare their teachers to educate them?

Step for a moment into the shoes of a student and you will recognize that if you are suffering an intensified state of stress or anxiety, you will probably be unwilling, or simply unable, to learn anything new until you feel safe in your place of learning. In a condition of heightened stress, you are more likely instead to protect and defend what you know and shut out or simply ignore what you don't know or can't control.

Cramming for a test in high school is an archetypal example of this condition. You marshal your needed material, you attempt to gain mastery over it by organizing and committing it to memory, you protect what you have mastered from anything that might threaten to challenge it or disturb your general knowledge base. It would be simply too scary to admit into this ordered *corpus* of understanding an unfamiliar perspective or an epiphany of new insight.

More generally, if students don't feel safe, they won't move, which is to say that in order to move or be moved—whether outwardly in physical activity or inwardly in soul and spirit—they need to feel safe. But this relationship between safety and movement can be reversed: movement can stir confidence (and a sense of safety) as much as safety can build confidence to risk engaging in movement. We are dealing with a symbiotic condition of "when-then," not a logical condition of "if/then."

We can say, therefore, that in educating teenagers (younger children, too) we need first to make sure they *move*. But here's the rub: whatever pressure an adult exerts on a student from without will inevitably create anxiety in that student, who will feel—rightly—the alien source of this pressure. Though in younger years children need to be steered toward healthy situations and protected from harmful ones, ultimately movement needs to arise from within, not from without.

In fact, all healthy movement arises from within, even if it is initially stimulated from without. This is the secret of the free human will, easily overlooked because clouded in unconsciousness and, among younger children, still largely undeveloped. With the exception of the reflex—an autonomic (and hence entirely unfree) reaction to the stimulation of the nervous system—healthy movement originates from within the human being, even if it is in response to outer guidance. Only when the kid moves will the kid learn.

By the time of high school, guidance from without must give way to inner self-direction and a sense of confidence if something is to be regarded as "learned." As in honing the skill of riding a bicycle, you cannot claim to have learned how to ride if your training wheels are still attached.

Though the development of this inner self-direction is gradual, by the time of adolescence it holds the key to successful high-school education. And yet no age group is more prone to paralysis born of anxiety than is puberty. For this reason, adolescents need their teachers to be skilled in three roles, or what I will call the "3PC's" of the high-school educator:

- Teacher as pedagogical coach
- Teacher as pedagogical counselor
- Teacher as pedagogical compass

As pedagogical coach, a teacher deals with *how to develop practical skills,* helping teenagers find purpose in work and confidence in conducting themselves in the world. This is why in high school the most trusted teachers are often the ones who can tell you how to do something yourself. Driver's ed instructors, gym and athletic coaches, practical arts instructors, computer techies, nurses and medics: these are the faculty and staff members who most easily garner a teenager's respect. And notice how coaches, of whatever discipline, are generally big on "safety first."

As pedagogical counselor (not to be confused with psychological therapist), a teacher deals with *how to handle feelings,* or more precisely how to sort out the confused skein of human sentiments that so easily tie teenagers up in paralyzing emotional knots. Good counselors know to use feelings as opportunities for learning; to pose questions rather than supply answers; to jointly come up with strategies rather than provide ready-made solutions. They, too, are committed to creating a safe environment for the unfolding of their students' emotional life.

As pedagogical compass, a teacher deals with *how to think,* but again not by providing answers but rather by helping students develop leading questions that will help them discover uncharted terrain for themselves. A good compass indicates direction quietly and steadily, albeit vibrating slightly and adjusting constantly on an acute needle point to changes in orientation.

In all three roles, the teacher's secret to success is to educate by stirring the student to move, whether that movement is physical or bodily, psychological or emotional, spiritual or mental. The teacher sets up the safe conditions in which the student can dare to try, to fail, to learn, and in this way to become motivated increasingly from within, free of outer prodding.

From Binary and Relational to Tri-une Understanding

In a binary way of seeing, the world is comprehended in pairs of "either/ or." William Blake, in a letter to his friend Thomas Butt, identified this way of seeing as the approach of reductionist science, or what he famously called "Single vision & Newton's sleep." On this view, movement—both inner and outer—is accounted for in the logic of cause and effect, and indeed, purely physical events, like a rock falling to earth, can be adequately described by the laws of causality or "if/then." (Even Albert Einstein, with his theory of relativity, would agree that the earth is more the cause of attracting a falling rock than the rock would be the cause of attracting a rising earth.)

Once we shift from mineral and mechanical objects to living or organic beings, however, the laws of logic no longer provide an adequate account of the phenomena. Now we need an understanding based on relational "when-then" (sometimes called "both-and") ways of thinking. Chaos theory, field theory, quantum theory, "flow" theory: all are attempts to comprehend the world in terms of "when-then" relationships rather than simply causal "if/then" connections. This approach shifts us away from the study of things as objects into a study of things as processes, and, in so doing introduces an element of movement (for instance, "flow") that is not essential to an understanding of material objects, even if they are set in motion. You don't need to see a car in motion in order to understand how a car works. The same cannot be said of a river or a growing plant or an animated worm. A river not in motion is no longer a river but rather a stagnant cesspool no longer able to do what a river is supposed to do; a plant that is not growing (or decaying) is a lifeless specimen, deprived of the essential characteristics of a living organism; a worm that is not able to wiggle is a sterile fossil—a noun, no longer a verb.

When we come to studying phenomena in their spiritual, metaphysical, or eschatological nature, we need to shift once more into a broader, more all-encompassing form of understanding that needs what I am calling tri-une thinking, which, to put it in its most abstract form, requires not simply two terms of if/then causality, nor even the relational terms of when-then, but rather three terms that have the relation of "when-and-when: THEN!" In this view, we study phenomena not only in terms of their polar complementary relationship ("when and when") but we watch for a third term that arises out of these two terms as a new "...THEN!" that transcends both of them while embracing each of them.

Before considering some examples of this way of thinking and its relationship to the training of high-school teachers, we need to be clear what is not meant by tri-une thinking. This mode of thinking is no additive model in which two or more elements are combined to yield some third element that simply contains aspects of both elements in a new configuration. For instance: it does not take tri-une thinking to say that a little white plus a little black yields a new shade called gray.

Nor is tri-une thinking meant to be a way of reconstituting an original whole that has been broken into its constituent parts. This is what was supposed to have happened for Humpty Dumpty, but, as we know, "all the king's horses and all the king's men" failed to glue him back together again. As any child knows, Humpty Dumpty is a living, fluid—indeed, a very oversized fluid—integrated organism, not a static lifeless mechanism of separate parts.

So, what is "tri" and what is "une" about tri-une thinking? And how does this thinking help overcome anxiety through movement? The essentials of this way of thinking are dramatically captured in *Man on Wire,* a documentary film shot by the French tightrope walker Philippe Petit, who during the hazy dawn hours of August 4, 1974—a quarter-century before the events of 9/11—unrolled a steel cable between what were then the unfinished Twin Towers of the World Trade Center in Lower Manhattan and then, carrying only a 50-foot long pole, proceeded to walk back and forth eight times across this swaying metal rope. At the high point of this film, *Man on Wire,* you see Petit setting off on his daring stunt by first gingerly stepping off the edge of one of the towers with an anxious, taut expression. After a few tentative steps, however, a new look comes over his face: his brow relaxes, his posture straightens, the hint of a radiant smile creeps across his countenance—and he is launched across the 200-foot-long wire strung between the towers roughly a quarter-mile up in the air. On both sides of him, to the left and to the right, lie the risks of a precipitous fall, but thanks to these polar complementary forces (assisted by the long pole), a dynamic balance is created that allows him to glide with seeming effortlessness from one tower to the other. Notice again, that both immanent dangers, of falling to the left or falling to the right, are needed for this third direction—straight ahead—to open up. Petit does not wobble or lurch from left to right or right to left: his gait is confident, his step safe and steady, his destination ahead leading in a quite different third dimension of space.

Rudolf Steiner offers countless examples of this tri-une way of understanding in a deeper way all manner of phenomena: in the constitution of the human body (birth and death), in the working of the human soul (sympathy and antipathy), in the healthy operation of the threefold social organism, in the relationship of the good to two polar complementary principles of evil—at one pole the luciferic, or what Aristotle calls the evil of "too much"; at the other the ahrimanic, or what he calls the evil of "too little"—to say nothing of artistic practices including the art of healing and the art of education. In each of these examples, we are dealing with three elements, but the third arising from the first two is of quite different order of being. Good is of a different order than the two forces of evil which it transcends; love represents the transcendence of antipathy and sympathy (as sympathetic parents must know when they release their children into free adulthood); life embraces birth as well as death while transcending both.

And what about the "une" in tri-une? In reconciling opposite poles in a transcendent third term, we experience the overarching unity of this relationship. In the case of *Man on Wire,* Philippe Petit enters an entirely new yet fully encompassing universe when he sets out across the cable strung between the Twin Towers. In the examples supplied by Rudolf Steiner, "death" is subsumed under the overarching term "life" rather than being set in opposition to it, just as the "good" embraces rather than opposes "evil" in its double guise, and "love" includes the harsh gesture of antipathy—perhaps better known as "tough love"—along with the more commonly accepted gesture of gentle sympathy.

In the language of the Romantic poets (and also of Rudolf Steiner), the practice of this kind of disciplined thinking is described as being the cultivation of imagination as a mode of cognition: that is, not as a flight of fancy but as a coherent way of knowing the lawful inwardness of things. Others call this practice metaphorical thinking or holistic thinking (by means of which a greater whole is perceived to transcend any of its parts) or holographic thinking (when that greater whole is revealed in each of its constituent members). Whatever its name, tri-une thinking bridges polar complements and, while retaining both poles, moves into a higher and more dynamic order of being.

It is time now to bring together two leading thoughts: the one, that movement, unfolding in a safe space, is prerequisite to learning; the other, that dynamic tri-une thinking promotes this kind of flexible movement in thought by developing the capacity to discover a third term arising out of two polar complementary elements, yet transcending them both. But it takes work, constant work, to think in this way, since it requires the exercise of imaginative inner activity that cannot be imposed from without; it can only arise as a free deed ignited from within. Like any worthy human endeavor, it proceeds in gradations of intensity, and it is to these stages that we now turn.

Practicing Tri-une Thinking

Goethe was perhaps the poet and scientist who offered the closest thing to a protocol for cultivating this mobile tri-une thinking. To be sure, he was not a systematic writer, and the four steps that follow are not to be found anywhere in his rambling body of work. And yet I hope he would concur with the suggestion that tri-une thinking unfolds in these steps:

1.   Take up an object of study and submit it to careful phenomenological observation. Resist the urge to explain it or infer or speculate. Goethe's first admonition is: "Hold to the phenomenon. It itself is the lesson!" Indeed, Goethe was skeptical of all hypotheses, which he called "lullabies that teachers use to sing their pupils to sleep." Instead, he encourages the observer to relate the object of his study to its polar complement. Perhaps his most famous example of this exercise is to be found in his study of plants, which begins with a careful observation of the rose in its gestures of expansion from seed to leaf, contraction from leaf to bud, a further expansion into blossom and contraction into hip, and culminates in a final expansion into pistil and stamen. Goethe calls this initial stage of study the apperception of *Polarität*.

2.   In observing these objects of study, pay special attention to the play of their polar complementarity. The risk here is that one falls back all too easily into binary thinking that results in the juxtaposition of logical opposites, rather than perceiving genuine polar complements. In the example of the plant study, Goethe reframes the conventional logical opposition of expansion and contraction into two polar complementary gestures, which give rise to a third term that recasts both earlier poles in a new dimension. Goethe calls this second stage of what I am calling tri-une thinking *Steigerung*, a term I prefer to translate (admittedly without the authority of any

dictionary) as the activity of "potentizing"—as, for instance, in the preparation of homeopathic remedies.

3. Discern, if you can, that transcendent third term, which may—or may not—arise out of the play of polar complements. You may feel reassured that you have actually apprehended this third term if it is a complete transformation of the two terms out of which it has come and is now manifest as something of an entirely new order of being. In studying light and dark as polar complements, for instance, Goethe demonstrates that the color spectrum, when viewed through a prism or even through squinted eyes, appears *between* light and dark (not simply as the breakup of the light, as Newton would have it). And this band of color is of an entirely new order of being: there is neither black nor white in the rainbow. Goethe calls this third step the apperception of *Metamorphose*.

4. A fourth step should be added here: if this third stage is achieved (and often it is not, even if one has accurately identified the play of a genuine pair of polar complementary conditions), then take a moment to give thanks. Like all growth and development, this form of thinking becomes more successful if its cultivation is bathed in a warm glow of gratitude.

There are many ways for teachers and prospective teachers in training to practice these four steps. In each of the examples that follows, thinking is first lifted from a world of physical objects to their etheric, organic, or systemic nature. In educating teenagers, starting with seventh grade and extending through the senior year of high school, we move from initial "object" thinking to "process" thinking, in which the laws of causality ("if/then") are superseded by the lawfulness of relationships ("when-then"). This move is akin to shifting attention from localized organs in the physical body—brain, heart, liver—to the dynamic etheric processes or systems of sense awareness, circulation, and digestion. But by the last two years of high school, we try to go beyond a systems approach to a genuinely tri-une way of thinking, in which out of polar complementary elements within these processes or fields a third element arises that transcends them both:

•   In biology, take any two organisms that enjoy a symbiotic relationship (a plant and an animal, for instance, or two plants or two animals) and follow in close observation their polar complementarity until they reveal—or do not reveal, since each will be uniquely different—some transcendent third reality. One way to prepare the imaginative leap needed to arrive at this third term is to transform careful observations of the two complementary terms (in words, but also in sketched drawings) into a parable that reveals the law-fulness of their relationship. What, for instance, are they able to do in symbiosis that neither partner in the relationship can achieve on its own?

- In embryology, set in juxtaposition the richly polar complementary qualities of ovum and sperm, then with a high-resolution stereo-scope—or the eye of imagination—follow their mutual dance or "PCAC" (pre-conception attraction complex) before sperm and ovum are united and both of their nuclei dissolve in a momentary hiatus of creation. Thereafter, there arises the beginnings of a new organism (no longer a cell) that far transcends anything ovum or sperm could have accomplished on its own. *

- In physics, study magnetism or electricity and see what arises from the relationship of so-called positive and negative terminals or from forces of attraction and repulsion.

- In the study of Shakespeare's plays, juxtapose the characters of Ariel (who flies too high) and Caliban (who grovels too low), or Guil-denstern (a voyager from the Persian East) and Rosencrantz (who is headed off to the Western island of Britain) and see if a third term—not just another character, however—arises between them that makes deeper sense of their roles in *The Tempest* or *Hamlet*.

- In history, discover what can come to birth—though, tragically, it rarely does—when social forces of left and right, rich and poor, master and slave, dependent and independent, Atlantic and Pacific, Kaos and Kosmos are not simply related to each other or pitted against each other but when both of these complementary terms are transcended in some third transformed reality.

- In listening closely to music, hear beyond the juxtaposition of musical notes the intervals that arise *between* the notes—a new

---

* For a thorough treatment of this process, see the essay by Jaap van der Wal, "Human Conception: How to Overcome Reproduction," in *Trailing Clouds of Glory: Essays on Human Sexuality and the Education of Youth in Waldorf Schools,* ed. Douglas Gerwin (Chatham, NY: Waldorf Publications, 2014), pp. 96-114.

and higher musical reality utterly dependent on the simultaneous sounding of two or more notes and yet transcending their "note-ness." An interval is not the addition of notes; it is the transcendence of notes.

The experience of moving from the apperception of polar complements to the discernment of their transcendent third term is akin to viewing the metamorphosis of a flat scrim curtain lowered before the stage of a theater: when the lights shift, we look no longer at a two-dimensional screen but *through* the screen to a fully three-dimensional stage scene beyond it.

The Purpose of Teaching

Ultimately, as high school teachers, we want our students to be alive in their thinking, sensitive in their feeling, responsive in their deeds. Develop in them a living, moving tri-une way of thinking and we promote in them these qualities of soul.

However, as educators we teach truly only what we have ourselves struggled to make our own to a certain level of proficiency (not to be confused with perfection). The teacher who has had to wrestle with the principles of mathematics in order to grasp them has an unfair advantage over a math genius; the experiment that a science teacher strains to get to unfold properly will be remembered more vividly than the flawless demonstration performed by a confident expert. So, too, the more a teacher takes up the arduous discipline of tri-une thinking, the more likely will this struggle inspire students to attempt this mode of cognition, either during their final years of high school or much later when they are adults.

With this mode of thinking we lift slightly the veil that normally conceals, on the one hand, the occult lawfulness of nature and, on the other, the hidden wisdom embedded in the events of society past and present, however dreadful or promising they may seem at first appearance. Seeing through the veil cast over life-in-nature and life-in-society by means of tri-une thinking bestows on us a renewed sense of confidence, since this cognitive practice discerns beyond the apparent randomness of life its lawful purpose and wise destiny. And the discovery of purpose, the discernment of destiny, is perhaps the most potent healing medicine for anxiety, since anxiety is fueled primarily by fear of an unknown future.

In the practice of tri-une thinking, like the juxtaposition of compacted logs and expansive air, we experience how it is "fuel, and absence of fuel, together that make fire possible."

16. Adult Learning

Most of this book is about adult learning, but in this chapter I intend to dive in particular into the findings of a couple of scholars and thinkers that can help us improve our understanding and practice, particularly in Waldorf teacher education. Argyris and Knowles are two pre-eminent leaders in overcoming barriers to adult learning and the science of how adults learn as opposed to pedagogy, learning as it pertains to children.

In his foundational book, *Knowledge for Action,* Chris Argyris addresses a variety of topics that can inform our practice in teacher education. His language and terminology are not what some may be used to, but it is good to learn new modalities of expression as part of our professional development. What follows is a sampling of a few key points followed by my commentary:

> 1. Action and Learning
> Learning occurs when we detect and correct error. Error is any mismatch between what we intend an action to produce and what actually happens when we implement that action. It is a mismatch between intentions and results. Learning also occurs when we produce a match between intentions and results for the first time (p. 3).

Some teachers think they are doing one thing in the classroom, but what is actually happening is another matter. This not only makes the case for mentoring and peer observation, but also for self-awareness and the need to constantly examine one's own practices. Humans have an infinite ability to think something and therefore believe it is happening. This is a danger also for Waldorf teachers in training, especially those who receive a great deal of theory without much time in internships, where there is a natural corrective in the responses of children.

> 2. Defensive Routines
> The use of defensive routines learned early in life is reinforced by the organizational cultures created by individuals implementing strategies of bypass and cover-up. These strategies persist because

organizational norms sanction and protect them. Once this occurs, individuals find it rational to hold the organization responsible for the defensive routines. Thus, there is a circular self-reinforcing process, from the individual to the larger unit and back to the individual (p. 21).

The Waldorf-oriented person will of course immediately recognize the biographical influences in "defensive routines" as long-held tendencies arising from hereditary and environmental factors. The interesting part in the first section of the above citation is how organizational cultures, our schools, can actually aid and abet these habits by providing shelter in a family-like organizational culture. Individuals do not spend much time in an adult education organizational culture, but it is worth questioning whether our centers and institutes provide undue "sanction and cover-up" for defensive routines and old habits in how we work together.

The other aspect of the above quote that is worth further consideration is the notion of "circular self-reinforcing" processes. How would this look in teacher education? A person might arrive at our doorstep with a certain biography that includes childhood experiences in schools. These experiences might include assumptions and coping mechanisms. Now, in a classroom with adults, this person may look for peers and ideas that confirm those assumptions regarding education and even carry them into an internship. Then, because these notions are deeply ingrained, the intern may look for confirmation in the children. This then informs his/her theoretical outlook…thus the circular, reinforcing cycle.

Argyris goes on to say that these defensive routines often lead to behavior that is outright dysfunctional, leading over time to disconnection between colleagues, secrecy, and even cover-up. This has a huge impact on school effectiveness and teacher morale. Errors persist and the tendency is to avoid embarrassment, thus there is an incentive to cover up. Interestingly, Argyris says that some organizational "rituals" and routines can serve to lull people to sleep and restrict the surfacing of what is really going on in some classrooms. The status quo can become a safety blanket.

One way to help turn things around is to make adult learning and defensive routines discussable in meetings, and to foster an organizational culture in which challenging questions are welcomed. Rather than fragmentation and avoidance, issues can be brought forward in the right context and in a setting that allows for candid conversation. It can be a big support to the future career of a teacher if group discussions during training model some of these qualities in a positive way.

3. Single- and Double-Loop Learning

Since an error is a mismatch between intentions and actual consequences, it is important to bring about change. Simply addressing
external behaviors involves "single-loop learning" that only gives
the appearance of change, and the individual will soon revert back
to the old behaviors. "The second way to correct errors is to change
the underlying program, or master program" that the individual used
to produce the actions (p. 50).

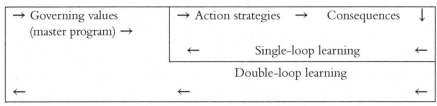

For the Waldorf teacher, we can translate this in terms of transforming old habits through self-development in a teacher-education program.
Anthroposophy provides many exercises and practices to dig down into
the "master program" of preconceived notions about oneself and teaching. Adult educators may want to consider more intentional articulation
of "why" we work with these exercises. It may be that some students see
engagement with anthroposophy as acquiring new terminology, or simply
attaching new concepts in a vast philosophic framework. This can lead to
more "single-loop" behaviors such as "talking the talk" in the right circles
without much fundamental change from within. To paraphrase Martin
Buber, this can become an "I-it" relationship to anthroposophy. It is more
helpful when one can develop an "I-Thou" relationship that challenges
the core of one's being in active engagement through practices, not just
discussion.

4. Theories in Action

Early in our research, my colleagues and I learned that there were
two types of theories in action. One was the theory that individuals
espoused and that comprised their beliefs, attitudes, and values.
The second was their *theory-in-use*—the theory that they actually
employed....it was a major surprise—given our view of human
beings as designing organisms—to find out that there are often
fundamental, systemic mismatches between individuals' espoused
and in-use designs (p. 51).

In other words, we often don't do what we say. Even more serious for
teacher development, some lack the ability to see the mismatch between

what we think we are doing in the classroom and what is really happening. We may have all sorts of pedagogical theories in our heads, but what is actually happening in the classroom may be a different matter entirely. These *theories-in-use,* part of what Argyris calls Model I learning, are often internalized and taken for granted (p. 54). Our teaching can flow from these rote behaviors in an automatic, reactive way that lives below the surface of consciousness. In contrast, Model II action strategies are subject to conscious inquiry and the learner is willing to have them tested and evaluated by others. "As a consequence, defensive routines that are anti-learning are minimized and double-loop learning is facilitated. Embarrassment and threat are not bypassed and covered up; they are engaged (p. 55).

These issues often come down to a teacher's willingness to have visitors, observers, and mentors. Some are more comfortable with this than others, which is also related to inherent social intelligences described in another chapter. But mentors are crucial in surfacing key questions after having observed a class. These questions can stimulate new ways of looking at "what just happened in the class" and increasing self-awareness through self-observation. By stepping out the comfort zone of *espoused theories in use* into new *theories in action,* the teacher not only acquires new skills, but also rebuilds what Argyris calls "governing values" or what I would call their deep-seated habits arising out of personal biography and learned behaviors. The task of the teacher educator is to stimulate a kind of break-out from the past, a fundamental *Umstülpung,* a turning inside-out that allows for new beginnings. Our classes and the structure of internships need to provide multiple opportunities to turn things upside down, to break out of the single loop of the past.

We promote double-loop learning and fundamental change through:

1. Classroom questions that encourage new perspectives.

2. Small-group work that allows for questioning of assumptions and intimate dialogue.

3. Artistic activities that take adults out of their natural comfort zone. We sometimes have tears when doing clay modeling, painting, or playing the recorder, which outwardly can be uncomfortable for all, but actually can be a sign that change is afoot!

4. Speaking is particularly close to the sense of self, the ego; and the art of speech formation can be particularly uncomfortable and yet awakening for the adult learner.

5. Internships and practica, for all the reasons mentioned above, are an ideal way to break out of old habits and single-loop learning and achieve a breakthrough. There is nothing more exhilarating than a lesson well taught! But the practice of reflection right after the lesson is invaluable learning. One could say the soul is broken open by the children, and the future teacher can find her footing on new ground.

6. Research, when done or facilitated skillfully, can also help the learner break new ground. Finding a focusing question, conducting interviews, doing a literature review, sifting out responses to a survey and reading new source materials can stimulate new perspectives. But most of all, if the question is deep-seated, if the line of inquiry arises out of biographical and professional passion, research can provide abundant opportunities for double-loop learning.

7. Our advising sessions are also crucial in supporting the kind of adult learning described in this chapter. In the confidence of a one-on-one conversation, it is possible to probe, question, guide, and challenge in a way that allows for greater self-awareness and double-loop learning. I have found the "return conversation," in which there is follow-up a few days later, to be invaluable. A few nights' sleep in between the meetings can enhance perspective on both sides of the dialogue.

There are of course many, many more opportunities in adult education programs to promote the processes of new learning, and they cannot all be listed here. But one might say in summary that those in leadership and instructional roles are there to facilitate awaking. It is not a matter of pedagogy as it is when teaching children, but rather a whole new art form: it is andragogy.

Malcolm S. Knowles, who died in 1997, is often called the Father of Andragogy. He was one of the world's leading scholar-practitioners of adult learning. He was able to rise above the many cross-currents of his time and point the way toward a more dynamic democracy through his emphasis on the importance of understanding adult learning as opposed to pedagogy. In his book, *The Adult Learner: The Definitive Classic in Adult Education and Human Resource Development,* he writes:

Pedagogy is derived from the Greek words *paid*, meaning "child" (the same stem from which "pediatrics" comes) and *agogus*, meaning "leader of." Thus, pedagogy literally means the art and science of teaching children. The pedagogical model of education is a set of beliefs. As viewed by many traditional teachers, it is an ideology based on assumptions about teaching and learning that evolved between the seventh and twelfth centuries in the monastic and cathedral schools of Europe out of their experience in teaching basic skills to young boys. As secular schools organized in later centuries, and public schools in the nineteenth century, the pedagogical model was the only existing educational model. Thus, the entire educational enterprise of U.S. schools, including higher education, was frozen into this model. Systematic efforts to establish adult education programs in this country, initiated after World War I, also used this model because it was the only model teachers had. As a result, until fairly recently, adults have by and large been taught as if they were children (Knowles, p. 61).

What is andragogy? According to Knowles and others, it revolves around a core set of adult learning principles:

1. The learner's need to know
2. The self-concept of the learner
3. Prior experience of the learner
4. Readiness to learn
5. Orientation to learning
6. Motivation to learn (p. 3)

These, of course, are influenced by the learner and situational differences, and the goals and course content of the program. Andragogy works best when it is adapted to fit the uniqueness of the learners and the particular situation and subject at hand. The implications for this in Waldorf teacher education are manifold, as the following pages will show. But one obvious one is the difference between those who are already standing *within a vocation*, as in our summer sequence programs and Transdisciplinary Healing Education M.Ed. as opposed to those in Foundation Studies or entering teacher-education programs, where many are sorting different career options. Andragogy, as outlined in the six points above, encourages us to take an initial inventory of the learner's prior experience, motivation, readiness to learn, etc. Advisors may want to spend more time assessing these factors *at the start of a program*.

Knowles describes the adult education process as one in which learners seek to become aware of "significant experience: Recognition of significance leads to evaluation. Meanings accompany experience when we know what is happening and what importance the event includes for our personalities"(p. 169).

Knowles has Gessner, another author, articulate the way adult education instructors really need to not only understand these basics of andragogy, but also develop new techniques:

> I am conceiving adult education in terms of a new technique for learning, a technique as essential to the college graduate as to the unlettered manual worker. It represents a process by which the adult learns to become aware of and to evaluate his experience. To do this he cannot begin by studying "subjects" in the hope that some day this information will be useful. On the contrary, he begins by giving attention to situations in which he finds himself, to problems which include obstacles to his self-fulfillment. Facts and information from the differentiated spheres of knowledge are used, not for the purpose of accumulation, but because of need in solving problems. In this process the teacher finds a new function. He is no longer the oracle who speaks from the platform of authority, but rather the guide, the pointer-out who also participates in learning in proportion to the vitality and relevance of his facts and experiences. In short, my conception of adult education is this: a cooperative venture in non–authoritarian, informal learning, the chief purpose of which is to discover the meaning of experience, a quest of the mind which digs down to the roots of preconceptions which formulate our conduct; a technique of learning for adults which makes education coterminous with life and hence elevates living itself to the level of adventurous experiment (Gessner, 1956, p. 160)(Knowles pp. 38-39).

In short, we need to "co-create" with our learners through goal-setting, discussion of obstacles, constant reflection and (self-) evaluation, and above all, harvesting and sharing of life experiences.

Knowles cites Gessner and Lindeman in outlining five basics of adult learning theory:

1. Adults are motivated to learn as they experience needs and interests that learning will satisfy.
2. Adults' orientation to learning is life-centered.
3. Experience is the richest source for adult learning.
4. Adults have a deep need to be self-directing.
5. Individual differences among people increase with age (p. 40).

This brings up a significant challenge for many who are used to practicing pedagogy instead of andragogy: Waldorf teachers in particular are used to being an authority figure in a classroom with children, whether it is the early childhood teacher meticulously preparing a nurturing environment, the class teacher, or the high school subject specialist. We often stand on Mount Olympus. Yet when these authoritarian, teacher-centered habits are carried over into working with adults, we run the risk of holding back healthy adult development, just as teaching a six-year-old as if she were a 14-year-old would be inappropriate and even unsuccessful. It is even worse when the pedagogue carries these classroom habits into the sphere of parent-teacher work. Many of our challenges with parents, I feel, are because teachers continue to practice pedagogy instead of andragogy when working with the adult community, colleagues, and parents, in a school setting.

> Authoritarian adult education is marked throughout by regimentation demanding obedient conformity to patterns of conduct handed down from authority. Behavior is expected to be predictable, standardized....Democratic adult education employs the method of self-directing activity, with free choice of subject matter and free choice in determining outcomes. Spontaneity is welcome. Behavior cannot with certainty be predicted and therefore is not standardized. Individual, critical thinking is perhaps the best description of the democratic method and it is here that the gulf is the widest between democracy and the authoritarian system (*Journal of Adult Education*, XI, 3, June 1939, pp. 244-245)(Knowles, p. 43).

> Noted clinical psychologists such as Freud, Jung, Erikson, Maslow, and Rogers made significant contributions to the study of adult learning. Freud identified the influence of the subconscious on behavior; Jung introduced the idea that human consciousness possesses four functions: sensation, thought, emotions, and intuition; Erikson provided the "eight stages of man"; Maslow emphasized the importance of safety; and Rogers conceptualized a student-centered approach to education based on five "basic hypotheses." Developmental psychologists provided knowledge of characteristics associated with age (i.e. physical capabilities, mental abilities, interests, attitudes, values, creativity, and lifestyles), whereas sociology and social psychology provided knowledge about group and social system behavior, including factors that facilitate or inhibit learning (Knowles, p. 71).

The chart below provides a helpful comparison between pedagogical and andragogical approaches to learning:

Element	Pedagogical Approach	Andragogical Approach
1 - Preparing Learners	Minimal	Provide information Prepare for participation Help develop realistic expectations Begin thinking about content
2 - Climate	Authority-oriented Formal Competitive	Relaxed, trusting Mutually respectful Informal, warm Collaborative, supportive Openness and authenticity Humanness
3 - Planning	By teacher	Mechanism for mutual planning by learners and facilitator
4 - Diagnosis of Needs	By teacher	By mutual assessment
5 - Setting of Objectives	By teacher	By mutual negotiation
6 - Designing Learning Plans	Logic of subject matter Content units	Sequenced by readiness Problem units
7- Learning Activities	Transmittal techniques	Experiential techniques (inquiry)
8 - Evaluation	By teacher	Mutual re-diagnosis of needs Mutual measurement of program

Developed from Knowles (1992) and Knowles (1995) (Knowles, p. 116).

17. Characteristics of Teacher Educators
by Florian Osswald

These guidelines for qualities needed in teacher educators were published by Florian Osswald, co-leader of the Pedagogical Section at the Goetheanum, and his international working group in the Pedagogical Section Journal *in March 2020.*

We have reported twice in this journal on the working group established by the Pedagogical Section looking at teacher preparation and teacher education* with the intention to offer a set of essential principles or guidelines that Steiner Waldorf teacher-education programs can adapt in ways best suiting their situations and circumstances. This project now has a name—the International Teacher Education Project (ITEP). The working group continues to meet twice a year to consider feedback and suggestions to refine and extend the guidelines for teacher education that we have reported on in past journals.

We would like to take the opportunity here to report on a second area of our work—looking at essential aspects of being a teacher educator, those who teach teachers. As before, the word "teacher" indicates all those responsible for the education of children and young people under the age of 18. In discussion with experienced teacher educators from different programs in different countries, it became clear that there is no acknowledged set of requirements or consistent expectations for those who work as teacher educators, nor is there an accepted path of suitable preparation. It can be a case of being on hand in the right place at the right time, of knowing the right people, or having connections to secure initial invitations, especially in smaller centers. While this can lead to excellent educators being employed, it can appear ad hoc and to favor established groups of acquaintances.

Questions arose about whether a general "skill set" for teacher educators could be identified, guidelines which could then lead to a possible path of development and further study being established. It is unlikely that all teacher educators will excel in every area, and those mentioned

---

* Journals 63 and 65

below indicate processes that are taking place at all levels from initial to advanced. As with the teacher guidelines, they can be used to identify areas of strength and those that need support.

The aims of this project are that:

- Anthroposophically-based educational initiatives around the world have access to sufficient consistent and high-quality teacher-education programs to support their need for well-trained and well-supported teachers

- Guidelines are created for best practices in Waldorf teacher education that will help ensure quality, equivalency, validity, and reliability across teacher-education programs internationally

- These guidelines are culturally inclusive and appropriate, actively encourage diversity and respect for others, align with an anthroposophical worldview, are research-based, seek partnerships and alliances with others, are professional, and have contemporary relevance.

The position of a teacher educator is one of considerable influence and responsibility. Being a teacher educator presumes that all the qualities expected of a teacher have been worked through.* In some fields, deep knowledge and advanced practice will be expected. It is expected that these focus areas will continue to be developed through professional life. As well as areas relating to teacher development, guidelines for additional qualities or skills relevant to being a teacher educator are characterized below.

We offer these guidelines as work in progress. They have been refined to take into account feedback from colleagues in Asia, Europe, and Australasia; they will no doubt be refined further. As with the teacher attributes, they are listed in no special order. They are guidelines and point toward an ideal rather than minimum expectations.

Teaching adults

Dialogue and co-creation are essential to all learning processes. Teacher educators strive to improve their ability to support these in their teaching.

---

*   These are: Development of knowledge practices; The arts; Self-development; Teaching as inquiry; Basic knowledge; Teaching and learning; Expanded understanding of human nature; Education and societal change; Legal responsibilities, finances, and regulations; and Recognition of qualifications.

Of particular importance are the skills of self-reflection and listening. Teacher educators acknowledge that their students are adults and that they come with their own experience and knowledge, and thus take this into account in their teaching. They encourage students to search for and develop their own questions and to strive for teaching approaches through which conceptual understanding grows out of lived experience.

Teacher educators understand that the process of teacher education needs to be health-enhancing, to encourage resilience as well as mental and physical well-being.

Anthroposophy

Teacher educators have a living, personal relationship to the work of Rudolf Steiner. This relationship embraces contemporary discourse and advances in related fields of knowledge. Teacher educators are able to mediate their strivings in the work to students in ways that generate deep meaning, and they appreciate that a student's path toward anthroposophical understanding, like theirs, is individual and one of gradual transformation.

The future of Waldorf education rests, to a great extent, on the individual teacher's relationship to anthroposophy. Many student teachers learn to know anthroposophy through the way they see it lived by their teachers. Teacher educators are able to present anthroposophy as a spiritual knowledge practice that seeks to safeguard the dignity of the human being, establish its freedom and make tangible its essential connection to what is spiritual in the cosmos. They strive to give students a deep sense of the ethic of freedom inherent in anthroposophy, with its goal of enabling an individual, self-responsible approach to life. They help students explore anthroposophy as a key to a deep understanding of the developing human being.

The Contemporary Child

Teacher educators need to be in an active, dialogical relationship with contemporary children and/or adolescents. They must have a living sense of how children and young people are developing in today's rapidly changing world and the challenges that these changes bring in the life of families and relationships as well as to a school or kindergarten. A central aspect of Waldorf education is to be found in the pedagogical relationship between teacher and student. Student teachers should experience this relational pedagogical practice in their studies. This is possible when teacher educators are able to imbue their teaching with the immediacy of ongoing encounters with children and young people.

Context Sensitivity

Teacher educators are sensitive to context and strive to strengthen diversity and diverse approaches. They understand the time they live in, and they acknowledge the qualities and history of the place where they are active and the complex nature of their cultural and societal settings. They acknowledge their inherited values and strive to individualize them, to perceive and balance their own preferences, biases, and contradictions to help ensure that no students are discriminated against or favored above others. This is reflected in the goals and aims of each teaching program. Teacher educators strive to work in the present and have a clear understanding that the needs of the times change as do those of youth. Their pedagogical practice reflects this awareness of contemporaneity and is reflexive and adaptive to context.

Research

Working from a research-informed position profoundly strengthens the authority and effectiveness of a teacher educator. Being actively engaged in research strengthens any educator's qualification to encourage learning and growth in others. Therefore, teacher educators should contribute to the research environment and, where possible, engage students in their work. In addition to standard methodologies, the teacher educator can practice phenomenological and contemplative approaches that lead to an understanding of the spiritual qualities of phenomena. Research is often situational, and thus responsive to place and cultural context. It interacts with contemporary educational research and gains value when disseminated in effective and appropriate ways.

Collaborative Leadership and Professionalism

The teacher educator is able to work with confidence and consideration within the organizational culture and structure of their institution. Clear and reliable communication at all levels of the work is essential. As a mentor, the teacher educator exercises a duty of care in a professional and ethical manner. When engaging with colleagues, his or her work is founded on the principles and practices of collaborative leadership and individual accountability. Good social practices are demonstrated and actively encouraged in students. The teacher educator is aware that he or she is in a leadership role; they organize, administer, and manage the bureaucracy of teaching and assessment effectively and efficiently, being aware of financial aspects of the work as appropriate.

We hope that these guidelines are relevant to all those involved in preparing Waldorf teachers as well as those involved in ongoing teacher development. They may also be used to guide the development of teacher mentors and those who help induct new teachers into the profession.

We hope that publishing this initial set of guidelines for teacher educators will encourage conversation in this area, though it is work very much in progress. As we mentioned last time, throughout this process we are engaging with teacher educators and others worldwide to hear their opinions and questions so that additional viewpoints can be incorporated. We would like the process to be one of dialogue, and welcome feedback regarding these guidelines for teacher educators as well.

During 2020, members of the working group will present the teacher and teacher educator guidelines at conferences worldwide. We hope that this will encourage discussion so they can be further refined, and also that some institutions can begin to work with them and test them in practice. It is intended that a publication be produced later this year in which a wider circle of teacher educators will expand on the guidelines, unpacking them and giving interpretations of how they may be put into practice in different contexts.

18. Demoralized:
The Challenges Teachers Face

In her book *Demoralized: Why Teachers Leave the Profession They Love and How They Can Stay,* Doris Santoro shares her extensive research on the challenges facing the teaching profession.

> It is not hyperbole to say that the teaching profession in the United States is in trouble. Teachers are leaving the profession at rates that outpace retirements. Surveys indicate a high level of dissatisfaction, with only a slight majority saying they remain enthusiastic about their job. Teacher retention in public schools—a potential solution to the current teacher shortage crisis—has been on a decline since the late 1980s (p. 3).

After conducting many in-depth interviews, Santoro did some thorough analysis that led her to the term *demoralization,* "the inability to access the moral rewards offered and expected in teaching" (p. 8). By moral rewards, she means being able to respond to the needs of students and having the satisfaction of experiencing their success.

"Areas of dissatisfaction include concerns with the administration, ranging from lack of support to lack of [teacher] input and control over teaching decisions; testing and accountability pressures; dissatisfaction with the teaching career; or unhappiness with various working conditions" (p. 19). No wonder teacher retention becomes an issue, especially in urban or isolated rural schools where 30 percent or more of the students qualify for reduced price lunches because they meet the federal poverty guidelines. Schools with a majority of students who are from Black and/or Latinx backgrounds often have the highest teacher turnover rates, and thus lack experienced teachers: turnover is as high as 25 percent, according to Santoro.

> Low compensation is also a serious issue, but "the majority of teachers leave Arizona schools for reasons *other than salary.* The U.S. Department of Education's national survey results indicate that the most significant reasons teachers leave the profession are 'personal life factors' (38.4 percent) and 'other factors' (20.5 percent)" (p. 19).

Teachers are required to complete certification, but the growing use of alternative pathways has left some teachers feeling that their own educational sacrifices were not adequately supported. And those who enter the profession "leave at rates double or triple those of better-prepared educators. Therefore, identifying more shortcuts to the profession will prove shortsighted and ultimately ineffective. In contrast, identifying ways to make comprehensive teacher preparation affordable and rectifying profound disparities between teacher salaries in high-poverty, racially segregated schools and well-financed suburban schools could effectively target the disproportional attrition for teachers of color and the white teachers who work in those schools"(p. 20). In post-Katrina New Orleans, 70 percent of the teachers were Black, but by 2014 it was less than 50 percent. At the same time the proportion of inexperienced teachers rose, and there was disproportionate closure of schools that serve majority Black and Brown students.

There are also organizational considerations. Unlike in schools with site-based management (charter, Montessori, Waldorf), most teachers feel they do not have a voice in decision-making. "Gallup's *State of America's Schools* report describes the profession as 'vilified.' It describes the 'alarming' findings that, compared to twelve other occupations, teachers were the least likely to agree with the statement 'At my work, my opinions seem to count.' Teachers' ability to participate in decision-making at their schools and their professional autonomy have been correlated to job satisfaction and retention" (p. 27).

> Public school teachers are expected to do more with less; they are experiencing intensification. Intensification refers to the increased professional demands added to teachers' workloads without concomitant time provided to incorporate new expectations or any reduction in previous duties (p. 28).

In summary, the last 20-30 years have seen several key trends that have affected the teaching profession in public schools:

- Standardization
- Increased focus on core subjects/narrowing of the curriculum
- Prescribed curriculum
- Adoption of corporate practices/use of value-added measures
- High-stakes accountability for students and teachers
- Fast-track or alternative teacher licensure programs (p. 27)

For Waldorf teachers, one could make a similar case for common struggles:

- Carrying responsibility for school administrative tasks while trying to stay fully engaged with teaching and classroom preparation
- The expectation of being a "Renaissance person": trying to do everything well and often feeling inadequate (see next chapter, "Empathy and Self-Compassion")
- Tensions between faculty and board expectations
- Working with administrators who sometimes do not have a basic background or understanding of Waldorf
- Demanding parents
- Low salaries
- and more…

One can then ask, what can we do, individually and collectively? Doris Santoro and others draw our attention to the importance of "cultivating an authentic professional community" as part of a "re-moralizing" process: (p. 14)

> I define professional community as the other professionals who give meaning, purpose, and direction to teachers' work. These are the people that teachers seek out for advice, support, and collaboration. Professional community does not mean the professional learning community (PLC) that a school leader might direct to meet between 2:30 and 3:15, although in fortuitous instances, this might turn our to be such a resource. Almost always, authentic professional community is chosen by those who make up its membership (p. 125). In the authentic professional communities, teachers articulate and refine their professional values and accompanying practices in conjunction with colleagues and partners who seek to do the same (p. 126).

In an article reviewing research on the impact of professional learning communities on teaching practice and student learning, Vescio, Ross and Adams did an analysis of 11 research articles and concluded that "participation in a learning community leads to changes in teaching practice" (p. 83). One particular study done by Louis and Marks (1998) "documented that the presence of a professional community in a school contributes to higher levels of social support for achievement and higher levels of authentic pedagogy" (p. 83).

How does this manifest? A professional learning community contributes to a "fundamental shift in the habits of mind that teachers bring to their daily work in the classroom" and the professional culture of the school (p. 84). Specifically, the change in school culture includes:

- increased collaboration
- more focus on student learning
- enhanced teacher authority
- continuous student learning

In short, when the faculty of a school works as part of a professional learning community, student learning increases. In a world that values test scores, there has been some evidence of test scores in reading, writing, math, science, and social studies going up substantially over a three-year period, from 50 percent passing to as high as 90 percent (p. 86). Students learn better when teachers are learning together!

Although most schools have staff meetings, it is not the business of those sessions that fosters a PLC. Rather, it is the student-centered activities that make a difference: working together on new curriculum, discussing student needs, doing a study or activity together that is classroom-centered.

One aspect that I found particularly intriguing is the notion that a PLC enhances teacher authority. The "authorship" of lessons taught brings greater job satisfaction, and helps teachers find a voice in a profession that often undervalues their insights. Rather than imposed outside standards and learning outcomes, teachers who work together in a PLC are able to respond to the real needs of their students. That is one reason site-based management models are often so successful.

Increased collaboration can also rebuild teacher confidence and commitment to the profession. To use Santoro's words: "When an individual teacher's spirit or energy flags, authentic professional community supplies other colleagues who can continue the work until the teacher is restored. This continuity combats feelings of futility and the myth that one person can do good work isolated from others. Professional community can provide support and an opportunity to share acquired wisdom. Furthermore, when teachers act with professional community, the risk that individual teachers may bear in taking action for re-moralization can be shared and potentially minimized" (p. 125).

But do we need to limit the notion of a PLC to faculty and staff? We have only begun to explore the potential of engaging parents in a school's learning community. This may require that we move beyond traditional classroom-based study and curriculum standards, and start to take up issues that affect all members of the adult community in a particular school. For example, one could articulate a question for common study and conversation each term or school year. A few possibilities that would most likely interest parents as well as teachers:

1. How can we strive for greater understanding of diversity and advocate for social justice?
2. What does racism look like today, and how can a school address systemic racism?
3. How can curriculum address gender issues?
4. How can writing enhance learning?
5. What are the age-appropriate uses of technology?

The list of potential topics of mutual interest is endless. But the topics need not all be "academic." For example, parents could engage more in learning through doing when working with questions like, How can the arts enhance emotional intelligence? Imagine workshops in clay modeling, movement, drama, music, and painting! We can enjoy the discovery process by doing things together.

One potential outcome of a school-wide PLC is that we learn to know each other better. And when we know each other, we are more likely to collaborate successfully. In schools that depend on parents for funding and much volunteer time, a PLC can provide the foundation for sustainability.

Another outcome is greater empathy for the other. Next chapter: "Empathy and Self-Compassion."

See Appendix for additional citations from Santoro's book.

19. Empathy and Self-Compassion

In trying to predict teacher success, capacity for empathy could be considered a top priority. As with other "caring" professions, teaching involves deep commitment to the interests and well-being of others. As with nursing, hospitality services, and Peace Corps volunteers, teachers spend most of their on-the-job hours serving and supporting. It is hard to do that on a daily basis if one is narcissistic. When asked about their childhood teachers, most people cite individuals who took extra interest, went beyond the call of duty, and were able to motivate learning, often through strength of personality and empathy. (See "Listening to Our Teachers: Stories From the Classroom")

Warren Buffett, the successful investor, speaks of "lovable" people and how "you cannot make a good deal with a bad person" in a CNBC interview. The Oracle of Omaha came to this through 89 years of living and interacting with many, many people. A lovable person is often an empathetic person.

An empathetic person is able to step into someone else's shoes and see their perspective, and in doing so, is able to have a greater impact. An empathetic teacher is simply more effective.

> In a DDI study of more than 15,000 leaders across 20 industries, researchers found that the ability to listen and respond with empathy was the most critical driver of a team's overall performance (Buffett, CNBC interview).

Is the good teacher someone who is naturally empathetic, or can these qualities be fostered through professional development? This age-old nature/nurture question lives in many professions, and goes to the heart of vocation and choice of a career. Often a person who "fails" in the classroom goes on to be successful in another career, yet for the purposes of this book, one has to assume that there are individuals who are naturally gifted with the "lovable" grace of empathy, and others who can work to unlock those qualities with time and cultivation. Another chapter explores the topic of social intelligence, which is intimately related, but for this section I would like to further explore the curious relationship between the outer manifestation of empathy and a more inward notion of self-compassion.

I was fascinated to discover recent research and an article, "Self-Compassion Increases Self-Improvement Motivation" by Breines and Chen. The question is asked: "Can treating oneself with compassion after making a mistake increase self-improvement motivation? In four experiments, the authors examined the hypothesis that self-compassion motivates people to improve personal weaknesses, moral transgressions, and test performance. Participants in a self-compassion condition, compared to a self-esteem control condition and either no intervention or a positive distraction control condition, expressed greater incremental beliefs about a personal weakness (Experiment 1); reported greater motivation to make amends and avoid repeating a recent moral transgression (Experiment 2); spent more time studying for a difficult test following an initial failure (Experiment 3); exhibited a preference for upward social comparison after reflecting on a personal weakness (Experiment 4); and reported greater motivation to change the weakness (Experiment 4). These findings suggest that, somewhat paradoxically, taking an accepting approach to personal failure may make people more motivated to improve themselves" (Breines & Chen).

Although clothed in academic language, these findings demonstrate the crucial link between self-compassion and the motivation for change, which then would include all the exercises available through anthroposophy and other spiritual paths, and the cultivation of empathy as one of them! Self-compassion influences the growth of empathy.

Just in case one might regard the above study as an outlier, further evidence of this line of inquiry is available in an article in the Journal of Research in Personality, "An Examination of Self-Compassion in Relation to Positive Psychological Functioning and Personality Traits" by Neff, Rude and Kirkpatrick. From the abstract:

> This study examined the relation of self-compassion to positive psychological health and the five-factor model of personality. Self-compassion entails being kind toward oneself in instances of pain or failure; perceiving one's experiences as part of the larger human experience; and holding painful thoughts and feelings in balanced awareness. Participants were 177 undergraduates (68% female, 32% male). Using a correlational design, the study found that self-compassion had a significant positive association with self-reported measures of happiness, optimism, positive affect, wisdom, personal

initiative, curiosity and exploration, agreeableness, extroversion, and conscientiousness. It also had a significant negative association with negative affect and neuroticism. Self-compassion predicted significant variance in positive psychological health beyond that attributable to personality (Neff, Rude & Kirkpatrick).

Teachers are often idealists. They are in a profession with very few material rewards in terms of compensation and career mobility. It is their belief in a better society for the future, their love of the children, and their passion for the subject matter that motivates and inspires them to enter the profession. But these very same traits, this deep-seated idealism, also makes teachers susceptible to setbacks and failures. Their success is so intimately tied up with the success of their students that when faced with hindrances, teachers often take it hard. Feelings of doubt, frustration and negative self-worth can rise to the surface. Often the stimulus for frustration comes from without, such as helicopter parents, state standards, and dysfunction in governance and leadership.

The key, according to the last study cited above, is self-compassion, or the ability to forgive and move on. Learning from mistakes is one thing; harboring grievances and hurt is another. There is nothing worse than a cynical, hardened teacher "serving time" until retirement. Self-compassion, on the other hand, can lead to happiness and many other positives as reported above: "optimism, positive affect, wisdom, personal initiative.... exploration, agreeableness, extroversion, and conscientiousness."

It is interesting that one of the key words above is "extroversion." I have long wondered about Jungian soul types and the influence of temperaments on teacher success. One would like to believe that a good teacher could be either an introvert or extrovert, choleric, sanguine, phlegmatic, or melancholic. But we all know what a difference strong instances of these qualities can make in the classroom! The Myers-Briggs types are also fascinating, as they come in pairs: Extroversion-Introversion, Sensing-Intuition, Thinking-Feeling, Judging-Perceiving. Should teacher educators do an overview of these attributes at the start of a program? Or at least request that matriculating students do a self-inventory, readily available online? Another possible avenue of research would be field research on the intersection of the above characteristics with subjects taught, particularly on the high school level. Is an ISTP person more likely to align with science teaching, and an ESFJ person able to work better with drama? All this may seem intrusive, but when not working out of one's strengths, a teacher can easily fall into the self-blame trap, especially if not accompanied by a good dose of self-compassion.

All this also has physiological implications, as measured in a further study on how self-compassion can positively influence stress-induced inflammations (see Appendix for article from *Brain, Behavior, and Immunity*).

One of the challenges teachers face involves governance, both in independent and public schools. We tend to spend a lot of time and resources as a society on teacher education and constantly changing licensure requirements, but relatively little on leadership development. Yet a board president, school chair or principal can be crucial to a school's success. We all know of many such examples. Interestingly enough, leadership skills have also been increasingly linked to empathy, as seen in the fascinating article below from Development Dimensions International (DDI):

What's the Number 1 Leadership Skill for Overall Success?
Evan Sinar, Ph.D., Richard S. Wellins, Ph.D., and Matthew J. Paese, Ph.D.

There is one leadership skill that ranks far and above all others in determining your overall success as a leader according to a new High-Resolution Leadership report from Development Dimensions International (DDI), a pioneer in leadership assessment and development for 45 years.

Leaders who master listening and responding with empathy will perform more than 40 percent higher in overall performance, coaching, engaging others, planning and organizing, and decision-making, according to the research. The unprecedented report is based on the analysis of real behaviors in assessment center simulations from over 15,000 leaders across 300 companies in 18 countries over a decade.

"Being able to listen and respond with empathy is overwhelmingly the one interaction skill that outshines all other skills leaders need to be successful," said Richard S. Wellins, Ph.D., Senior Vice President, DDI.

DDI defines empathy as acknowledging others' feelings and circumstances when they express emotion verbally or nonverbally. Empathy involves letting others know that their feelings are understood and helps them to feel that their perspective is being taken into account.

"Each and every day, leaders have multiple conversations with a range of constituents. Each of these interactions will collectively determine their ultimate success as a leader," said Wellins.

The leaders who were highly successful in DDI's research were able to use empathy to understand key constituents' concerns, frustrations, and feelings. Using empathy is very important to defuse conflict and learn more about facts, circumstances and/or feelings.

"The research shows there is no other single leadership skill that is more important and yet, in today's culture, empathy is near extinction. I believe it is one of the most dangerous global trends of our time," he added.

THE DEATH OF EMPATHY

There is a wealth of research that shows empathy is on the decline, according to Wellins. With the advancement of technology, it has become commonplace to send an email or text and eliminate conversations altogether. "Many in today's workplace think sending an emoticon is equivalent to responding with empathy," said Wellins. "It just isn't so."

A study released by the University of Michigan reported that college students are 40 percent less likely to have empathy compared to 20 to 30 years ago. DDI's High-Resolution Leadership report found the same in today's workplace. Only 40 percent of frontline leaders were proficient or strong in empathy. Of the eight leadership interaction skills measured, listening and responding with empathy was one of the weakest.

This research documents the importance of empathy to overall leadership success, said Wellins. The good news is that soft skills, including listening and responding with empathy, can be learned and practiced.

BOOK SMARTS OR SOFT SKILLS?

The DDI research also evaluated whether leadership performance is impacted more by cognitive ability (IQ) or emotional intelligence (EQ). The findings showed that brainpower alone did a better job in predicting the more business-focused aspects of leader performance such as business savvy and financial acumen. However, soft skills related more strongly to performance in the people-focused competencies, such as leading teams and evaluating networks.

"The reality is that both brainpower and soft skills matter to overall leadership success. However, we cannot overemphasize the importance of emotional intelligence. Far more leadership failures are attributed to insensitivity than stupidity," said Wellins.

20. Personal Hygiene for Teachers

by Jennifer Hudziec

The concept and implementation of self-care has become a popular topic over the last few years. How we care for ourselves in a world that is increasingly fast-paced and constantly changing may feel overwhelming and impossible to manage. What I have witnessed in over twenty years of work as a holistic health care provider is that there is a difference between self-care and *soul*-care. These two forms of caring for ourselves have a symbiotic relationship; they work in tandem to provide us with the most completely empowered version of ourselves.

Many of us are aware of the most obvious and physically fundamental ways we can care for ourselves: partaking in a diet of living foods that are nourishing, getting restful and restorative sleep, being physically active with whatever form of movement speaks to us, practicing mindfulness while maintaining an overall attitude of gratitude, and limiting our media consumption. In addition, there is a plethora of external offerings such as spa treatments to help us feel cared for and appreciated.

Beyond these forms of self-care, however, is a realm of soul-care full of nuances that are often overlooked. Having clear belief systems and some connection to a higher power provides us with a well from which we source wisdom and guidance. Once sourced, how do we then move about the world with daily challenges that threaten to throw us off course? We establish a healthy practice of spiritual hygiene so we may maintain and sustain the vitality of our soul and thereby contribute to the well-being of the collective.

Our lives, being energetic in nature, change. The circumstances surrounding us shift. Our experiences with people vary from interaction to interaction. To bring the most alignment to our lives at any given moment, we need an energetic body that is healthy and resilient. We need to be able to meet our internal and external worlds with the clearest vision possible and to be self-aware enough to know when disharmony is occurring and how to adjust ourselves. Perfection is not the goal, but sustained effort is. Ideally, what we strive toward is operating within a narrower and narrower range of being thrown "off." We are striving toward having a solid foundation under us to hold us up when life fluctuates. We are striving toward having a clearer vision of who we are and being responsible for what we emit in the world. We are striving toward heightening our consciousness and living in reciprocity with the laws of the universe.

The spiritual hygiene suggestions below are great opportunities to take stock within ourselves for areas where we often have messy soul-care. Use them as prompts to self-evaluate/reflect on some areas where you may disperse your soul's vitality or as a reminder as to where you may replenish it.

Choice – This is one of the most powerful tools we possess. Every choice we make either empowers or disempowers us. Our choices may also mean the same for others. Making aligned choices for ourselves requires the practice of the "pause": taking a moment to consider how our decision will impact not just how we feel, but whether our choice will assist our spirit to live out its purpose and do no harm.

Boundaries – The implementation of personal boundaries can be a difficult business. Asserting ourselves to protect the power of our choice from a whole, healthy place is often difficult when it has either not been modeled for us or the messages we received were contrary to having boundaries. We tend to swing on a spectrum of either people-pleasing or being rigid and inflexible. Knowing ourselves (how we act, interact, and react) along with what cultivates healthy interactions and environments in which for us to flourish, is what fuels our ability to exert our No. This type of No comes from a healed place inside of us where we are aware that having boundaries is really about maintaining an active containment system. It is within this containment system that our personal power is replenished and we are less likely to feel depleted.

Triggers – The concept of triggers has gained a lot of traction in the mainstream over the last few years as educational spaces struggle to create environments that are trauma-sensitive. Taking an inventory of what jolts our nervous system and creates emotional distress for us is the first step in becoming aware of our triggers. The next step involves doing the inner, soul-level work to heal the trauma fueling those triggers so we can move about the world as spiritually resilient adults. In this way, we take care both of ourselves and our communities as we are less likely to react and more prepared to respond.

Limiting Draining Situations – This topic really falls under maintaining boundaries; however, it is important to speak to it specifically. Whether with our families, friends, colleagues, etc., it is important for us to have clarity around which situations in our lives drain our energy. People are capable of pulling on us energetically and, if we have not established a healthy boundary system (which is the first line of defense), we sense this pull deeply. The symptoms of becoming tired, frustrated, moody, or irritated after interacting in certain situations is evidence of situations that may not be healthy for us. In some cases, it is best to avoid these people or situations, but, more realistically, we need to place clear limits for ourselves around the amount of time we spend in environments that we find draining.

Space – The creation of unplanned space in our lives seems like a luxury, when truly it is a necessity. Placing value on a "wrinkle in time," so to speak, invites a ripple of unknowingness to penetrate our agendas allowing intuition, inspiration, and co-creation to flow through us. It is within this space that we often feel most connected to ourselves and the magical universe around us. We are reminded that our essence is a microcosm of the divine whole and, in this place, we embody true peace. Space may be unplanned and arise spontaneously when plans change or we feel inspired. For those who need more structure, the paradox of planning unplanned space in our routines works! No matter how it occurs, opening this portal in our lives is an imperative part of soul-care.

Spiritual Practice – In tandem with allowing space for ourselves, establishing a *regular* spiritual practice is a key component to spiritual hygiene. For some, partaking in a particular religious faith fulfills this requirement. For others who may never have had, or have left, a religious faith, forging a unique path can be daunting. This is where self-reflection comes into play. Asking yourself what your core beliefs are about the meaning of life, the nature of the universe, and your place within the great macrocosm are juicy starting points. Taking stock of what you are grateful for in your life (gratitude) and who/what you care about can also provide a basic framework to develop a spiritual practice. Next, setting time aside in your day (even less than 5 minutes!) to give thanks, connect to deeper truths, and send well wishes to others IS a spiritual practice. Releasing ourselves from the construct of what a spiritual practice should look like frees us from rigidity and allows for creativity. Regularity is the key.

Nature – We all benefit from nature in ways similar to that of allowing space. Spending quality time in nature provides us with the opportunities of dialogue and reciprocity. Our relationship with the natural world provides a steadfast friendship; she is the one who is always available to comfort our sorrows, offer solace, receive inspiration, and replenish our vitality. If we open our perceptive abilities, we can experience a rich dialogue with her beings (nature spirits) who offer wisdom and insight. Concurrently, when we deepen this relationship, the habits and patterns of how we walk in the world change. We may create shifts in our lifestyle such as supporting local farms, walking rather than driving, recycling, etc., which all help to tend the balance of the delicate ecosystem that we inhabit. In this way, we embody the spirit and practice of reciprocity.

Teachers have a huge role to fill in the lives of their students. Their task is not to be underestimated. Not only are they entrusted to impart knowledge, but they are constantly modeling for their students. This is not to say that teachers don't have bad days! They need as much vitality and grace as possible to conduct themselves and their class. The recognition and practice of good spiritual hygiene for the teacher ensures that a teacher's energetic body is vital enough to enter into a relationship with students first from a place of neutrality. Being in this place allows for more clarity when the teacher may feel triggered or experience boundary-pushing. It also allows for a clearer evaluation of situations and aligned decision-making. With regular soul-care, teachers are more precisely able to interrupt the environment and situations around them. The conclusions they draw may of course be subjective, but having a clear filter to begin with allows for deeper and more thoughtful reflection.

For students, teachers who are practicing both self-care and spiritual hygiene will model a more healthful life both in and out of the classroom. Students will see the implementation of solid, healthy boundaries. They will understand the power of their choices and how the choices they make will either empower or disempower them. Through modeling, they may become aware of their own triggers and seek out more qualified help to initiate deeper healing processes. Students will notice how a teacher is able to handle fluctuations and challenges while exhibiting groundedness and insight. Regular disciplined spiritual/soul hygiene is the foundation upon which all this is possible.*

* Note from Torin: In working with "triggers" and self care, I highly recommend readers take up study of the book *My Grandmother's Hands—Racialized Trauma and the Pathway to Mending our Hearts and Bodies* by Resmaa Menakem (Central Recovery Press, 2017).

21. Institute Expectations:
Three Articulations of Requirements
for Waldorf Teacher Education Programs

1. AWSNA (Association of Waldorf Schools of North America)

PROPOSED MINIMUM EXPECTATIONS FOR AWSNA INSTITUTES
GRADES PROGRAM

To receive and maintain AWSNA membership, institutes engage in these primary activities: collaborating with other Association members, and practicing the AWSNA Principles for Waldorf Institutes and AWSNA Policies and Practices for AWSNA Institutes. In addition, new member institutes agree to the minimum expectations outlined below, and current member institutes agree to these minimum expectations based on a phased implementation to be coordinated between the Leadership Council and the institutes.

As stated above, the minimum expectations identified in this document represent only one aspect of what it means to be recognized as an AWSNA member institute. Other aspects, which are fully articulated in the Membership Agreements, include a demonstrated commitment on the part of each institute to the AWSNA Principles for Waldorf Institutes through an annual site visit or a seven-year cycle of self-study and peer review.

Should a teacher-education institute wish to offer a program that does not fit the Institutes Grades Program Expectations as set out below, the Association will invite the institute to initiate a conversation with AWSNA's Teacher Education Network (TEN) for special consideration of its program.

MINIMUM EXPECTATIONS FOR INSTITUTES GRADES PROGRAM:

Grades teacher-education programs offered by AWSNA teacher-education institutes include coursework, fieldwork, and supplementary work, as described below. These expectations recognize the distinction between enrolled trainees who are already teaching in Waldorf schools (called practicing or "in-service") and enrolled trainees who are not yet teaching in a Waldorf school (called "pre-service").

Whereas coursework is designated in terms of hours, fieldwork is designated in terms of weeks (with an identified hour equivalency), to emphasize that fieldwork is undertaken in longer chunks of time—days and weeks—rather than during specific hours. Fieldwork entails being present not just during class, for instance, but also for transitions, recess, meetings, etc.

While this document outlines agreed minimum expectations for grades programs, institutes create programs in which the AWSNA Principles for Waldorf Institutes are living. For example, Principle #3 states: "Components of the teacher-education program include individual transformational...experiences." This statement implies that to fully engage in these programs, trainees need time extending beyond their course and fieldwork; and that programs need to provide this extended time in the way they are structured.

All institutes include foundation studies in their teacher-training programs, either as a prerequisite or as part of their coursework. Institutes that require foundation studies in anthroposophy as a prerequisite to their teacher training courses may count these offerings as up to 100 hours of coursework, as set out below. In addition, institutes are permitted to credit coursework from another recognized institution in accordance with their own documented policies on the transfer of credits.

I. COURSEWORK

In addition to at least 100 hours in foundation studies, whether undertaken as prerequisite or as part of their teacher training programs, Waldorf teacher-education institutes require a further minimum of approximately 400 hours of coursework facilitated by institute instructors in the following five areas, which are treated in roughly equivalent proportion:

  a. *Inner/Self Development* (for example, the study of foundational books and lecture cycles by Rudolf Steiner, individual exercises, artistic activities for the adult learner, etc.)
  b. *Human/Child Development* (for example, the constitution, health, and evolution of the human being)
  c. *Pedagogical Development/Art of Teaching* (for example, but not limited to...)
     • Curriculum content: literacy/numeracy
     • Teaching methodology: educational support, lesson planning,

artistic activities for the classroom, classroom management, differentiated learning
- Assessment methods: child observation and assessment

d. *Social/Organizational/Administrative Development* (for example school organization and leadership, adult group dynamics, parent work, etc.)

e. *General Development* (for example, special features of a course or program requiring extended time, additional time for areas a.-d., or including but not limited to the production of a play or preparation of a science experiment)

2. FIELDWORK

Waldorf teacher-education programs require a minimum of approximately six weeks of pedagogical observation and teaching practice if a trainee is "in-service" (already a lead or subject teacher in a Waldorf school), or approximately twelve weeks if a trainee is "pre-service" (not yet lead teaching in a Waldorf school). Fieldwork involves being present not just during class, but for transitions, recess, meetings, etc.

Fieldwork for "in-service" trainees includes six weeks of the following components across the grades program:
- Observing experienced teacher in a Waldorf classroom beyond one's own school (pedagogical observation)
- Lead teaching under the supervision of a mentor teacher in a different grade area; for example, lead teaching in the middle school if the in-service trainee is currently teaching in the lower school
- Lead teaching one's current class under the supervision of a mentor teacher for at least 50% of the practicum

Fieldwork for "pre-service" trainees includes twelve weeks of the following components:
- Observing experienced teacher other than one's lead or mentor teacher (pedagogical observation)
- Observing school days, including faculty meetings, parent meetings, extracurricular events, etc.
- Assisting lead teacher
- Lead teaching under the supervision of a lead or mentor teacher, for at least the equivalent of one full block
- Receiving regular mentoring

3. SUPPLEMENTARY WORK

Waldorf teacher-education programs require a minimum of approximately 200 hours (or six weeks) of additional institute coursework or fieldwork, or other work (independent projects, capstone, etc.) to be determined by each institution based on individual or program needs.

2. TEN (the AWSNA Teacher Education Network) has elaborated on the above guidelines as follows.
(Draft as of Oct. 12, 2016)

EXPECTATIONS OF A WALDORF TEACHER-EDUCATION PROGRAM

Waldorf education is based on particular insights into child development and world evolution made possible through Rudolf Steiner's spiritual research known as anthroposophy. A thoroughgoing familiarity with these insights is vital if one is to take up the vocation of becoming a Waldorf educator, whether in the early childhood, elementary, or high school years. In fact, one can more accurately characterize Waldorf education as being "the activity of a school or teacher working with the insights derived from anthroposophy" than being simply the application of so-called Waldorf methods or techniques.

The key areas of study and practice — each receiving roughly equal emphasis—in any Waldorf teacher-education program are essentially four:
- Inner/Self Development
- Human/Child Development
- Pedagogical Development/Craft of Teaching
- Organizational/Leadership Development
- General/Supplementary Development (of the areas outlined above)

Without the engagement of these transformative elements, methods and techniques will not provide sufficient basis for a Waldorf school or teacher. Given these four areas of emphasis, what are the experiences and activities that prepare an aspiring Waldorf teacher? Which foundational and teacher training courses will help a prospective—or indeed practicing—teacher connect with the vital transformative principles that constitute the essence of Waldorf teaching?

The Teacher Education Network of AWSNA has formulated an outline as a way of responding to these questions. The TEN offers the following overview as a general outline; it is meant neither to represent a

curriculum sequence nor to prescribe a precise course of study. The outline is described in four phases unfolding in sequence or, in many cases,
overlapping over extended periods of time:

I.   Foundational studies in anthroposophy and the arts
II.   Coursework in teacher education
III. Fieldwork (i.e., internship or practicum in a Waldorf school)
IV.   Supplementary work

Waldorf teacher training institutes that designate at least a portion of
the first phase (foundation studies) as being prerequisite to enrollment may
in consequence offer a program totaling 800-1,000 hours, representing
the equivalent of 20 to 25 weeks of course and field study; by contrast,
institutes in which foundation studies are embedded in their initial coursework may offer a program lasting up to twice that length of time.

Beyond the four phases laid out above, it is expected of all Waldorf
teachers that, once certified, they will continue their professional development with further ongoing courses and workshops to deepen their work
at all four levels.

I.   FOUNDATIONAL STUDIES IN ANTHROPOSOPHY AND THE ARTS

One important aspect of foundation studies is to develop the understanding that history tells the story of development in human consciousness. The awareness that our consciousness today is only one step in the
evolution of humanity is an essential underpinning of Waldorf education
and provides a context for the entire curriculum. To develop this awareness is in itself transformative, because it opens new possibilities for understanding oneself and the world.

As Waldorf schools, teacher preparation programs, and teachers, we
agree to start our study of human evolution with a consideration of the
picture that Rudolf Steiner painted of human history. In the context of
Steiner's backdrop, we weigh our experience and begin a continual testing:
How is this picture true today? We use the knowledge found in spiritual science, or anthroposophy, as a starting point or "working hypothesis."
If anthroposophy is not the starting point in this exploration, then we
are not operating as Waldorf teachers! Therefore, one of the foundations
of becoming a Waldorf teacher is to explore actively the basic tenets of
anthroposophy and its spiritual history of humanity. For aspiring teachers,
simply reading Steiner's books and voluminous lectures, or merely being
exposed to his ideas, is not sufficient. It is generally agreed that in actively

working with these anthroposophical concepts—for instance, through the practice of the arts—or in reflecting and sharing insights with fellow students, we develop a far more flexible understanding, while building as well the capacity to work together socially.

It must also be strongly emphasized that working with Steiner's ideas is only one part of an effective foundation for becoming a Waldorf teacher. Perhaps even more important are the capacities the teacher-training student will gain through working both with the arts and with exercises for inner development. Let us consider each separately, though ultimately they represent two side of a single coin.

<u>Working artistically</u>: Waldorf teachers are asked not only to work with the arts—clay modeling, painting, music, drama, speech, and, perhaps above all, eurythmy and Spacial Dynamics—but to work artistically also in all of their teaching. By actively working with the arts, aspiring teachers develop a flexibility of soul that enables them to develop enhanced powers of perception and imagination. To have the capacity to "perceive" what is needed in a given situation and to respond—to create artistically in the moment—is a necessity for every teacher, however mature or experienced.

<u>Inner development</u>: In addition to the flexibility and imaginative power that can be built through artistic activity, an essential characteristic of Waldorf teaching is that the teacher cultivates an inner life. No foundational program would be complete without focusing on the need for the teacher to know him- or herself and to be willing to continually work at both improving areas of weakness and embracing areas of talent and leadership. Meditation, basic soul exercises, biography work, and the development of healthy social skills all serve to help the teacher stand as a worthy role model and leader of children. It is not the complete mastery of one's inner life but rather an honest and forthright dedication to embracing the task of self-development that readies the teacher for the challenges of the classroom.

The Teacher Education Network has identified the following areas of study and experience as being the essential foundation for Waldorf teaching. It should be noted that there are many paths a student may take in exploring each of these areas. Again, it would be an unrealistic expectation for students to think they need to achieve full mastery of these concepts; some of these ideas may require lifetimes of work to be fully comprehended! The important fact is that students are exposed to these anthroposophical ideas and exercises and that they work with them in a holistic way, both socially and artistically. Through this kind of work, the capacities for self-transformation are built. These capacities constitute the fundament of Waldorf teaching.

We might also add that these foundational studies need to continue if they are to be of lasting value for teaching. Experience shows that both teacher and school benefit greatly when further opportunities for the exploration of these topics are made a priority.

The following areas of study are presented not as a catalogue of belief, but as areas of ongoing philosophical inquiry.

1. <u>Understanding the human being</u>

The twofold, threefold, fourfold, sevenfold, ninefold, and twelvefold aspects of the human being. The twelve senses. Especially the physical, etheric, astral, and ego aspects of the body, and the thinking, feeling, and willing aspects of soul.

Possible references: *Theosophy, Esoteric Science*

The stages of human development, especially the first twenty-one years of life. Aspects of the biography of a human life.

Possible reference: *The Human Life* (O'Neil)

Karma and Reincarnation: How would one teach differently if human development were seen in the light of repeated earth lives?

Possible reference: *Anthroposophy in Everyday Life*

The nature of thinking and free human activity. Rudolf Steiner's picture of moral intuition as the basis of true human freedom.

Possible reference: *Intuitive Thinking as a Spiritual Path: A Philosophy of Freedom*

The relationship of the human being to the hierarchies, including the School of Michael and its role in anthroposophy and Waldorf education.

Possible references: *The Spiritual Guidance of the Individual and Humanity; Harmony of the Creative Word; The Younger Generation; Anthroposophical Leading Thoughts*

2. <u>Influences in historical development</u>

Exploration of historical evolution of consciousness in terms of individual development and current circumstances. This inquiry could be through art history, literature, mythology, biography, philosophy, music, religion, mathematics, science, etc. Not only does this study form a basis for deeper insight into the Waldorf curriculum, it provides a great opportunity for the student to take another look at what s/he already "knows."

Inquiry into the influence of the Christ being on human evolution. Developing perspectives on the activity of the Christ being throughout history—in whatever culture, and separate from "religious fact"—frees the student both from the dogma of traditional religions and from the emptiness of the materialistic modern world. This study helps develop a language and outlook that are inclusive of all peoples.

Possible reference: *And Who Shall Teach the Teachers: A Colloquium on the Christ Impulse in Waldorf Education* (Gerwin, ed.)

3. Modes of understanding

Percept to concept: Thinking about thinking...

Observation and phenomenology: A way of understanding the material world. How can we develop a relationship to the natural world that does not deaden us to the spirit that created it? An emphasis on phenomenological science opens new possibilities for exploring the boundaries of natural science.

Possible reference: *The Wholeness of Nature* (Henri Bortoft)

Relationship to the rhythm of the year: What are the realities hidden behind our celebration of festivals? What has been lost in modern culture of the healthful benefits of a relationship to the seasons?

Possible reference: *The Festivals and Their Meaning*

Science, religion, and art: What is a spiritual scientific method? A religious mood? An artistic expression? Where is each appropriate?

4. Path of inner development

For example, the "Six basic exercises": Control of thinking, the will exercise, equanimity, positivity, impartiality, perseverance.

Eightfold path.

Meditation: What is a modern path of meditation?

Possible reference: *Meditation According to Rudolf Steiner* (Katz)

Rückschau: The daily practice of reviewing the events of a day—in reverse order of their occurrence—provides a foundation of strength in daily life.

Possible references: *How to Know Higher Worlds; Guidance in Esoteric Training; Esoteric Science; Intuitive Thinking as a Spiritual Path; Man on the Threshold* (B. Lievegoed)

5. Artistic experience as a path of self-development

Exercises in color, movement, form, tone, rhythm, and the Word.
Work with speech, painting/drawing, eurythmy, sculpture, music, drama,
and architecture.

6. Rudolf Steiner's life and work

Rudolf Steiner's autobiography: Chapters from *The Course of My Life.*

7. Evolution of consciousness and working socially in the modern age

Sentient Soul, Mind Soul, Consciousness Soul: How do we reach
beyond mere feeling and intellect?

The Threefold Social Organism.

Perspectives on Psychology
Possible reference: *Psychoanalysis and Spiritual Psychology*

Social and Anti-Social Forces
Possible reference: *The Challenge of the Times*

The Double
Possible reference: *Man on the Threshold* (B. Lievegoed)

The most important factor is that students engage in active research
within each of these categories and practice the various exercises. The
aspiring teacher must understand that an anthroposophical worldview is
based on disciplined inquiry. The aim is to consider all traditions, yet not
to get swept up in, for example, the intellectual abstractions of modern
science or the latest "New Age" fad. An anthroposophical approach invites
the student to look at what one thought one knew, but to look at it with
new eyes.

II.   Coursework in teacher education

Waldorf teacher-education programs expect a minimum of approximately 400 hours of core content and research facilitated by institute
instructors in the following five areas, each treated in roughly equivalent
proportion:

INNER/SELF DEVELOPMENT

The study of Rudolf Steiner's basic books and lectures, individual exercises, artistic activities for the adult learner, etc., including the themes of:

- Evolution of consciousness
- Karma, destiny, and biography
- Anthroposophical view of the human being
- Life and work of Rudolf Steiner

Artistic practice and skills development, including:

- Eurythmy
- Painting
- Drawing, Chalkboard
- Form Drawing
- Sculpture—Beeswax, Clay Modeling
- Woodworking
- Instrumental Music
- Singing
- Speech, Drama
- Handwork, Crafts
- Spacial Dynamics (Bothmer Gymnastics)

HUMAN/CHILD DEVELOPMENT

The constitution, health, and evolutionary stages of the human being, including the themes of:

- Child Development pre-birth to 21
- Developmental views (temperaments, sensory, polarities)
- Child's well-being (social, physical, nutritional, emotional, ethical)

PEDAGOGICAL DEVELOPMENT/ART OF TEACHING

Curriculum content, lesson planning, artistic activities for the classroom, classroom management, child assessment, etc., including the themes of:

- Overview of Waldorf education
- Development of education
- History and philosophy of education
- Curriculum indications and development
- Multicultural perspectives on curriculum
- Pedagogical indications and practices
- Method indications and practices
- Rhythms

- School and classroom culture
- "Child Observation" and study
- Formative assessment methods and practices

ORGANIZATIONAL/ADMINISTRATIVE DEVELOPMENT

School organization and leadership, adult group dynamics, social development, etc., including the themes of:
- Threefold social organism
- School organization
- School and pedagogical leadership, collaboration
- Professionalism and career development (including mentoring and evaluation support)
- Legal responsibilities (including mandated reporting)
- Work with colleagues
- Work with parents

GENERAL/SUPPLEMENTARY DEVELOPMENT

Special features of a course or program requiring extended time, such as the production of a play or preparation of a science experiment.

III. Fieldwork (internship/practicum) [6 – 12 weeks]

Waldorf teacher-education programs expect a minimum of approximately six weeks of pedagogical observation and teaching practice if a student is "in-service" (already a lead or subject teacher in a Waldorf school), or twelve weeks if a student is "pre-service" (not yet lead teaching in a Waldorf school).

Fieldwork for "in-service" students includes **6 weeks** of the following components:
- Observing experienced teacher in a Waldorf classroom beyond one's own school (pedagogical observation)
- Undertaking "staged" lead teaching of a class other than one's own
- Conducting "lead teaching" under the observation of a mentor teacher
- Receiving continued mentoring

Fieldwork for "pre-service" students includes **12 weeks** of the following components:
- Observing experienced teacher other than one's lead or mentor

teacher (pedagogical observation)
- Observing full school days, including faculty meetings, parent meetings, extracurricular events, etc.
- Assisting lead teacher
- Teaching under the supervision of a lead or mentor teacher
- Receiving continued mentoring

IV. Supplementary work [6 weeks]

Waldorf teacher-education programs require a minimum of approximately 200 hours (or 6 weeks) of additional institute coursework or fieldwork, to be determined by each institution based on individual or program needs.

3. The Alliance for Public Waldorf Education has outlined the following recommendations.

RECOMMENDATIONS FOR CORE COMPONENTS FOR TEACHER PREPARATION IN ALLIANCE MEMBER SCHOOLS

The Pedagogical Committee of the Alliance has identified eight major areas that are considered essential components of any teacher preparation program for teachers in an Alliance member school. Fieldwork is the ninth component; it is described separately below. Effective preparation is aligned with the Core Principles of Public Waldorf education.

This outline is offered as a guide for individual or institutional reference; the Alliance does not certify, endorse, or approve teacher-preparation programs, individual trainers or consultants, or institutions.

MAJOR AREAS OF TEACHER PREPARATION

Philosophy:
- Anthroposophy in context of modern thought
- Rudolf Steiner's life and works
- History and Philosophy of education

Child Development:
- Models of child development: Steiner and others
- Phases of child development
- Developmentally appropriate curriculum and education

Curriculum and Instruction:
- Early childhood: child and curriculum
- Grades: child and curriculum (main lesson scope and sequence includes: language arts, math development, science, social sciences, STEAM); "special subjects" (e.g. world languages, handwork, movement, music)
- High school: child and curriculum (main lesson scope and sequence includes: language arts, math, science, humanities, STEAM); "special subjects: (e.g. arts, world languages, crafts, movement, etc.)
- Multicultural adaptations: teaching who is in the room
- Methods
- Literacy (note that this is typically an area of special emphasis in teacher education)
- Technology in the classroom
- Classroom management
- Planning and record-keeping

Development of the Teacher:
- Teaching Presence: inner development, mindfulness, presence
- Arts for (inner) self-development
- Social, collegial, and group work
- Communication
- Leadership
- School governance and organization

Policy and Contemporary Issues:
- Contemporary issues in education
- Diversity and multicultural perspectives
- Equity and social justice
- Accountability
- Professional responsibilities, rights, and expectations
- School structure and culture
- Media literacy and technology ethics

The Individual Learner:
- Assessment
- Child Study
- Archetypes and polarities
- Trauma-informed education
- Educational support, including remedial work
- Special education/special needs

Arts in education:
- Role of the arts
- Teacher as artist
- Arts curriculum

Research:
- Independent reading and study
- Research methodologies
- Independent project/capstone/action research/thesis (determined by program requirements, ideally linked to practice)

CORE COMPONENTS, LENGTH AND WEIGHTING (DOES NOT INCLUDE FIELD EXPERIENCE; SEE BELOW FOR RECOMMENDATIONS)

A range of clock hours or percentage of time has been allotted to each key component, allowing flexible design based on the strengths and needs of individual programs. *Note: this means that percentages do not add to 100%.*

Overall length is given in classroom contact hours; although traditional higher education is assessed in units or credit hours, this does not translate well across academic, practical arts, inner work, and arts classes.

FOUNDATION STUDIES

A common feature of traditional Waldorf teacher-preparation programs, this is not specified as a stand-alone requirement, although its important role is acknowledged.

Typical options for fulfillment include but are not limited to:
- Applicants demonstrate prior study and knowledge of Steiner's work and artistic activity;
- Program offers coursework in fundamentals of anthroposophy;
- Equivalent foundation studies subjects are woven throughout the program if not taught separately.

Recommended guide: 100 hours

TEACHER EDUCATION, OVERALL LENGTH REQUIREMENTS

Core components are embedded in the following areas:

400-500 hours:
- Inner work and self-development, 10-15% of total program (may be partly covered in "foundation" studies)
- Human/child development, 10-25% of total program

- Pedagogical development/art of teaching, 25–40% of total program
- Social/organizational/administrative aspects, 15–25% of total program
- Arts and teacher as artist, 10–15%
- Additional topics (e.g., assessment, Child Study, trauma-informed education, educational support, archetypes and polarities), 8–15%
- Independent research, e.g., capstone or another project, 5–16%

Online Learning

Several aspects of teacher preparation may be delivered online. These include the more academic subjects (e.g., human development, educational philosophy) and seminar classes.

All teacher preparation programs must include a substantial face-to-face component. As this is a changing, dynamic sector of adult education, "substantial" is not specifically defined.

Field Experience: Pre-service (trainee teachers with no prior training or teaching experience)

12 weeks to 2 full semesters (standard in many conventional teacher-education programs):
- Programs are responsible for ensuring that placements take place with an experienced, trained Waldorf teacher in an established school.
- Combination of observing (class and child), assisting, participating in the full life of the school, solo teaching, mentoring.
- Must include experience in an Alliance member school.

Field Experience: In-service (students with prior non–Waldorf teacher training and teaching experience)

6 weeks to a semester.
- May be fulfilled though traditional, internship, or apprenticeship models.
- Includes observations in a range of grades.
- On-site mentoring by master teacher.
- Observations, mentoring, and coaching from program.
- Demonstrate participation in full life of school.
- Supported by seminar, practice-based classes (can be online).

Mentoring, Evaluation, and Professional Development

These are essential elements for effective teacher preparation.

- For trainees, mentoring is a shared responsibility of the host school (must be able to provide an experienced supervising teacher) and program (must be able to provide observation, mentoring, coaching, and evaluation).
- Evaluation must include feedback on the placement from the supervising teacher plus program-based evaluation.

Mentoring and support are essential during the first years of teaching; this is a responsibility of schools. Ongoing professional development is an expectation. It is anticipated that this may be achieved through a combination of on-site faculty study, workshops and conferences, and summer enrichment or certificate courses.

Many years of experience demonstrate that development of a teacher continues well beyond completion of any certificate or qualification. Any preparation program is inevitably introductory in many areas. New teachers continue to develop their skills in the classroom and need support in order to do so. Ongoing professional development and support are essential to the deepening of teaching.

Whole-school trainings

- Must meet the minimum core requirements.
- Must include additional emphasis on leadership, school structure, faculty meetings, school culture, governance, etc. in an Alliance member context.

Resources and Texts

The selection of resources is the responsibility of each program. Resources and texts must include core knowledge, demonstrate an understanding of contemporary issues in education, the needs of teachers, students, and schools, and an awareness of requirements of public education.

Commentary and Questions

This author is grateful to AWSNA, TEN, and the Alliance for doing so much work in considering the key components of Waldorf teacher education. The overview represented in the documents above provide foundational considerations not only for the institutes, but for the many schools that seek qualified teachers. At the same time, the guidelines leave considerable freedom, which is as it should be. We cannot become like the regulatory agencies that specify quantifiable hours for each segment, for, as we all know, curriculum taught by one person can be very different when taught by another. Efforts to highly regulate often end up suppressing the very initiative we so need in education today.

Looking at the broad strokes of the documentation above, we see major categories. In the AWSNA and TEN expectations we have:

- Inner/Self Development
- Human/Child Development
- Pedagogical Development/Craft of Teaching
- Organizational/Leadership Development
- General/Supplementary Development (of the areas outlined above)

In the Alliance recommendations we have:

- Philosophy
- Child Development
- Curriculum and Instruction
- Development of the Teacher
- Policy and Contemporary Issues
- The Individual Learner
- Arts in Education
- Research

Both describe foundational studies, field experience and supplementary work. There are also slight divergences, as the Alliance recommendations, for good reason, include the Policy and Contemporary Issues more explicitly, listing contemporary issues in education, diversity, equity and social justice, accountability, professional responsibilities, school structure and culture, media literacy and technology ethics. Taken together, these documents form a solid foundation for the work of teacher education.

Weaving between the categories and language are questions that each program needs to address on a continuing basis:

What is the relative balance and proportional emphasis and time spent on the different categories? The Alliance gives percentage ranges, but much remains up to each institute and program. How much anthroposophy? How much curriculum vs. skills work in math and language arts? How are the arts balanced with the rest of the coursework and with each other? How much time is devoted to fieldwork? Research? Inner development?

In a healthy situation these matters are dealt with through vigorous conversations followed by consistent practices. In less ideal situations, the answers to the above questions come from singular individuals who happen to be teaching in the institute at a given moment in time. Here one has the need to find the delicate balance between accepting the talents of particular faculty and building a consistent set of program expectations that can survive any particular biographical phase of the institute (see core principles and other related topics in "Future Pathways" chapter).

Historically, my impression is that program emphasis has also changed according to the demands/needs of the schools. The "classic" forms of Waldorf teacher education with year-long, full-time foundation years, lots of general curriculum work, arts, and anthroposophy have given way in some instances to more focus on grade-specific preparation and skills. Post-training needs are now addressed by consultants and online instructors with specialized fee-for-service programs. All this is natural, but little research has been done on the effectiveness of various programs and delivery models in terms of school success: student learning, enrollment, parent satisfaction, etc. We need to look at what we are offering in teacher education and assess the impact on schools, celebrating success and recognizing shortcomings that call for change.

In the absence of sufficient research on these matters, I am left with simple means of evaluating where we have been and where we need to go. For thirty years I have read student evaluations of individual courses at Antioch and the Center for Anthroposophy, have heard large- and small-group feedback, have interacted extensively with schools, heard anecdotal commentary from practicing teachers, and listened to colleagues in teacher-education programs describe their impressions of how we are doing. I have also been stimulated by the research for this book and the survey responses from our wonderful alumni (see next chapter). All this goes into the chapter that follows the alumni responses: "Future Pathways for Waldorf-Teacher Education," in which I attempt to lay out new directions for the work ahead.

22. Listening to Our Alums

Summary of Alumni Survey #1

From July to December 2019, the Center for Anthroposophy distributed a survey to Antioch New England and CfA alumni with the aim of updating contact information and measuring interest in the formation of an alumni association. Hard copies were distributed in our summer programs, after which electronic copies were sent out. In all, 191 individuals completed the survey, and 300 corrections were made to our database.

The response to forming an alum association was positive, and the alumni were aligned in their goals and needs. Below is a summary of a few key questions, in each case reporting just the top responses:

1. *How would an alum association best support you?*
   Keep me connected to my cohort   130
   Help me contact colleagues teaching similar grades
   and subjects   124
   Allow me to share teaching resources   113

2. *What would be your preferred means of communication within the association?*
   Email   117
   Dedicated website   52

3. Would it be helpful to have short bios of alumni to see who has taught specific grades/subjects to share experiences?   92

4. Would it be helpful if members of an alum association provided support for non-teaching issues, such as
   parent work, governance?   98

5. Most pressing issues:
   Differentiated earning   85
   Working with parents   75
   Mentoring and evaluation   78
   Specific subject areas   62

6. How would you like to meet?

    Face to face on weekends, regionally   123

    Some offered to lead regional workshops, others to serve as school reps. The notion of school-based representation replaces the more traditional class reps, since teachers do change schools and keeping up with contact info can be challenging.

Summary of Alumni Survey #2

The next step in the process was a more comprehensive survey of alumni in 2020, asking for assessment of their teacher-education program in light of subsequent service in schools. Some of the results are featured below:

Who Responded: Response rates from alumni from both the CfA high-school program as well as Antioch's year-round and summer-sequence program were remarkably consistent, at 10-15 percent of graduates. Some others joined in as well, such as a one-time cohort we had in the great state of Maine, and a few from the Healing Ed program. Years of experience varied from 2 to 20+ years in the classroom since graduation, and 13% were themselves graduates of Waldorf schools.

Why Waldorf? When asked why they were drawn to Waldorf teacher education, respondents shared comments such as:

    Creativity, freedom, emphasis on teaching the whole child and the school environment.

    My interest in child development and the social mission of Waldorf schools.

    I was working in a Camphill Community and wanted to be a teacher.

    The Waldorf graduates I met told me about their education and I was inspired. The curriculum stuck with me, and the spirituality of the education.

    I wished to pursue a career change from engineering/business. Wanted my family to join the Waldorf community.

    I was inspired by the unique gift Steiner brought to the world and an educational approach that gives each child the ability to look at life with utter freshness....to expand the horizons of human experience and become inclusive.

    I wanted to know about and understand what lay behind and at the heart of the education I myself had received.

When I was looking for a school for my son, I decided to teach at the same school to understand the education better.

The community—the friendly, wise and welcoming nature of those who are involved in the movement, and the fruits/family aspect of seeing well-rounded children and very involved teachers and parents.

And there were practical considerations too. These included finding a delivery model that suited full-time work, the need to move from assistant to full-time work in the future, referrals from trusted friends and alumni, and the reputation of the program in question.

Graph 12: How well were you prepared for teaching in certain key areas? (A low number means well prepared, higher numbers mean less well prepared.)

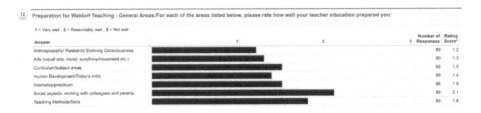

Graphs 13, 14, 15: We then asked the Goldilocks question for alumni from the year-round program, the summer sequence, and the high school training program: too little, just right, or too much?

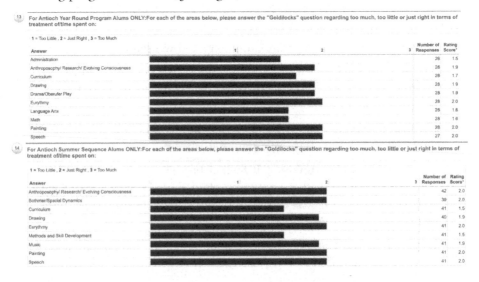

For CfA High School Program Alums ONLY:For each of the areas below, please answer the "Goldilocks" question regarding too much, too little or just right in terms of treatment of/time spent on:

1 = Too Little , 2 = Just Right , 3 = Too Much

Answer	1	2	3	Number of Responses	Rating Score*
Anthroposophy Human Development				25	1.9
English Literature				15	2.0
Fine Arts & Art History				13	1.9
History & Social Studies				14	2.0
Life Sciences & Earth Science				13	1.8
Mathematics				15	1.8
Physics & Chemistry				12	1.8
Social Relations/Administration				19	1.5
ProSem II (Research)				20	1.9
ProSem III				17	1.7

Reflections on Responses by High School Alumni

It is heartening to see that a great number of high-school respondents singled out the significance of artistic practice, both in the context of their training as well as in their own lives, as essential to the task of becoming a Waldorf teacher. It is not always easy to persuade high-school teachers to take the risk of plunging into an artistic activity, especially if they come with no prior experience of it or little native skill in learning it. To see a middle-aged high-school science teacher struggle with needle and thread in an exercise of sewing a little being of felt and fabric, and then at the end to treasure this hard-won accomplishment, will disarm even the most skeptical academic observer. That said, some of the most compelling demonstrations of eurythmy, for instance, or striking sculptural forms on display during the final assembly of the summer program, can be attributed to these artistic neophytes.

Not surprisingly, the high-school trainees singled out mentoring as one of the most helpful aspects of their professional development, mostly in the schools where they were teaching, but also during the time of the summer program. Many highlighted the help they received from seasoned colleagues, as well as from fellow participants in the training; others pointed up the insufficiency of this aspect of the program. Though more work needs to be done in this area, as one high-school trainee correctly observed, the mentorship of high-school teachers has been expanded since the early days of this program, now in its 25th year.

Waldorf teachers, as we know, do not grow on trees. In many cases, they do not of themselves go for training and then seek a position in a high school. More likely, as quite a few mentioned in their individual narrative responses, they are drawn to Waldorf education because they were seeking a school for their own children or because someone *asked* or *encouraged* them to join the high school faculty. This tells us that, as a school movement, we need to be on the lookout for strong and dedicated teachers and help them find their way into our high-school classrooms.

Consistent with responses from trainees in the Antioch elementary school program, high-school trainees singled out the non-academic aspects of life in a Waldorf school, such as work with colleagues and parents, as requiring more attention in their training. This need has been identified by AWSNA's Teacher Education Delegates Circle—a consortium of seven full-member institutes and a further seven associate member programs—as requiring much more "air time" in our programs. Even (some might say "especially") experienced teachers new to Waldorf schools struggle with the way the schools run their meetings, handle communications with parents and colleagues, make (or neglect to make) decisions. While as teacher trainers we cannot—indeed, should not—anticipate the shortcomings of the schools where their graduates will end up teaching, we can do more to provide graduates with a bigger toolbox to address these issues.

From the responses we received, it would seem that high-school respondents are pretty happy "Goldilocks" when it comes to the quality and content of their academic courses and subject-specific seminars. It was reassuring to see that if they deviated from the "just right" rating, the average of their responses strayed toward the "too little" rather than toward the "too much" pole. When asked to rate various aspects of the program on a scale of 1 ("poor") to 5 ("excellent"), with very few exceptions the number of respondents selecting the top score exceeded any other numerical rating.

Reflections on Responses from Antioch Alumni

It is striking how many similarities there are between alumni of our high school program and those who graduated from our elementary teacher-education programs at Antioch. Even though faculty, schedules, and of course, content were different, some of the same strengths and needs emerged from both groups:

Strengths of the Antioch Programs:
- Anthroposophy courses
- Arts in general, but particularly painting and eurythmy
- Internships, practica
- Research courses and masters projects
- Aspects of curriculum work
- Mentoring and advising

Challenges that need to be addressed:

- Social issues such as working with parents, colleagues, and school governance
- Methods and skills courses, especially math
- Some of the arts

Individual responses in interviews and follow-up conversations surfaced some interesting nuances to the above:

It was not that we did not have enough curriculum course work, but too often the focus was on "philosophy of curriculum" and why we do what we do rather than the "how and specific methods." In regard to the social issues, some wondered how one might do more to prepare for working with parents and administration when still in the program and *before* being immersed in the life of a school. Some wondered if these aspects would best be covered toward the end of the program, or even as post-graduate workshops such as in Renewal offerings. Others asked that we please not lessen the high-quality experience received in the areas of strength to accommodate the identified needs.

Taken together, the two surveys point to the opportunity for alumni to network and serve one another through more frequent communication, regional gatherings, and sharing of expertise. There is also a realistic tone of what is actually possible in terms of alum work given the high demands on the time of the average teacher.

One final note: both surveys were designed and conducted *before Covid-19*, and while they should not be discounted in any way, the world is not the same. Alum preferences for regional gatherings, for example, might now give way to zoom and other virtual ways to connect. We will all have to wait a bit to see how things settle down and what pathways will be most possible in the years to come.

23. Future Pathways for Teacher Education

In an earlier chapter on "Information Overload," there was a description of the different levels of teacher preparation:

- Yearlong—gathering and digesting of materials (physical)
- Monthly—working rhythmically to prepare and sequence entire blocks (etheric)
- Weekly—organizing specific lesson plans and threading the transitions of one learning unit to the next, like juxtaposing the movements of a piece of music (astral)
- Daily—pulling it all together, revising in the light of the last lesson, and polishing delivery and specific activities, risking something new and untried (ego)

With these in mind, we need to look at the future of teacher education in a way that honors all four levels. For when we do, we can draw forth *the whole human being in the creative process of becoming a teacher.* What can we do in teacher education that works with the yearly, monthly, weekly, or daily rhythms? Can we take these seriously, rather than just jump to discussion of cost-effective delivery models?

We need to bear in mind that the whole trend in civilization today is to back-end things into the astral and ego realm: just-in-time delivery of goods is matched by just-in-time preparation. Amazon can do one-day delivery, and most of us are grateful to get things so quickly. But when the same mentality is transferred to teacher education, we have too much emphasis on attending one-week grade-specific courses (astral) and Googling answers the night before teaching (ego). When this becomes a habit, we remain more on the surface of things and hinder the acquisition of real knowledge that with time can mature into wisdom. And wisdom has throughout history been the fount of true learning.

The reverse can also be true: a teacher who prepares a complete lesson a year ahead at a summer intensive course can find that it hardens into "concrete form" prematurely.

So, as with so much in Waldorf education, there are few rules but many things that flow out of artistic practice:

- With the 24-hour cycle: day and night, light and shadow;
- With the 7-day cycle: the complementary six planetary styles, plus the radiant sun-style that shines through them all. How to teach on a Monday, a Tuesday, etc....and how to weave in the mood of Saturn when we don't teach on Saturdays!
- With the 12-month cycle: the twelve perspectives of the zodiac; perhaps also the four archangels of the seasons (*The Four Seasons and the Archangels*, GA 229, is a great resource for teachers in this latter regard, especially the fifth and final lecture).

Thus *one of the essential components in designing teacher-education programs of the future has to do with how we harness the laws of* **time**.

The second key component is working with the notion of **space**. This has to do with location of course, but also with where face-to-face courses are located. For years, the Antioch University/Center for Anthroposophy summer courses have taken place during July on the High Mowing/Pine Hill Waldorf School campus in New Hampshire, giving us not only consistency of location, but also Waldorf classrooms where children learn all year long. Their creativity lingers into the summer and helps us hold the space. For example, the location on 200 acres at the top of Abbot Hill has been a source of stability and nourishment to countless teachers in our summer programs.

Spatial considerations also have to do with travel, and we have found that long before Covid-19, travel had become more challenging for some, as it usually entails leaving family and children at home for several weeks. However, the program most impacted has been our Keene-based residential program, with fewer students being able/willing to relocate.

Conversely, our "extension" programs, such as the Explorations and Building Bridges programs, have done relatively well. In these sites, the classes are held at a regional school over a weekend once a month (etheric rhythm). Students have minimal travel and food/lodging is often not an issue. In our Yuba, CA cohort in the 2019-20 school year we had 26 students from six local schools and some local instructors, but at least one faculty member had to fly in from a distance each weekend. In our summer programs in Wilton, NH, we have both students and faculty traveling a variety of distances, some even internationally.

In our Explorations Program (foundational studies in arts and anthroposophy) we also use a weekend model, but with fewer hours than Building Bridges. Host schools have been happy to open their doors to our students, many of whom are also parents, administrators, and beginning teachers at the school. Tuition is relatively low, and our local coordinators help with recruitment, preparing the classrooms, and attending to social dynamics such as potluck meals. One really senses a productive partnership between an institute and the host school.

So in terms of spatial considerations, we have an interesting interplay between "center and periphery." How much can be done on the periphery, how much needs to be done out of the home base?

With the use of Zoom these last two years for our Explorations program (once a month to supplement the weekend face-to-face sessions) we have both a center and periphery at work simultaneously. Presentations and small-group discussions (but not large-group discussions) have worked well in this format, especially when it is balanced with lots of eurythmy, painting, clay modeling, and other arts in the weekend sessions. Many colleagues feel that it is essential that the face-to-face experience needs to happen *before* the virtual sessions.

Going forward, we need to look at how much more can be done virtually and what needs to be retained for face-to-face coursework. Teachers are currently evaluating their spring 2020 experiences during the Covid-19 crisis and will have valuable learning to share with us all in the months ahead.

Given what we know now, and given the content of the preceding chapters on topics related to teacher education, what can we do to reform our current practices? Having looked at some key themes covered in preceding chapters (Adult Learning, Group Work, Social Intelligence, etc.) how can we begin to design a new framework for anthroposophically inspired adult education going forward?

I would like to suggest it is time to establish **Core Principles for Waldorf Teacher Education.** Each center for adult learning should be free to refine their own, but this is a beginning list upon which to build:

1. We aim to support the development of new capacities (such as imagination, inspiration, intuition) that can help the teacher take initiative and deliver compelling instruction.

2. We work out of a view of the human being articulated in anthroposophy in general terms and in *The Foundations of Human Experience* (given by Rudolf Steiner) in particular.

3. Waldorf teacher education recognizes the difference between

pedagogy and andragogy, and uses methods appropriate to adult learning.

4. We recognize the importance of balancing group work with lectures, seminars, and presentations in our classes.

5. We value the development of social intelligences because teaching involves active engagement with children, parents, and colleagues.

6. We realize that most change and development in adults occurs through individual initiative, and thus we support ethical individualism and self-directed learning.

7. Although it may not always be immediately visible, we recognize that teaching is destiny learning.

8. We practice discernment in admissions, advising, and recommendations to schools. Teaching is a vocation, and not everyone is suited for that calling. We may sometimes need to advise alternative careers, with the comment, "You do not yet seem ready to teach," leaving open the future none of us can determine. (And some of those I have had most concerns about have ended up surprising everyone!)

9. In an age of increased stress and societal demands on teachers, we support practices that include meditation, personal hygiene, and self-compassion.

10. Education is essential to social renewal, and teacher educators strive to serve as leaders as they aim to engage in the larger issues of our time.

11. Teacher educators engage in research so they can better serve as advocates for Waldorf education, our schools, and the renewal of education.

12. We value the striving for balance between theory and practice, coursework and fieldwork.

To be continued...

Partnerships

Another foundational element to teacher education is the partnership between institutes/centers and schools. I would like to suggest that *implicit partnerships, where they existed in the past, now need to be made explicit. The future of Waldorf teacher education rests in the hands of an active, well-articulated partnership between schools, institutes, and like-minded organizations* (Camphill villages, biodynamic farms, community-supported agriculture, local arts organizations, etc.). Some considerations for possible MOUs (memorandums of understanding) might include the following.

The institute will provide:

1. Faculty who work out of the core principles of teacher education and see their work as a distinct profession.
2. A program that is recognized by AWSNA and the Teacher Education Delegates Circle of AWSNA (institutes), as well as non-Waldorf accreditation agencies when possible.
3. Professional best practices in teaching and the general administration of the program.
4. Fundraising for scholarships through grant applications to foundations, donors, and alumni.
5. Faculty will be hired who can successfully deliver distant courses, write reports to colleagues upon completion, and review student evaluations of their courses.
6. The institute will work actively to realize the expectations and guidelines of AWSNA and the Alliance in regard to teacher education, and will represent their programs in the appropriate national and regional meetings of these professional associations.
7. Through Antioch University in particular, faculty will engage in regular discourse with thought leaders in higher education outside the Waldorf movement.

The partner school will provide:

1. A welcoming site for the teacher-education program free of charge.
2. Local adjunct faculty to teach in the program who meet the standards of the institute (CV and phone interviews required before hiring someone as an adjunct).
3. Active recruitment from the school community so the program is well enrolled.
4. A local coordinator (job description available) to attend to logistics on the ground in exchange for a 50% tuition discount.
5. Use of classroom space, at least one seminar-style classroom, and one space suitable for movement and/or arts classes.
6. Some help in raising scholarship funds locally.

Creative Tensions in Teacher Education

As with many other things in life, there are numerous creative tensions in the realm of teacher education. A few of them include:

1. The aim to offer as much coursework as possible vs. the costs of time and money when programs are too long (shorter, closer, cheaper vs. wider, stronger, deeper).
2. The need to establish a solid foundation in anthroposophy and the arts vs. the desire of many practicing teachers (and schools) to acquire skills and curriculum materials for immediate use.
3. The importance of group work that develops future colleagueship skills vs. the growing need for individual advising and self-directed learning.
4. The benefits of face-to-face residential learning vs. virtual instruction and support.
5. "Academic theory" vs. "artistic practice."
6. The value of a cohort model in which students experience learning in the context of a group over time vs. electives and out-of-sequence program plans that allow for greater flexibility.
7. The need to uphold standards in admissions of trainees to teacher-education programs vs. the growing need of schools to replace an entire generation of teachers.
8. Keeping tuition as low as possible vs. sustaining a core faculty at the institutes that strive for professionalism in adult education and can offer a full spectrum of subjects throughout the program, rather than offering courses on weekends or during vacations or "on the side" while holding down full-time school positions.
9. Time needed in internships/practica/field work vs. time for coursework.
10. The balance of subject-specific coursework (especially in the high-school trainings) vs. general Waldorf teacher education, including the practice of the arts (especially those one is not being trained to teach to students of any age).

To be continued...

Having named some of the creative tensions in the above points, it might be helpful to go into more detail in one area, as an example of the sort of conversations that we need to conduct with schools and institutes:

Face-to-face residential learning vs. virtual instruction

With Covid-19, many have used Zoom and online instruction more than ever before. We have found that there are many advantages/opportunities with virtual classrooms: low-cost delivery; chance to connect with students around the world; opportunities to present visuals and materials most classrooms could not usually access; less of a gap between home and school; breakout group conversations that can facilitate learning; and much more.

There are also still advantages to the face-to-face learning we have practiced for so long: more in-depth human-to-human engagement in which one can read body language and catch nuances of meaning; robust, full group conversations; more physical activity; hands-on art instruction in which a teacher can actually assist individuals; a greater sense of "the group"; a balance of formal learning vs. the little asides that happen in any classroom between students; and much more.

So the question becomes, how can one find the right balance between the virtues of online and face-to-face? How can one construct programs that employ the advantages of multiple modalities while minimizing the pitfalls? Finally, how can learning be sequenced with both modalities in mind?

All the creative tensions that exist in teacher education afford opportunities to revisit core principles and establish common groups in a more conscious way. For example, with the creative tension of online vs. face-to-face, one might consider the importance of place. Ancient traditions in a variety of cultures have valued the sacredness of place. New Grange in Ireland, Stonehenge in England, Chartres, Mecca, Matrimandir in Auroville, India, the great pyramids in Egypt and Mexico are all examples of special places that have the power to move human beings, to lift them up. Even a special tree in the woods can become a friend that nourishes and supports contemplation and learning.

So how can we maximize the power of place in both face-to-face and online learning? Hosting a summer session in a Waldorf school has so many benefits. Even when the children are not on campus, their energy, artwork, and joy linger in the classrooms and the general environment.

Can we become more and more intentional in terms of programming? Which courses work best in a residential session face-to-face? What works best online? Regarding a sense of place for online, it may not seem as significant, but after many Zooms lately, it seems that some things still matter: which room and backdrop, which chair, lighting, visuals and opening/closing rituals? All these and more matter, not only to participants but also to the instructors' and participants' preparation, focus, and comfort with the session. How does virtual learning work for introverts vs. extroverts? What aspects of learning can best be enhanced virtually, and which need to be reserved for face-to-face intensives, either in a central location or regionally?

These abovementioned considerations lead me to propose a model for Waldorf teacher education going forward that is based on the double helix, or to be more precise, multiple versions that span some of the creative tensions mentioned above. Thus, for each of the "pairings" mentioned, we can design a double helix: face-to-face and virtual, central campus-based courses and regional workshops, more academic instruction and arts courses, etc. Rather than a quantitative, sequential approach by semester, we could put more emphasis on the pairings and creative dynamics as students move through a course of study. Thus the double helix as a metaphor:

We know that the double helix portrays the double-stranded DNA molecule which was discovered by Francis Crick and James Watson in 1953 and then elaborated by Maurice Wilkins, who shared their 1962 Nobel Prize. The role of Rosalind Franklin was not fully acknowledged until later.

> The double helix describes the appearance of double-stranded DNA, which is composed of two linear strands that run opposite to each other, or anti-parallel, and twist together. Each DNA strand within the double helix is a long, linear molecule made of smaller units called nucleotides that form a chain. The chemical backbones of the double helix are made up of sugar and phosphate molecules that are connected by chemical bonds, known as sugar-phosphate backbones. The two helical strands are connected through interactions between pairs of nucleotides, also called base pairs. Two types of base pairing occur: nucleotide A pairs with T, and nucleotide C pairs with G. (https://www.nature.com/scitable/definition/double-helix-277/)

So each "rung" of the DNA helix was composed of a pair of bases joined by hydrogen bonds. Thus one has multiple connections in an amazing, elastic form!

Without going further into either the science or history of the double helix, there is value in simply living with the shape and wonderful dynamics of the image. There is so much to discover from a phenomenological vantage point. I have asked several colleagues to help me "open my eyes" to ask the question: What can we observe?

At first glance one can observe a kind of double staircase, two strands moving up or down. The overall impression is one of movement and life. There is a connection between the two strands as indicated, left/right, right/left. There is also movement between inner and outer, with the stands twisting as they progress.

From observation, can one then begin to bring some understanding arising from the above sense impressions?

1. It seems that the two strands are in both *in relation* and *stand as polarities,* and there is a creative tension between the two.

2. The observed movement and vitality speak to life forces and etheric rhythms.

3. As with the image of the snakes on the Mercury staff used in medical and healing modalities, there is a suggestion of change and transformation. The staff is triune, thanks to the vertical straight line around which the two curves entwine. A similar gesture can be derived from the third lecture of *Balance in Teaching* with a schematic depiction of what Steiner calls the sculptural/visual forces swirling downwards from head to limbs and the musical/auditory forces swirling upwards from limbs to head.

4. Many of us have done the spiral rod exercise in eurythmy: beginning below and with a slight rotation of the wrist, one turns the copper rod and raises the arm and then goes back down. The spirals grow up and then tend to contract downwards again. The wrist is like the bars in the diagram, connecting the spirals. The external two points of the copper rod move the double helix in space!

5. We know that it matters if we move right to left (counterclockwise) or left to right (clockwise), either with the rods or in circle activities with children. I was always told as a class teacher that the young ones need to move *with the sun* (left to right) and the older ones after the 9-year change can move *with the earth rhythm* (right to left).

6. This spiral in the helix is a miniature form of a much larger natural

phenomenon known to us as a vortex, seen in whirlwinds, tornadoes and whirlpools, but also in outer space (the Great Red Spot on Jupiter or the polar vortices of Venus). Dolphins and whales blow out bubbles that form into rings as they reach the surface. The faster the vortex bubble ring spins, the more stably it travels.

7. Thus the double helix is a force of nature and of life. It goes to the very core of all that lives and moves.

Might we imagine creating teacher-education programs that capture the structure, life, and vitality of a double helix? If so, what would they look like?

There is much in the above observations that can and should be discussed among adult educators, but one fundamental archetype is the notion of the sun/earth reality mentioned above, which is connected to culture (passing on the legacy of curriculum and more) vs. creating a "reverse cultus," a new community experience with each group of adult learners. One way to "translate" this is to distinguish those activities that are incarnating, self-directed, done more on a solo basis (in front of my laptop in my office) vs. those activities that build community through multidimensional activities, those course elements that depend highly on human-to-human collaboration and have a high degree of the "unexpected." For future reference, I will refer to these two aspects as self-directed vs. professional learning community. (The reader may want to look at the chapter on the "third space" in *Organizational Integrity,* as elaborated on work done by Henry Barnes.) How can we work with these in teacher education?

Aspects that lend themselves to self-directed learning:

- Research projects
- Assignments that are mainly individually driven, often asynchronous: essays, color journals and individual paintings/drawings, completing main lesson books, preparation for solo teaching in an internship, individual advising, individual student "reports" (as opposed to a group effort), Master's thesis, individual program plans, etc.
- Individual advising
- Presentations of students' individual projects in class
- One might say from a color point of view that many of the above aspects work with the blue side of the spectrum, and encourage reflection and the night cycle of learning

Aspects that lend themselves to teacher education through the development of a professional learning community:

- Conversations in all courses (trios, seminar-style discussions, and more)
- Most of the arts, especially movement, singing, and speech
- Activities that have a strong connection to a particular physical site and sense of *returning to a familiar place,* as that reminds the group of shared experiences and memories from previous sessions (and nourishes the etheric)

My dear colleague and adjunct in our Antioch and Building Bridges programs, Colleen O'Connors, has shared with me a possible threefold structure of future teacher education. She distinguishes between activities that are mostly willing, those that are mostly feeling, and those that are more reflective as follows:

WILLING	FEELING	THINKING
speech	music	foundational readings
sculpture	painting	methods/didactics
eurythmy	eurythmy	meditation

And she then indicates that the willing activities above could best be offered regionally and at school sites, the feeling courses are best served in larger community experience such as a summer residency, and the thinking/reflective activities might lend themselves more to virtual learning.

All these considerations are simply meant as food for re-imagining our delivery options. And all of the above can be turned upside down—even the double helix, but also the threefolding just mentioned. One needs will in meditation, feeling and thinking in speech, etc. But these considerations are meant to encourage readers to ground future work in a renewed art of andragogy and what Rudolf Steiner called a "profound and loving understanding of the human being" (p. x, *Rudolf Steiner in the Waldorf School*).

Given the aspects described in the chapters of this book and the topics in the above pages in particular, I propose that going forward, teacher-education programs work with a double helix design for program delivery: one strand for face-to-face, site-based, mostly experiential learning, and one strand running parallel for online, more individualized, self-directed learning. The two strands would be closely coordinated (the horizontal connectors in the double helix image) and intimately connected so that even within individual courses, there would be both virtual and experiential components that would track the movement of the student through a particular theme of study.

In short, I am suggesting that because of all the factors described in the pages above, including the creative tensions and notions of adult learning, we redesign all our courses to be double-looped in this way. Even an art course, which for all the reasons described should remain 90% experiential and face-to-face, there could be an accompanying strand that moves virtually with the progression of lessons. For example, the painting class might have instruction and asynchronous activities before, during, and after the residency that bring historical and diverse cultural aspects to the student's attention.

Another example might be a course I have taught for years that could be converted to the double helix approach (indeed, some aspects are already in place):

Research for Self-Development Course

RESIDENTIAL STRAND	VIRTUAL STRAND
Welcome, orientation, expectations	Reflections afterwards
Group norms	Summary
Self-development exercises, trios	Trio sharing over weeks
Introduction to research	Reflections
Finding your question	Listing of questions
Research presentations and	Use of online forum and
spontaneous group conversations	further sharing in trios

The division of time for the above course in the residency would be 90% face-to-face and 10% virtual. One might say, why bother for 10%, but the group would have had a chance to get used to the virtual environment, and individual questions that arise can be brought to the group for support, say after a weekend break. Then when everyone goes home after the residency, the proportion would go to 90% virtual and 10% face-to-face (peer counseling), with the research project done at a distance with some individual phone time/Skype etc. and some site visits by faculty, especially for the practica and internships.

Some might see this as only a minor departure from present practices, but there are a few aspects that are new:

1. Online and face-to-face from day one of a program.
2. Placing courses in residencies based on the lens of the above adult education best practices, not just what has been done in the past.

This would emphasis the "retreat" aspect even more.

3. Shortening the residencies, possible with the above, lowers costs to the students and the programs.
4. Working more consciously with the yearly, monthly, weekly, and daily rhythm thanks to the double helix imagination, engaging dimensions of both time and space.

Next, I propose that given the arrhythmic nature of today's world, the need for personal hygiene and many other factors, we put much more emphasis on the monthly rhythm in programming.

This might mean a once-a-month (Saturday) virtual session that would feature several courses not only for check-in and progress reports, but some inspiration and new content. Then, once or twice a year, the Saturday session could be replaced by a regional face-to-face meeting, perhaps in conjunction with a public lecture and another weekend session already planned for Explorations or Building Bridges. So, for example, there might be a mini-retreat weekend in D.C., which begins with a Friday evening public lecture open to the school community, followed by Saturday and Sunday parallel meetings of two cohorts, one in the Explorations or Building Bridges program, and the other a meeting of teachers in training and/ or alumni in that region. At least portions could be live-streamed. This could have a festive atmosphere for those who can be there physically, with shared lunches and some "on the town" cultural or sporting event on Saturday evening.

Next, I propose that an institute consider establishing semi-permanent distant sites that would host these weekends and serve as models for school/institute partnership.

For Antioch/Center for Anthroposophy, it would make sense to have a Waldorf school site in Santa Barbara, Seattle, Cincinnati, and, of course Keene, NH. These sites would be within the 50-mile radius allowed by the Higher Learning Commission (accreditation for Antioch University). It would be great if we could do one in the southeast as well, such as in Chapel Hill or Atlanta. The virtue of such sites is that students get to experience a Waldorf school (importance of place), meet more practicing teachers (some can do their internship visitation days ahead of and after a weekend) and can find one another again in the human encounter of face-to-face classes.

Next, I propose the institutes and schools redesign the financial model used to pay for programs.

The AWSNA loan program was a start in the right direction, but we need to ramp that up significantly, work on *pay-forward options*, and increase loans and scholarships so anyone suited for admission can pursue Waldorf teacher education, eurythmy training, Spacial Dynamics and other pathways without financial hardship. These financial reforms are long overdue, and there are those in social finance that can help us work out specific proposals and find partner-cosponsors. The goal would be that the tuition costs are eventually shared equally between the sponsoring school, the individual student in training, and the institute through their fundraising efforts and endowment funds. Ideally, schools who benefit from our graduates would also help pay off student loans over time with each year of service rendered by the newly minted teachers.

This financial aspect is intimately connected to the "partnership" component, as the schools and institutes need to see themselves as one enterprise in support of teacher education and post-training mentorship, and we will need the help of AWSNA and the Alliance to strengthen this work. Collaboration is no longer a nice word; it is now a necessity. And we may even want to "merge" all the Waldorf training institutes into one umbrella organization with separate local sites offering complementary programs.

We need to establish a new global approach to all our anthroposophically based adult education programs, even while still delivering place-based, local residencies. Jaimen McMillan and other visionary leaders in the field have been doing international programs for years, and through the strength of uncommon inspiration (and considerable personal stamina) have modeled a global reach. We now need to do this not just based upon singular individuals (I well remember the visits of globetrotters such as L. Francis Edmunds, Rene Querido, and others), but through the use of virtual learning platforms that connect multiple time zones around thematic programs. Our Center for Anthroposophy Waldorf high-school program, for instance, is ideally suited to go global, with a balance of yearly regional gatherings complementing virtual courses open to all and allowing economies of scale. But we need to begin by thinking internationally. And the resources are simply not there for each center to build and maintain brick-and-mortar buildings. We need to move Waldorf teacher education out of a "physical" orientation into the etheric plane in which we are united through common rhythms and best practices.

Finally, I suggest we launch a Practicing Destiny Program to prepare future adult educators working out of anthroposophy.

Again, details are already being developed, also with Pedagogical Section leaders at the Goetheanum, but it is essential that we recognize that working with adults is a profession that needs recognition, support, and preparatory programs/apprenticeships. I hope this book can contribute to this calling.

In his signature course for pioneering Waldorf teachers in 1919, Rudolf Steiner carried several themes throughout the fourteen lectures, now known as *Foundations of Human Experience:*

1. The human being has three aspects:
   a. A soul aspect that works through sympathy and antipathy (lectures 1-5)
   b. A spirit aspect that works with states of consciousness (lectures 6-9)
   c. A physical body aspect that works with the morphology of forms (lectures 10-14)
2. Metamorphosis and transformations (examples found on pages 155, 185, 194 for example)
3. Use of a comparative methodology (examples on pages 121, 128, 133 etc.)

These fundamental approaches need to become ever more firmly grounded in both our pedagogy and our andragogy. How can our courses and programs build the soul/spiritual "muscles" so our future teachers can work with metamorphosis and transformation in every lesson? How can we work with adults so that we use a comparative methodology and characterize (rather than define) each aspect of the curriculum so it is a living experience that moves and grows with diverse cultural experiences and ever-fresh impulses arising from the teacher's inner life and active research? How can we work with soul, spirit, and body as described in the original fourteen lectures so that the image of the human being is complete in our classrooms? How we work with these elements, not just in an educational concern, has a great deal to do with our future social interactions. How we see each other (and ourselves) influences how we behave and treat one another.

So, although I am proposing much innovation in the above pages, my final suggestion is that *as a movement, we also go back to our "roots" and a meditatively acquired knowledge of the human being.* We no longer have the luxury of simply being an attractive "alternative" education. We now need to bring the utmost intentionality to all we do, and our work in teacher education needs to be grounded in core principles that are unshakeable, even as we bend and grow to meet the times in which we live. Just as with a strong tree, we can have both our roots and trunk *and* our moving branches and leaves. Flexibility within rootedness is a virtue.

When we are able to fully process the great tragedies of 2020, especially Covid-19 and racialized trauma, those of us active on behalf of Waldorf education will need to not only "read" the signs of our time but also implement a host of changes in our schools and programs, and thus move forward with new focus.

1. We need to be more "Waldorf" than ever before.
2. We need to tap into our own creative forces with enthusiasm.
3. We need to focus more on the *individual path of self-education* and less on the personality-driven, inspirational lectures of the past (although we still need the nourishment that comes with inspiration and spiritual substance).
4. We need to slow down (stay-at-home has been a powerful lesson for many).
5. We need to embrace change and the adventures ahead without fear, knowing our children are bringing us fresh impulses out of the future to help us along.
6. To make place for the new, it is okay to embrace "nothingness" and a state of not knowing as the seedbed for innovation.
7. There are those who call themselves Waldorf teachers or students of anthroposophy, and there are those who are working out of similar spiritual streams but have not identified themselves by enrolling children in our schools or doing one of our programs. The latter are our sisters and brothers. Rather than continually doing "outreach" to get them to come to us, let us build bridges that are invitational and *let us cross those bridges so we can meet our natural partners by reaching out to them.*

At the very beginning of the beginning, Rudolf Steiner spoke of the good spirits that want to help us realize the founding of Waldorf schools and an entirely new form of education. Today we need to call on these good spirits as never before, and in particular the being of Michael. Those working in education today are in so many ways servants of archangelic beings, but these beings are now waiting for us to call upon them *so they can become more active in our lives.* The spiritual worlds are filled with unimaginable strength, courage, and resources that are just waiting for our invitation.

For those willing to serve the future of humanity by dedicating their lives to education, there is no better way to serve than by responding to a call to teach.

24. Listening to our Teachers, Part 1:
Advocacy Through Research

Many professions seem to be held in higher regard than teaching. Although one might ask for a second opinion from a doctor, few in the medical profession receive as much feedback as do teachers. Parents can at times be very demanding. In local district meetings, superintendents often have to argue strenuously for even minor increases to school budgets, yet the public has no say as to what arrives in a medical bill. At times, teachers are buffeted by new state standards, parental expectations, and differentiated learning needs of their students. It is no wonder fewer teachers are entering the profession (see chapter on "Demoralized").

One way forward is to increase advocacy for education by truly listening to our teachers. They, in turn, need to work on verbal and written articulation so that they are heard. In a recent Building Bridges Program for public Waldorf teachers in California, each student developed a research question through a year-long process of reflection and winnowing. What started as a random collection of "wonderings" ended up being a focusing question that was deep-seated, and often personally and professionally acute. (See my book *Silence is Complicity* for more detail.) Then, with question in hand, each participant spent four months doing research, reading, interviewing, journaling, etc., culminating in a paper and final presentation. Having had the pleasure, over many years, of coaching this process I am always astounded at the passion these teachers bring to their research questions. Often they realize afterwards that this process was not a mere academic exercise, but something with deep biographical roots and vocational implications.

When our teacher-researchers present in the summer session in Wilton, NH, we often have an additional audience of other students and even faculty. Their short 15-minute presentations are seen as a highlight of the session for many. After several presentations, we often break into multiple groups, each facilitated by the author of the particular topic that had just been presented. Students and faculty wander from group to group, asking questions and entering into spontaneous conversations. Afterward, those who have presented are glowing. They have been able to address a theme of deep concern, and the audience has validated their months-long research. They are now advocates for school renewal.

The next pages contain four of the papers submitted in the 2019-20 cycle. Although there are many excellent papers submitted each year, these were selected because of the particular topics chosen and their relevance to the theme of this book. One senses in each one a call to teach, a deep commitment to the work of schools, and the hope that teacher voices can make a difference.

The Effects of Silence on Teacher Well-Being
by Chelsea Nealy

ABSTRACT

This research study seeks to answer the question: *Can an increase in silence during a teacher's workday leave the educator with a greater sense of well-being?* To explore this question, a microscopic view was taken on the concept of silence within and outside of education. Research was conducted on the science of silence, its modern-day perception and use, and the willingness and reluctance of educators to use it in their classrooms. Recent studies, statistics, and empirical data were used, as well as philosophical lectures from Rudolf Steiner dating back to 1904. It was concluded through Part I of this research that silence plays an important role in the development of the brain, specifically in areas of creativity and memory. It was also found that living in noisy environments increases the risk of the development of anxiety, depression, and physical ailments. The value of silence on the well-being of the human was established, and Part II will seek to specifically determine if these practices (when used in the classroom) will increase the well-being of an educator, as it relates to career satisfaction.

THE EFFECTS OF SILENCE ON TEACHER WELL-BEING: PART I

I first became interested in the effect of silence on educators years ago during my second year in teaching. At the time, I had a brand-new baby girl and lived with my husband and our two-year-old daughter. That school year, I found myself avoiding the staff lounge specifically to avoid conversation. I sat in my classroom alone and absorbed the silence, inadvertently branding myself the school hermit. After school, I would often drive out of my way to go home and sit on my couch in silence for fifteen minutes, before getting back in the car to pick my children up from daycare. Why was I going to such great, and odd, lengths for a few minutes of quiet? I knew that I lived a chaotic life, and was trying to avoid noise, but I did not know the deeper reasons why. I did not research this question at the time; however, it always stuck with me in the back of my mind.

Years later, I became a teacher at a Waldorf-inspired public charter school. For the first time, I was part of a school community that examined the soul of the educator. In staff meetings, in my Waldorf certification program, and in daily conversation with my colleagues, the topic of teacher fatigue was discussed and debated. Through our conversations, it became clear how many of our complaints were outside of our control, and they left me questioning what I *could* do to combat this fatigue. It dawned on me that my need for silence, the one that had been living in me for so long, could possibly be connected to this very issue.

I wondered: *If I have more silence throughout my day as a teacher, will I have more energy at the end of my workday?* And this small wondering grew into a larger question: *Can an increase in silence during a teacher's workday leave the educator with a greater sense of well-being?* This question became the focus of my research.

There has been an overwhelming amount of research dedicated to determining effective teaching methods and finding what works best for students, but far less research has been done on methods that benefit the teacher. In December of 2019, a simple Google search of "caring for the students' well-being" produced 3.85 billion results. A similar search of "caring for the teacher's well-being" produced only ten percent of that amount. Specifically working with the concept of silence in the classroom, the vast majority of anecdotal and data-driven research centers around its effect on the students and their academic performance. However, the overlooked issue of teacher well-being is more important than ever before and deserves a close examination of its own. For, without the health of the teacher, the class system itself is harmed.

To begin the study of how silence affects teacher well-being, the general value of silence for any given person must first be examined. For Part I of this study, I learned about silence both within and outside the realm of education. I studied the current scientific research on how silence affects brain chemistry and the physical human response. I read translations of Rudolf Steiner's lectures to find out his beliefs about silence and its restorative value. Finally, I found schools and educators who are using silence as a teaching tool for student success and well-being.

Part II of *The Effects of Silence on Teacher Well-Being* will include practical advice for how to incorporate non-verbal teaching and dedicated silence into the school day, along with an action research study that monitors stress and anxiety levels in teachers throughout their journey to achieve a quieter classroom.

Teacher Turnover

Research conducted by Gallup in the 2017-2018 school year concluded that almost half (48%) of teachers in the United States are "actively looking for a different job now or watching for opportunities" (McFeely, 2018). If this number seems unusually high, a second source might remove any lingering skepticism. An independent survey conducted by PDK International, a professional association for educators, supports the statistic. In their 2019 poll of 556 public school teachers from across the U.S., it was found that 50% of respondents have considered leaving the profession (Hess, 2019). The number of teachers who follow through with their desire for a different career is lower, but still staggering; it is currently estimated that 44% of new teachers leave the profession within the first five years (Will, 2018).

These figures clearly indicate that there is a high level of career dissatisfaction among educators. The good news is that teachers have not been withholding or mysterious about their reasons for departure. Using umbrella concepts, it is commonly cited among a variety of sources that teachers feel overworked, underpaid, and not respected by society. While there is no silver bullet for all the maladies of the teaching profession, and many of the concerns are completely outside of the educator's control, one problem area that can be addressed by the teachers themselves is the feeling of being overworked—with an emphasis on the word *feeling*.

The Nature of Teaching and Educator Burnout

Teaching, by those who have done it, is often compared to being on stage. Similar to a Broadway actor, a good teacher has the rapt attention of her audience, her performance has been mentally (and sometimes physically) rehearsed, and a variety of predicted reactions have been carefully calculated. The performance must be interesting enough to hold the attention of the audience, but not so enthusiastic as to be cheesy or unrealistic. Unlike a Broadway production, however, the teacher must be able to change direction at any given moment without losing poise. Student behavior, pop-ins from administration, fire drills, a lack of understanding that requires re-teaching, all require pivots in the lesson. Also unlike a Broadway production, the audience must be included in the process. In a great lesson, the teacher draws knowledge out of the students through their own voices and volition. To do this successfully is a delicate dance that requires peak awareness and heightened sensitivity on the part of the teacher. She does this dance on her metaphorical stage day after day, and every word out of her mouth, every movement made with her body, is on display.

A primary tenet of anthroposophy, the spiritual philosophy behind Waldorf education, is the idea of soul forces. The soul mediates between the physical body and the spirit and is comprised of the thinking, feeling, and willing. Thinking represents the head, feeling the heart, and willing the hands (Association for Anthroposophic Psychology). The teaching profession draws on all three soul forces each and every day. Physically, the teacher is on her feet, standing before the class and walking around observing and assisting students. The Waldorf teacher incorporates movement into the rhythm of the lesson, and she models proper posture throughout the day. Emotionally, teachers are tied to their students as if they were actual family. We care for our students deeply, and, when they struggle, we struggle. When they hurt, we hurt. Teaching is a caregiving role, and it often leaves the educator drained of her own feeling force. The willing is affected by any effort to restrain or hold back one's natural instincts. In teaching, words are chosen carefully and censored for appropriateness. Frustration that is felt during a lesson going poorly is held back, and patience and gentility are displayed instead. Facial expressions are suppressed, smiles sometimes forced, and uncertainty masked. Again, it is a performance—and it is exhausting.

Qualitative reports regarding educator exhaustion can be found in any school faculty lounge, and their sentiment is backed by hard data. In 2017, the American Federation of Teachers conducted a survey, titled the *2017 Educator Quality of Work Life Survey*. Educators were asked a variety of questions relating to their job satisfaction and feelings of general well-being. When asked "How often is work stressful?" 61% of the respondents stated that they feel stress at their job "always" or "often." This figure is more than double that of the general population, in which 30% of the respondents felt stressed. The same survey also determined that a majority of teachers have less enthusiasm for their job than they did when they began (AFT, 2017).

When a teacher suffers in this way, as so many teachers are currently suffering, the soul forces are not being replenished, and burnout is likely to occur. One active contributor to the weakening of the soul forces is today's culture of "more is more."

The Pervasive Lack of Silence in Today's Culture

Numerous studies have examined the current level of stimuli in the lives of Americans, as compared to that of previous generations. With the

influx of smartphones, wireless earbuds, and other devices, it is a rare occasion that one finds oneself in a state of silence. In previous decades, opportunities for quiet contemplation, reading, or simply "zoning out," came
frequently—while waiting at the DMV, sitting on the commuter train, or
even lying in bed preparing for sleep. These moments of empty space have
been filled to the brim with technological distractions, many of which are
auditory. In the 1970s, the average American was exposed to around 500
advertisements per day. In 2019, this number has climbed to approximately
5000 per day (Holmes, 2019). It can only be estimated what percentage
of these advertisements are auditory in nature, but considering that a user
must typically watch a video advertisement before many online activities,
and that most Americans are essentially carrying around televisions in their
pockets, it is fair to assume that the percentage is notable.

In recent years, trends in education have also led to more high-stim-
ulation learning environments. Collaborative group work, invigorating
classroom discussions and debates, the use of songs for memorization, and
high-energy center activities are all considered best practice in today's classroom. While they certainly have merit and there is research to back up their
validity, it is worth noting what they have replaced. Sustained silent reading
and quiet individual classwork are now rarities in the American classroom.

Scientific Findings

As it is pointed out in 3M's educational video "The Science of Silence"
(2018), quiet environments and products are generally seen as being of
better quality than noisy ones. A quiet hotel room is assumed to have
high-quality windows and walls. A quiet car is perceived to be expensive
and luxurious. Conversely, a noisy air conditioner or refrigerator causes
worry and disdain. It is built into our nature as humans to value quiet, and
for good reason. Biologically speaking, our brains need quiet to thrive.

In the 1970s, a team of psychologists conducted a study of children who
lived in a noisy building in downtown Manhattan. Even on the eighth
floor, the noise from the interstate below was at a constant 66 decibels, just
lower than a running vacuum (Sheikh, 2018). The psychologists learned
through their study that the children who lived on the lower, noisier floors
struggled with learning to read in comparison to the children who lived
on higher floors of the same building. They also had difficulty distinguish-
ing between similar sounding words, such as "thick" and "sick," which
indicated a damaged ability to process verbal language.

Since this study was conducted, there have been numerous others that have linked noise pollution to "increased anxiety, depression, high blood pressure, heart disease, and stroke" (Sheikh, 2018). Citing a few notable examples, Knvul Sheikh of BrainFacts.org writes:

> Even small increases in unwanted ambient sound have significant effects. In 2011, for example, scientists studying people living near seven major European airports found that a 10-decibel increase in aircraft noise was associated with a 28 percent increase in anxiety medication use. Another study found that people living in areas with more road traffic noise were 25 percent more likely than those living in quieter neighborhoods to have symptoms of depression. (Sheikh, 2018)

If an increase in noise, even of an ambient nature, has been proven to decrease the mental health and well-being of those exposed, it stands to reason that more exposure to silence will have a positive effect on the well-being of the "listener." Scientists have begun to support this notion.

When silence was first studied scientifically, it was almost by accident. Scientists were not looking at silence as an individual entity, but rather as a lack of noise. Studies such as the one above identified the danger of noise to brain development. To explore the idea further, silence was used as a baseline and control. As research continued, however, it was discovered that silence was not actually a control, but an experience all its own with surprising benefits.

In 2013, Imke Kirste, a Duke University regenerative biologist, was examining the effects of sounds in the brains of adult mice. She separated her mice into four exposure categories: music, baby mouse calls, white noise, and silence. Like other scientists, she was using silence as her control and was not expecting for it to produce any kind of result. As it turns out, all of the sounds had short-term neurological effects, but none of them were long-lasting. She found, by happy accident, that the mice who were exposed to two hours of silence each day had significant growth in their hippocampus, the brain region responsible for memory (Gross, 2014). The mice that were given silence during their day had far better neurological results than any of their counterparts.

Silence has also been shown to increase the brain's ability to self-reflect. In 2001, a group of researchers published a seminal piece to their work highlighting the activity of the prefrontal cortex during times of silence. They found that a "resting brain," free from cognitive activity, is actually perpetually active and continually scanning the environment and gathering information. Much of this activity is subconscious, and it is repressed when performing cognitive tasks. The act of self-reflection and deep, personal connection to self is an act performed by the prefrontal cortex and requires a lack of stimuli to properly perform. "Freedom from noise and goal-directed tasks, it appears, unites the quiet without and within, allowing our conscious workspace to do its thing, to weave ourselves into the world, to discover where we fit in. That's the power of silence" (Gross, 2014). Rudolf Steiner, the father of Waldorf education, seemed to know this information intuitively. Exactly 100 years before this study was published, Steiner explored the same idea of connection to self through intentional silence.

SILENCE IN THE WALDORF PEDAGOGY

Waldorf education is unique in that it not only prepares students academically, but it also nourishes the soul forces of children throughout their development. Jessica Moore, a kindergarten teacher at Maine Coast Waldorf School, wrote a poignant article about the young child's need for quiet environments. She points out that the young child is an "open sense organ," into which all the sensory stimuli of the world are poured. While a child can close his or her eyes if a light is too bright, there is no effective way to shut off hearing. In fact, we are listening even as we sleep. It is the one sense that humans have no control over. She goes on to offer suggestions for quieting the world of the small child, both at school and at home (Moore, 2016).

Excess stimuli and their negative effect on the development of the young child are widely discussed in Waldorf education, and steps are taken to prevent it. Media guidelines are given and explained to parents, classrooms exist without screens, and "cell-phone–free zones" are created. Waldorf schools are known for having hushed, reverent ceremonies. A "breathing" is present in lessons and in the daily rhythm to create a balance between the frenetic and the calm. Waldorf teachers are trained to care for these soul needs of their students, but are far less often taught how to care for themselves.

Perhaps Waldorf schools should refer more often to Rudolf Steiner's beliefs about the rejuvenative power of silence, and apply his theories in faculty meetings and trainings. Steiner often spoke of silence as a meditative force, though he did not use that word at the time. In his 1904 lecture,

Vom inneren Leben, Steiner said to his Berlin audience, "In pondering the demands of everyday life, it becomes clear that it is an impossibility to completely free one's mind from outside impressions. To do so, it becomes necessary to set aside a short period of time every day…and thoughts that connect us with finiteness and transitory matters must be silenced" (Steiner, 1904). More than 100 years ago, before the arrival of modern-day technology, he said this. The vast majority of the population was still riding in horse-drawn carriages, news broadcasts existed only in print, and yet, people were feeling overwhelmed and distracted by the rigors of their daily lives. This goes to show that the responsibility for achieving a peaceful inner life lies with the individual and nowhere else. Educators cannot control what goes on around them, but they can control what goes on within them.

As a way of relinquishing this hold on the stresses of the present, Steiner recommends sitting with oneself, even for five minutes a day. During this time, one must consciously sort and separate one's thoughts. As a thought comes into the light, one should ask oneself if that thought is "transitory in nature," or in other words, temporary. If it is, then the thought should be gently released to live somewhere else. Over time, one can train the brain to not dwell on transitory thoughts, and one should, as "such thoughts have no value for inner development" (Steiner, 1904). Examples of these temporary, time-sensitive thoughts include: *Do I have all of my materials ready for tomorrow's lesson? Should I grade those reports tonight, or spend time with my family? Will my students be prepared for the test?* These thoughts, though important for daily functioning, are only important within a set time frame. It will not matter in five years or even a month from now if you graded the reports on Tuesday or Wednesday. During the time of silent contemplation, these types of thoughts have no place. "When such silence has been produced in the soul and for a while all our surroundings, be they of the era, the nation, the race or the century we live in, are subdued and eliminated, the soul will begin to speak of its own accord" (Steiner, 1904). In order for any human to have a healthy well-being, one must be able to hear one's own soul.

Steiner speaks again of silence to an audience in Copenhagen, Denmark in 1923. It is nearly two decades later than the lecture referenced above, though there were many in between. The world has changed quite a bit since the 1904 lecture. World War I has come and gone, motor vehicles are now commonplace, and radio news is in every household. It is a louder world, indeed. In this lecture, Steiner uses a metaphor to describe how one can distance oneself from the din of daily life and step into a place of deep inner thought. Imagine yourself, he said, in the center of a roaring city. From this place, visualize yourself walking outward until you are five minutes removed. Imagine, then, that you travel five minutes further, and five minutes further after that. You hear the tumult of the metropolis fading with each step. You eventually find yourself at the foot of a great forest. You are far from the city now, and the dense trees provide cover and insulation from the outside world. You walk deep into the forest until you reach the center. You can no longer hear the city at all. You have reached a state of zero. From here, however, you can travel even further—beyond zero. You can travel deep into the silence of the center of your mind and soul, into a negative space. It is here that "one can awaken in the deep silence of the soul to a higher stage and clarify what life on earth is" (Steiner, 1923). "When this inner void has been created, man is able to receive the prompting of his inner being" (Steiner, 2008, p. 27).

Steiner has painted an important picture of why silence is important for development of the inner being, but one is left wondering: *What does this look like in a modern-day classroom?* How can the philosophy of silence be used in a practical way?

Becoming Comfortable with Silence in the Classroom

Present-day Americans are notoriously uncomfortable with silence. "Awkward silence" is a phrase known to all. But how can one reap the benefits of silence without first becoming comfortable with it? To become truly at ease with silence, educators must first themselves recognize its purpose and value. Once this is achieved, they must then obtain buy-in from their students. After all, in order for a room to be silent, all of its inhabitants must be invested. Finally, the act of silence must be practiced routinely and rhythmically.

In his article "Sanctioning Silence in the Classroom," Charlie Wesley, who served as an assistant professor of English at Daemen College, discusses the reluctance of educators to use silence as a tool in their teaching. He explains how, especially to a new teacher, the silence that often follows a question can be nerve-racking. *Is my lesson boring? Do the students not understand the question? Am I not being clear?* These are a few of the many questions that might run through the mind of a novice educator during those moments of quiet. And so, what does this teacher do in response? He fills the silence with explanation, prompting, or a rephrasing of the question. This, however, is a missed opportunity for genuine learning. As Wesley notes, "just as often, silence denotes the process of thinking—genuinely mulling over something" (Wesley, 2013).

Patricia Owen-Smith, a professor at Oxford University, echoes the sentiment shared by Charlie Wesley. "We are a culture that fears silence, and teachers fear it as much as anyone. Professionally socialized to both value and bestow words, many of us see silence in the classroom as a failure to disseminate knowledge or generate dialogue and activity" (Owen-Smith, 2018). After 20 years of teaching, Patricia decided to change her high-energy, self-admitted "frenetic" approach. She heeded the research that indicated "chronic activity, and the accompanying stress, leaves little space for creativity, introspection, compassion, and emotional understanding" (Owen-Smith, 2018), and decided to begin each class day with five minutes of pure silence. She noted that at the beginning of each semester, her students would show great discomfort, annoyance, and skepticism when asked to sit silently and focus on their breath for five minutes straight. The students fidgeted, fiddled, and painstakingly waited it out. As the weeks went by, however, the students not only became comfortable with the silence, but they even began to look forward to it. From there, she integrated more and more silence into her lessons. It helps to think of silence not as an "absence," but as a "presence with a clear purpose and agency" (Owen-Smith, 2018).

If this purpose and agency aids in the well-being of our world's educators, then it is certainly worth pursuing.

CONCLUSION OF PART I AND PREVIEW OF PART II

Part I of *The Effects of Silence on Teacher Well-Being* established the question: *Can an increase in silence during a teacher's workday leave the educator with a greater sense of well-being?* In 2019, the importance of this question cannot be understated. Teacher turnover rate is at an all-time high, and career satisfaction among those who are still teaching is abysmal. Today's teachers feel stressed out and anxious as they fight through the myriad of issues facing the United States' educational system. If there is a way for teachers to reduce their stress levels and increase their general sense of well-being, then the retention of good teachers will be within reasonable grasp.

Rather than asking an overworked teacher to add something more into their already packed days, the idea of subtraction is presented. Specifically, the subtraction of sound. Part I of this study established the restorative value of silence on those who experience it. Be it from a spiritual or scientific perspective, the statistics behind the benefits of silence are indisputable. Whether the benefits of silence are enough to increase a teacher's overall sense of well-being is yet to be determined. And if they are, how much silence needs to be included in a school day to produce meaningful results for the educator? Part II of this study will seek to fully answer these questions.

Methodology: A sample group of educators will be given tools and training to begin using silence as a teaching method in their classrooms. A baseline will be established for their general stress and anxiety levels at the beginning and end of each workday. As the educators implement the techniques in which they are trained, their stress and anxiety levels will be tracked, producing both qualitative and quantitative data.

Our teachers are crying out for help. Perhaps the solution is to make no sound at all.

REFERENCES

3M. (2018, August 3) *The Science of Silence* [Video file]. Retrieved from https://www.youtube.com/watch?v=Zx9g7D2jCdk

AFT (American Federation of Teachers) (2017). *2017 Educator Quality of Work Life Survey.* Retrieved from https://www.aft.org/sites/default/files/2017_eqwl_survey_web.pdf

Association for Anthroposophic Psychology [Accessed Dec. 2019]. *Anthroposophic Psychology, What Is It?* Retrieved from https://anthroposophicpsychology.org/Anthroposophic-Psychology-What-is-It

Gross, D. (2014, Aug. 21) *This Is Your Brain on Silence.* Retrieved from http://nautil.us/issue/16/nothingness/this-is-your-brain-on-silence

Hess, A. (2019, Aug. 9) *50% of teachers surveyed say they've considered quitting, blaming pay, stress and lack of respect.* Retrieved from https://www.cnbc.com/2019/08/09/50percent-of-teachers-surveyed-say-theyve-considered-quitting-teaching.html.

Holmes, R. (2019, Feb. 19) *We Now See 5,000 Ads A Day...And It's Getting Worse.* Retrieved from https://www.linkedin.com/pulse/have-we-reached-peak-ad-social-media-ryan-holmes/

McFeely, S. (2018, Mar. 27) *Why Your Best Teachers Are Leaving and 4 Ways to Keep Them.* Retrieved from https://www.gallup.com/education/237275/why-best-teachers-leaving-ways-keep.aspx.

Moore, J. (2016, Oct. 10) *The Young Child's Urgent Need for Quiet.* Retrieved from https://www.mainecoastwaldorf.org/2016/10/10/young-childs-urgent-need-quiet/

Steiner, R. (1904, Dec. 15) *Vom inneren Leben*. Retrieved from https://wn.rsarchive. org/GA/GA0053/19041215p01.html

Steiner, R. (1923, May 14) *The Eternal Soul of Man From the Point of View of Anthroposophy*. Retrieved from https://wn.rsarchive.org/Lectures/ES5278_ index.html.

Steiner, R. (2008) *Esoteric Cosmology: Evolution, Christ & Modern Spirituality, 18 lectures in Paris, May 25-June 14, 1906*. Hudson, NY: SteinerBooks.

Wesley, C. (2013, Sept. 5) *Sanctioning Silence in the Classroom*. The Chronicle of Higher Education. Retrieved from https://www.chronicle.com/article/ Sanctioning-Silence-in-the/141369

Will, M. (2018, Oct. 23) *5 Things to Know About Today's Teaching Force* [Blog post]. Retrieved from https://blogs.edweek.org/edweek/teacherbeat/2018/10/ today_teaching_force_richard_ingersoll.html

Foreign Language Teaching for
Social Justice in Waldorf Schools
by Thea Bieling

ABSTRACT

Teaching foreign languages was one of the many foundational subjects that Rudolf Steiner recommended as a core component in his educational model. This research explores the relationship between the specific indications from Steiner's lectures and today's concept of social justice and considers approaches to teaching social justice in schools today, asking the questions: Can social justice be taught in foreign language programs offered to grades one through eight, while still maintaining Steiner's vision for teaching foreign language? And what modern-day educational standards address the main social components Steiner included in his foreign language curriculum?

CORE PRINCIPLES OF WALDORF EDUCATION

When the first Waldorf school was established by Emil Molt in 1919, it was founded as a social act in response to the devastation of World War I (Steiner, 1922). The adult generation at the time was recovering from the trauma of war and and was fixed in their nationalistic beliefs, encouraging Steiner to focus his attention on the new generation of children in the hopes of improving society as a whole (Steiner, 1922). It was Steiner's belief that a practice of empathy could begin in the classroom, through safe, loving, thoughtful interactions between teachers and students. The implementation of empathy in education was seen by Steiner as the foundation for peacemaking on the international level, and an order of the highest importance (Steiner, 1922).

Today, one hundred years after the creation of the first Waldorf school, the Association of Waldorf Schools of North America (AWSNA) identifies seven core principles that guide Waldorf education. They include: 1) The image of the human being as a spiritual being informs every aspect of the school; 2) Waldorf schools foster social renewal by cultivating human capacities in service to the individual and society; 3) Anthroposophical understanding of child development guides the educational program; 4) Waldorf schools support freedom in teaching within the context of the school's shared agreements; 5) The conscious development of human relationships fosters individual and community health; 6) Spiritual development in support of professional growth is an ongoing activity for the faculty, staff, and board; 7) Collaboration and shared responsibility provide the foundations of school leadership and governance (AWSNA, n.d.). The implementation of these core principles in Waldorf schools has the potential to strengthen communities and to provide a comprehensive picture of Steiner's original vision of education. Steiner's timeline for implementing his educational goals only extended through the twelfth grade because the founding of a university was not feasible at the time the first Waldorf school was created (Steiner, 2000). For this reason Steiner stated: "We must provide our students by the time they leave with the necessary qualifications for whatever further education will be suitable for them when they go out into life" (Steiner, 2000, p. 117). This combination of developmental, spiritual, cognitive, practical, and community education is why Waldorf has been referred to as an education for the "whole child" (Forrer, Salusso & Silvestry, 2000).

STEINER'S GOALS FOR FOREIGN LANGUAGE TEACHING

Anthroposophical scholars agree that the theme of world citizenship occurs primarily in the foreign language lessons where students are given the opportunity to develop an intimate feeling for a foreign language and to learn skills to speak in that language, and are later invited by the teacher to express themselves using their newly acquired language (Forrer et al., 2000). Offering foreign languages to public school students from the first grade on was a revolutionary idea in early 20th century Germany—where the first Waldorf school was founded—and today can still be seen as a "radical social and cultural act" (Wiechert, 2013).

In *Teaching Foreign Languages*, Dahl (2014) states: "The purpose of Waldorf education is to support the development of children and young people with the aid of the subject matter" (p. 58). Foreign language lessons are uniquely designed to encourage openness and awaken interest for what is foreign to oneself (Forrer, et al., 2000). Through this process of discovery, foreign languages "lose their foreignness as we become more familiar with them" (Dahl, 2014). According to Steiner (2000), "an extraordinary amount can be learned from the way a people or a tribe speaks. Entering consciously in a living way into the framework of language, we can learn a very great deal from the genius of language itself" (p. 59). This element of Steiner's educational model stimulated the development of a social consciousness of the individual and cultivated an interest in others through the assimilation of language (Forrer, et al., 2000).

FLEXIBILITY

Offering foreign languages in Waldorf schools predisposes young children to internal and external flexibility. This versatility positively impacts children throughout their lives, especially with respect to their social abilities (Forrer et al., 2000). Essential to Steiner's original vision of education is offering at least two foreign languages from grades one through twelve (Steiner, 1995). These languages must have diverse linguistic origin, providing students the opportunity to develop different thought processes through the integration and expression of language (Forrer et al., 2000). Each language invokes a unique vision of the world, which is expressed through the use of vocabulary, the formation of sentence structure, the use of grammar and pronunciation, and the evolution of the language itself. Within each of these foundational elements of language lie distinct ways of thinking, which if not explored can lead to hardened ways of being. Language learning is a process of exposure and repetition and is by its very nature self-affirming; therefore, the reinforcement of ideas through language can easily solidify and perpetuate a specific worldview (Dahl, 2014).

Children are born with a special ability for language learning, states Dahl (2014): "Not every person can be a good botanist, musician or mathematician but every newborn baby can learn to speak any language in the world to perfection; young children possess as many keys as there are languages" (p. 9). Dahl references the 21st century German philosopher Peter Sloterdijk, who described national language as "a world-giving instance," in which "each new life is tattooed with the patterns of national language" (p. 15). Dahl then goes on to say in his own words: "As newborns, and later as young adults we are at the mercy of the patterns of thinking contained in every language" (p. 15). Dahl suggests that nationalistic tendencies may be developed by speaking disparagingly about speakers of other languages, proposing that the antidote to this is to "liberate our perception, thinking, values and action from a system of orientation defined by our national language" (p. 18). The balance that can come from learning to speak additional languages is an "inner emancipation" (p. 16) and an opportunity to genuinely relate to more than one group of people from an early age.

DEVELOPMENT OF EMPATHY

The development of empathy is at the heart of teaching foreign languages in Waldorf schools. Waldorf schools approach foreign language instruction through language immersion in the classroom, with the goal of students relating to and better understanding the perspective of others. Children as young as six years old learn a foreign language, as soon as they enter school (Steiner, 1924), for it is during these formative early years that they are most able to learn new linguistic material. The capacity to imitate and willingness to follow their teacher guides the process of learning for the young child (Forrer et al., 2000). It is through this going-along-with that students are exposed to a perspective that is different from the one accompanying their mother tongue (Dahl, 2014). It is this very experience that is the birthplace of empathy. According to *Psychology Today* (2019), the definition of empathy is as follows:

> Empathy is the visceral experience of another person's thoughts and feelings from his or her point of view, rather than from one's own. Empathy facilitates prosocial or helping behaviors that come from within, rather than being forced, so that people behave in a more compassionate manner ("What is Empathy?" n.d.).

While empathy is an emotion that, by definition, has no action involved, it is a prerequisite for compassion, kindness, and tolerance, all of which are action-based. Empathy is a feeling that is imperative for true goodwill and positive action. This clarity is important because it is from the feeling realm that Steiner wanted his teachers to deliver their curriculum, knowing that through a true connection to feeling the children would make a positive impact on the world (Forrer et al., 2000). Dahl (2014) believed that "with every emotionally accompanied sound they assimilate, the pupils start to identify with a foreign consciousness, a foreign will, with foreign mental attitudes; this is active tolerance" (p. 18). Empathy serves as the foundation to an "inner knowing," which guides the children into young adulthood and beyond. Steiner's foreign language curriculum broadens its focus as the children grow, giving them opportunities to reflect on their surrounding environment. They begin to learn right from wrong, to identify the difference between just and unjust situations, and understand their role and responsibility as world citizens (Dahl, 2014).

Steiner's developmental model suggests that young children are one with their family and their environment, perceiving themselves as connected to their surroundings. It is not until around nine to ten years old, in the third and fourth grade, that they begin to experience themselves as separate from one another and their environment, creating a new self-concept (Steiner, 1922). A defining moment in foreign language education comes when the children begin to write, usually around the fourth grade.

This was offered by Steiner as a reflection of the children's inner experience of separation from their environment. In this way, without explicitly describing this process, foreign language teachers begin to identify the parts of a sentence and how they join to make a whole (Forrer et al., 2000). This teaching allows the children to see that they too are part of the whole of their family, their community, and humanity, though they may feel separate. This moment connects the children with a greater consciousness and a greater awareness of the world, helping them to recognize their place within the society. The theme "from the whole to the parts" continues in grades six through eight, incorporating verb conjugation, adding increasingly complex grammar, and discussing literature that meets the development of the students' analytical minds (Forrer et al., 2000, p. 16). This reflective method facilitates the theme of looking outward and assessing the world. This is where the seeds of empathy, which were planted in the early years of foreign language instruction, begin to take root.

SAFE AND PRODUCTIVE LEARNING ENVIRONMENT

Steiner envisioned the foreign language teacher embracing the students wholeheartedly, creating a safe environment in which the children could be receptive to new, foreign material (Dahl, 2014). Dahl speaks of an "atmosphere of trust" between child and teacher: "Speaking a foreign language in the artificial situation of a foreign language lesson develops more easily to the extent that the element of warmth is tangible for the child" (p. 20). Steiner's educational model calls for astute teachers to attune themselves to the needs of the students, allowing the students to lead the process of discovery based on their readiness for new topics (Steiner, 1922). Wiechert (2013) spoke to the demanding nature of foreign language teaching: "Language teachers—probably more than any other teachers—need presence of mind, a sense of humor, empathy, the ability to respond and a good sense of time. They [have] to be able to create a relaxed and productive atmosphere and a mood of expectation" (p. 6).

The topic of mental, emotional, and physical classroom safety has since been backed by the research of Brené Brown (2017), empowering teachers to create a "culture of courage" in their classrooms that may be the "only safe space" a child has to learn ("Daring Classrooms"). Brown highlights the discomfort and vulnerability involved for teachers and students in creating these "brave spaces." When describing the safe learning environment of the classroom, Brown paints a picture in which the students are like turtles without shells, cautioning: "The minute they [armor themselves and] put the shell back on they're protected...from their teacher, or their peer, or whomever, but no learning can come in, because [without] vulnerability, [there is] no learning." According to Brown, this armoring is an all-too-common occurrence in education. Students who feel unsafe, either emotionally or physically, withdraw from the learning environment, again either emotionally or physically, and may or may not return to participate fully. Though Steiner's approach was not research-based, his insight into the vulnerable nature of learning is clear in his indications of how to best succeed in the classroom.

From the Whole to the Parts

Teaching in totalities is one way Dahl summarized Steiner's approach to bringing the entire essence of a language to the students. Foreign language teachers rely on the imaginative life of children to engage them in story and activity and to take them on a journey into another culture. It is essential that the teacher bring a wealth and richness to the lessons, by teaching vocabulary, folklore, songs, rhymes, and games in the context of the students' lives, allowing them to connect to the material. Instead of teaching words in isolation, Steiner suggested foreign language teachers teach vocabulary in full sentences. Within this framework, the first three years of foreign language instruction is completely oral. The children learn to speak, rhyme, act, play, and sing the language without ever writing a word (Forrer et al., 2000). Teachers rely on the inherent imitative and imaginative capacities of the young child to lead their classes.

Forrer (2000) describes how primary language acquisition includes the process of connecting sounds with objects. Children learn to speak when they are able to imaginatively picture the object and repeat the word that goes with it. Steiner called this process "forming a mental image." "It is through these mental images that we learn to express thoughts, at first in a simple way and then with more complexity [...this allows] the child to have a total experience of language," Forrer describes (p. 19). As previously mentioned, it is not until the fourth grade that students are introduced to writing and very basic grammar in foreign language classes. This timing is a reflection of their developmental phase of increasing self-awareness and separation from their environment, bringing awareness to the "parts" within the "whole" of a sentence, in synch with the students' awareness of their "individuality" within "society." This theme of adding academic intricacy in correlation with the students' social and emotional growth continues through the twelfth grade, increasing complexity to meet the analytical mind of the developing young adult (Forrer et al., 2000).

DEVELOPMENT OF PERCEPTUAL ABILITY

Foreign language learning requires a significant amount of cognitive ability, and yet it requires an equal amount of "perceptual ability" (Dahl, 2014). Dahl explains that the emotions a child experiences when learning their mother tongue form a specific perceptual ability. This ability is extended when a child learns to speak more than one language. One of the main goals of language learning is the ability to hear the articulation and subtle differences in sounds and intonation patterns within a particular language. Such subtle differences in sound often have distinct differences in meaning. The ability to clearly perceive these subtleties is a process of growing both hearing and listening capacities in students.

As humans we can never entirely experience what it is like to live another's experience, and so the development of perceptual, hearing, and listening skills becomes essential in order to best understand and relate to others. When speaking to an audience of teachers at the SXSW (South by Southwest) Education Conference in 2017, Brown reminded teachers of the importance of listening in education. She cautioned that those who belong to "majority culture" in whichever location they are teaching have been given the societal privilege of power. According to Brown (2017), those who are members of "majority culture" were never taught to inquire about others because their reality aligns with the dominant culture. When someone is not challenged to communicate outside of their culture, they will have a weaker, less developed perceptual ability (Dahl, 2014). This creates a lack of awareness about those who have less privilege and societal power, resulting in blindness to the needs and experience of those who are at a disadvantage. This can be problematic when creating an inclusive learning environment with students of diverse backgrounds and needs. Brown recommends those who hold societal power learn to listen and build their perceptual abilities. It is only through listening to others that we are able to close the gap in worldviews and experiences. This connection between people of diverse backgrounds was Steiner's goal for foreign language teaching, thus setting students up for internal development of empathy and the development of perceptual abilities from an early age (Dahl, 2014).

SOCIAL-EMOTIONAL LEARNING (SEL) APPROACHES

Many efforts have been made to deliver competent and compassionate individuals into the world through educational programming since Steiner's time. In 1994, the Collaborative for Academic, Social, and Emotional Learning (CASEL) was formed in an effort to establish "high-quality, evidence-based social and emotional learning (SEL) as an essential part of preschool through high school education" ("What is SEL?" 2019). Social and emotional learning is the process through which children and adults understand and manage emotions, set and achieve positive goals, feel and show empathy for others, establish and maintain positive relationships, and make responsible decisions (CASEL, 2019). CASEL identifies five areas of competencies for the success of children's learning that include: self-awareness, self-management, social awareness, relationship skills, and responsible decision-making. With respect to foreign languages, Steiner's approach directly addresses two standards as defined by CASEL: social awareness and responsible decision-making. Social awareness is the ability to "understand the perspectives of others and empathize with them, including those from diverse backgrounds." According to Steiner, this is the foundation for foreign language learning (Dahl, 2014). Social awareness develops into responsible decision-making as Steiner's curriculum progresses into the middle school years. CASEL defines responsible decision-making as "make[ing] constructive choices about personal behavior and social interactions, based on ethical standards, safety, and social norms" (CASEL, 2019).

Today, we see various school programs that prioritize socio-emotional learning from the moment students enter the classroom, and while parallels can be drawn between these programs and Steiner's approach to education, very few programs are as free in their interpretation of the lessons as Steiner's approach. Steiner gave freedom to the teacher to decide when, where, how, and whether each lesson was delivered, which sharply contrasts with the strong movement by present-day research-based programs to provide a structured step-by-step approach to incorporating socio-emotional lessons.

Steiner knew that students learn best when loved and cared for by trusted adults, and he placed great responsibility on the teachers to meet these expectations. His model, in line with SEL principles, relies heavily on the exchange between the students and the teacher as the foundation for the learning process (Dahl, 2014). If this groundwork is properly laid,

Steiner believed the students would be open to immersing themselves in a new culture through the lens of language. The greater the ability of the teacher to bring the warmth of their being and true love and caring for their subject and the students, the greater the assimilation of the subject material will be.

SOCIAL JUSTICE

The social justice movement has attempted to illuminate lost historical perspectives for the ultimate goal of greater understanding and empowerment of those who have been oppressed. Waldorf schools have been teaching social justice values for one hundred years (AWSNA, 2018). "Social justice is a concept that originates in philosophical discourse but is widely used in both ordinary language and social science, often without being clearly defined" ("Social Justice: History, Theory and Research," 2010). According to Jost and Kay, the American Psychological Association suggests social justice can be defined by the integration of three practices within a society: distributive, procedural and interactional justice:

> Social justice [is] a state of affairs...in which (a) benefits and burdens in society are dispersed in accordance with some allocation principle; (b) procedures, norms, and rules that govern political and other forms of decision-making preserve the basic rights, liberties, and entitlements of individuals and groups; and (c) human beings...are treated with dignity and respect not only by authorities but also by other relevant social actors, including fellow citizens. A social justice system is to be contrasted with those sytems that foster arbitrary or unnecessary suffering, exploitation, abuse, tyranny, opression, prejudice, and discrimination (Jost & Kay, 2010).

REASSESSMENT OF HISTORY

A large part of the social justice movement, which gained momentum in the 1970's (Zinn, 2015) has been the reassessment of history and the presentation of hidden histories. This process of historical excavation has revealed viewpoints that have been systematically disregarded throughout human history. Zinn claims that too much history is written "from the point of view of governments, conquerors, diplomats, leaders" (p. XV). His *A People's History of the United States* sides with the losers, the downtrodden, and the underdog. It is a book "disrespectful of governments and respectful of people's movements of resistance" (p. XVI). A parallel can be drawn between this effort and the importance Steiner (2014) placed on foreign language learning:"All the words in a language are not a collection of labels for things which exist outside language but in their totality they are the sum of events which the people of a language has experienced and come to terms with in its history" (Dahl, 2014, p. 24). This comprehensive view of culture honors the history and totality of a society and its origins.

In retelling history, another goal of the social justice movement has been to reframe the concept of important historical figures. In an effort to move away from the standard of white male as all-important, efforts have been made to embrace the histories of ordinary people (Zinn, 2015). In the introduction of *A People's History of the United States*, Anthony Arnove references the film director Ava DuVernay:

> The impression too often perpetuated in history books and in popular culture is that you have to be a president, someone special, or White to have an important idea or to achieve major accomplishment. This is an idea that disempowers citizens and should not be propagated further (p. XV).

SOCIAL JUSTICE IN THE WALDORF MOVEMENT

Recent efforts have been made to integrate present-day concepts of social justice into the educational approach and organizational structure of Waldorf schools. The theme of AWSNA's 2018 annual conference was Social Justice: Exploring Race, Place, Class, and Gender. In its letter to the community, AWSNA (2018) referenced the upcoming 100th anniversary of the founding of the first Waldorf school as a call to reassess and deepen values of Waldorf education on a global scale, as well as an opportunity to look toward the future with creativity, innovation, and enthusiasm. The importance of the AWSNA mission to strengthen Steiner's vision of an educational approach based on human values and social consciousness is highly relevant in an increasingly divided and disconnected world:"There is an urgent need for change before the divisions that separate us from each other, our environment, and our community grow deeper and wider" ("Letter to the Community"). In the social impact campaign, AWSNA emphasizes the need for human values in education: "Humankind needs self-aware people with a strong sense of purpose, concern for others, and the capacity to be in service to the world." The core values of the AWSNA campaign for the growth of Waldorf education over the next one hundred years are: 1) to inspire a strong sense of self; 2) to respect the dignity of each human being in every encounter; 3) to develop capacities to meet an ever-changing world; 4) to cultivate empathy and concern for others...to make a difference; 5) to nurture and protect childhood; and 6) to embrace diversity and practice inclusion.

Steiner's developmental approach to education provides a carefully considered arc of building the emotional capacities for empathy that can later develop into moral action. According to this approach, the explicit action associated with social justice would come into being in grades 9 through 12, when the students have formed themselves as individuals and are interested in putting their skills to work in the world (Dahl, 2014). For this reason Steiner's model prepares students for real-world situations by introducing them to foreign language instruction at an early age. After years of exercising their empathic abilities, they have developed the skills needed to effectively act on social justice issues as young adults.

Conclusion

In summary of this research, Rudolf Steiner's mission of creating an educational program centered around the need for compassionate citizens in the world was the birth of Waldorf education. The connection Steiner makes of teaching basic social emotional qualities through the languages is one of genius. While other schools are implementing SEL programs with explicit lessons on how to treat one another, Steiner created the foreign language curriculum to allow this experience of others to develop naturally and implicitly. We see the foundation for building empathy primarily in the foreign language classes where students are guided through a process of learning what it is like to step into a reality that is different from their own. This goal is achieved through the development of a perceptual awareness that the students hone over the course of their twelve years of foreign language study. Foreign language teachers follow the same developmental trajectory as all the other teachers in a Waldorf school, offering the children more information when they are ready and in the way they are ready to receive this information. Determining when children have the capacity to handle the next set of lessons may be called an art form in itself. Foreign language teachers must be highly aware of their students and their needs in order to successfully guide this process.

A combination of current social justice efforts and Steiner's views can serve to inform teachers and schools who strive to represent the most comprehensive and balanced summary of the dynamics creating our world. It could be said that the foundations for social justice education are laid from the time the child enters the foreign language program at a Waldorf school, in that children are exposed to stories and cultural traditions that allow the child to step into an empathetic space from an early age. It is through this greater awareness of the world and other communities that we start to develop a strong sense of morality. This inner knowing of right and wrong is what Steiner hoped to cultivate in children from a young age, providing a foundation for action later in life. Steiner's indications for teaching foreign languages are an excellent guide for effectively cultivating empathy and social justice principles in students in grades one through eight.

REFERENCES

Arnove, A. (2015). Introduction. In H. Zinn, *A people's history of the United States* (p. XV). New York, NY: HarperCollins Publishers.

Association for Waldorf Schools of North America (AWSNA). (no date). AWSNA Principles for Waldorf Schools. Retrieved from https:// www.waldorfeducation.org/waldorf-education/in-our-schools/awsna-principles-for-waldorf-schools

Association for Waldorf Schools of North America (AWSNA). (n.d.). Letter to the community. Retrieved from https://resources.finalsite.net/images/ v1544552326 /waldorfeducationorg/ebvidnpvk9jlrovtbmy5/AWSNA_ AR18_Full_v8_DIGITAL.pdf

Brown, B. (2017). Daring classrooms. [Video file]. Retrieved from https:// brenebrown.com/videos/sxsw-edu-2017-daring-classrooms/

Collaborative for Academic, Social, and Emotional Learning. (2019). What is SEL? Retrieved from https://casel.org/what-is-sel/

Dahl, E. (2014). *Teaching foreign languages: The Steiner Waldorf school approach.* (Christian von Arnim, Trans.) Edinburgh: Floris. (Original work published 1999)

Forrer, E., Salusso, C., Silvestry, E. (2000). *Senderos: Teaching Spanish in Waldorf schools.* Chatham, NY: Waldorf Publications

Jost, J. T., Kay, A. C. (2010). Social Justice: History, Theory and Research. Retrieved from https://psycnet.apa.org/record/2010-03506-030

Psychology Today. (n.d.). Empathy: What is empathy? Retrieved from https://www. psychologytoday.com/us/basics/empathy

Steiner, R. (August 24, 1922). Spiritual Ground of Education: The Organization of the Waldorf School, Lecture VII. Retrieved from https://wn.rsarchive.org/ Lectures /GA305/English/APC1947/19220823p01.html

Steiner, R. (1995). *The Kingdom of Childhood: Introductory Talks on Waldorf Education.* (Helen Fox, Trans.) Hudson, NY: Anthroposophic Press

Steiner, R. (2000). *Practical advice to teachers: Fourteen lectures.* (Johanna Collis, Trans.) Great Barrington, MA: Anthroposophic Press.

Wiechert, C. (2013). Cosmopolitan goals and ways of achieving them. *Journal: Pedagogical Section at the Goetheanum, Special Edition Midsummer 2013, 48,* 4-12.

Zinn, H. (2015). *A People's History of the United States: 1492–Present.* New York, NY: HarperCollins Publishers.

The Essential Components of an Assessment Program in Grades 1-8 in a Public Waldorf Charter School Setting
by Jennifer Hoover

ABSTRACT

This paper explores how Waldorf charter schools can effectively meet testing mandates from the government and document student learning using formative assessment practices in a way that fulfills accountability needs while maintaining the heart of the Waldorf pedagogy. This paper categorizes assessments into four categories: formative learning, formative diagnostic, benchmark or interim, and summative assessments. Assessment programs that are well-rounded integrate all four types of assessment. Traditionally, private Waldorf schools do not implement summative type assessments and rely heavily on student observation and reflection of lessons to determine student learning, or assessments *for* learning. Charter schools are mandated to administer standardized summative assessments annually, or assessments *of* learning. Additionally, charter schools are required to give accountability reports to their authorizing entities that describe in detail how student learning is assessed and what standards are taught in each grade. This paper describes how Waldorf charter schools can rely almost entirely on assessments *for* learning and if done well, the assessments *of* learning will have similar results.

THE ESSENTIAL COMPONENTS OF AN ASSESSMENT PROGRAM IN GRADES 1-8 IN A WALDORF CHARTER SCHOOL SETTING

Good assessment can lead to transformation in both teaching and learning. Assessment has received a bad reputation, as it is often a political hot topic. Waldorf schools are typically exempt from high-stakes standardized tests from the government. With the development of the charter movement in the early 1990s, the private Waldorf school pedagogy has entered the public-school realm. There has had to be some give and take as a result of more government oversight, namely in standardized assessment. Recently there is a movement for more accountability to the government from charter schools. While charter schools are granted more freedom and flexibility than public schools, they are held to high accountability standards to ensure student learning and can face closure when standards are not met. A systematic and whole-child approach to assessment is key when developing an assessment program for Waldorf charter schools for accountability purposes.

Traditional Waldorf View of Assessment

Testing, and, more specifically, standardized testing, are increasingly identified as sources of a host of ills that afflict contemporary education (Zachos, 2004). Although the cause of these woes is not actually testing and standardization, the real problem is far deeper and more widespread. The true culprit is the non-educational uses of tests, a very unhealthy practice. According to Zachos, the "integral part of dealing with the problems that are associated with testing is the adoption of sound testing process" (p. 7).

A study completed in 2010 looked at how Waldorf teachers prepared lessons and assessed student learning across several domains: cognitive, affective and social, psycho-motor, and aesthetic (Ireland, 2015). The teachers that assigned curriculum-embedded work such as worksheets, tests, quizzes, or portfolio evidence, were able to give a real-time picture of what the student is learning. The curriculum-embedded assessments are used to observe and record student progress across several domains and multiple modalities. The private Waldorf school community has the opinion that student learning can be assessed without high-stakes testing, like standardized state tests.

According to Ireland, Waldorf pedagogy maintains the notion that the purpose of education is for students to find meaning and purpose in their lives, to become global citizens and have respect for all of humanity, and to be able to make informed and thoughtful decisions. The purpose of assessments is to motivate students, to evoke inquiry and excite curiosity by engaging them with the materials in a multitude of ways and modalities to elicit questions and dialogue.

Traditionally, in the early years of Waldorf education, no letter grades are given because grades may hamper enthusiasm for the learning process (Zachos, 2004). In the upper grades, teachers give tests and quizzes to further engage with lesson content, to allow the students to realize what lesson content they grasped, and for the teacher to evaluate what content was understood and what content should be retaught (Ireland, 2015). Assessments are nearly always formative in the Waldorf private school setting, as learning is never static because students are always growing and changing. According to Ireland, summative test results cannot be used to support teaching and learning for those being tested. However, Ireland suggests that post-instruction tests may support some learning if test results are provided to students with detailed feedback regarding specific learning goals, but they cannot influence instruction because instruction on the topic of interest has already come to an end (Zachos, 2004).

Learning, from an anthroposophical perspective, is "a process that transforms the whole person and thus changes the way we are and how we act, and that has to do with making and sharing meaning about the self, others, and the world" (Rawson, 2015). From this perspective learning can be assessed in two ways. The first method of learning can be evaluated by assessing whether the learner possesses the knowledge, or an assessment *of* learning. The outcome is paramount, and it can be measured quantitatively. In the second method of assessing learning, the process is what counts and is done through careful watching and observation. This is an assessment *for* learning. In Waldorf education, both types of learning and both types of assessment are necessary. The learning method we teach first, and which one we privilege and reward, is what requires careful thought and consideration. Assessing only the cognitive academic achievement lowers the value of everything that children do. Careful observation and understanding of each individual student allow educators to appreciate the general process of learning and development. Rawson (2015) explains that "These general principles are not norms but are archetypal processes that are expressed differently depending on the individual" (p. 32).

A balanced approach to assessment must look at both the teaching and the outcome of the teaching. This involves a cycle of reflecting on, in, and for teaching. As stated by Rawson, this means:

> Reflection on is retrospective, looking back at what happened. Reflecting in or while teaching involves noticing how children respond and intuitively knowing how to respond pedagogically. Reflecting for teaching involves planning, anticipating, and preparing lessons. The purpose of assessment is to give the students reflections and suggestions in a form and in such a way that the students understand what the next concrete step needs to be (p. 34).

Assessments in the Waldorf setting tend to be ipsative-reference assessments (Rawson, 2015). In this type of assessment, the student is evaluated against themselves (personal best) from their previous performance (Thayer, 2017). According to Rawson, this is the most relevant way to assess individuals in classes with a wide range of abilities. This type of assessment does tend to be highly subjective in nature (Thayer, 2017).

Mitchell, Gerwin, Schuberth, Mancini & Hofrichter (2008) said that "It is the birthright of every child to enjoy a healthy childhood that involves free play, loving warmth, and healthy child-centered rhythms—the unfolding of which will be transformed later into cognitive and moral capacities that become sources of strength in adult life" (p. 22). Therefore, assessments should not focus simply on the performance of students but on the efficacy of teachers (Mitchell et al., 2008).

PUBLIC CHARTER WALDORF SCHOOLS

Waldorf schools were able to move into the public sector with the creation of charter schools, or public schools of choice. Charter schools are afforded the freedom to provide innovative education through a reduction of regulation and to provide choice and access to different types of schools (Beaven, 2013). As public institutions, charter schools are subject to political controls that restrict freedom of practice (Lamb, 2015). These controls are evident in requirements for a type of student assessment that is incompatible with the Waldorf model of human development and that may impose restrictions on curriculum and teaching (Beaven, 2013). There is a struggle to provide free access to public education utilizing Waldorf principles, while having to subject students to assessments that are at odds with the Waldorf pedagogy. There must be a compromise with these two concepts.

Charters face intense scrutiny in the current political climate. It no longer works for schools to say, "I know the students are learning because I observe it." Schools are asked to "prove it" with evidence constantly. Waldorf teachers know that children are learning because of the inherent observation that is critical and integral in Waldorf education, but Waldorf charter schools have the burden of backing up these observations with concrete data. There is a way to perform these tasks while preserving what is essential in Waldorf education.

Charter schools have the option to provide a distinctive curriculum or environment not offered by the local school district, or to serve a specific student population (Lamb, 2015). Some charter schools provide curriculum that is specialized, and, in the case of Waldorf charter schools, incorporate educational methods traditionally found in independent schools. In exchange, charter schools are held to stronger accountability requirements based on student scores on state-mandated standardized tests. Charter schools can face closure if scores are not to their authorizing district/ organization's standards.

The worst-case scenario is when a Waldorf school has no evaluation culture other than state assessments (Rawson, 2015). When a student is used to working with meaningful forms of pedagogical evaluation and reflection throughout the school in age-appropriate ways, external tests play a much less significant role in the minds of students, families, and even teachers. Evaluation compares and assesses abilities, competencies, achievements in relation to standards, or self-determined goals. Assessments can be a diagnostic tool in accompanying the learning process. In the form of self-evaluation, assessments can enable the development of self-knowledge and learning competence.

Types of Assessment

There is quite a bit of disagreement on the types of and categorization of assessments. For the purposes of this research, assessments will be categorized into four types as described by Sparks (2015). According to Sparks, the four types of assessments are: formative learning assessments, formative diagnostic assessments, benchmark or interim assessments, and summative assessment. A well-rounded assessment program at any educational organization should have all four types of assessment in order to capture an accurate picture of each student.

Formative Learning Assessment

Formative learning assessment is the process of teaching students how to set goals for their learning, to identify their growth toward those goals, to evaluate the quality of their work, and to identify strategies to improve. Individual students measure themselves against the learning outcomes/ expectations. This is an ongoing type of assessment and can be used for daily lessons or long-term projects. The feedback is immediately given. This type of assessment is used to help students internalize the learning goals, reflect on learning, evaluate the quality of their work and develop strategies to improve their work and understanding. The strategies used to assess are self-evaluation and metacognition, analyzing work of varying qualities, developing one's own rubric or learning progressions, writing laboratory or other reflective journals, peer review, etc.

FORMATIVE DIAGNOSTIC ASSESSMENT

Formative diagnostic assessment is a process of questioning, testing, or demonstration used to identify how a student is learning, where her strengths and weaknesses lie, and potential strategies to improve that learning (Sparks, 2015). This type of assessment focuses on individual growth. The way students answer gives insight into their learning process and how to support it. This is an ongoing type of assessment that is often part of a cycle of instruction and feedback over time. Results are immediate or very rapid. This assessment is used to diagnose problems in students' understanding or gaps in skills and to help teachers decide next steps in instruction. The strategies used in formal diagnostic assessments include rubrics and written or oral test questions, and observation protocols designed to identify specific problem areas or misconceptions in learning the concept or performing the skill.

BENCHMARK/INTERIM ASSESSMENT

Sparks (2015) asserts that benchmark or interim assessment is a comparison of student understanding or performance against a set of uniform standards within the same school year. This type of assessment may contain hybrid elements of formative and summative assessments, or a summative test of a smaller section of content, like a unit or semester. These are used to evaluate individual students or classes and occur intermittently, often at the end of a quarter or semester, or a midpoint of a curricular unit. Results are generally received in enough time to affect instruction in the same school year. This type of assessment gives educators something to track student progression toward their long-term learning goals.

Depending on the timing of assessment feedback, this may be used more to inform instruction or to evaluate the quality of the learning environment (Sparks, 2015). These assessments tend to be a condensed form of an annual summative assessment, e.g., a shorter term paper or test. They may be developed by the teacher or school, be bought commercially, or be part of a larger state assessment system.

SUMMATIVE ASSESSMENT

Summative assessments are outcome assessments and evaluate performance (Sparks, 2015). These assessments compare the performance of a student or group of students against a set of uniform standards. The educational environment, which includes teachers, curricula, education systems, and programs, is who is being evaluated. Summative assessments evaluate one point in time, often at the end of a curricular unit or course, or annually at the same time each school year. The purpose of summative assessment is to give an overall description of students' status and evaluate the effectiveness of the educational environment. Summative assessments are standardized to make comparisons among students, classes, or schools.

Traditional and Authentic Assessments

Traditional assessments are administered to assess the acquisition of knowledge and skills (Mueller, n.d.). Tests usually consist of selected-response items (multiple choice tests, true-false, matching, fill-in-the-blank, label a diagram, etc.) and occasionally some constructed response items (e.g. short essay). No new knowledge is constructed within the test.

Authentic tasks are assignments given to students designed to assess their ability to apply standard-driven knowledge and skills to real-world challenges (Mueller, n.d.). A task that asks students to perform is considered authentic when students are asked to construct their own responses rather than select from ones presented, and when the task replicates challenges faced in the real world. Authentic tasks are not just assessments. In contrast to traditional assessment, these tasks encourage the integration of teaching, learning, and assessing.

In the traditional assessment model, teaching and learning are often separated from assessment. A test is administered after knowledge or skills have been acquired in traditional assessment (Mueller, n.d.). In the authentic assessment model, the same authentic task used to measure the students' ability to apply the knowledge or skills is used as a vehicle for student learning. Table 1 distinguishes the differences in attributes between traditional assessment and authentic task.

Traditional Assessments	Authentic Tasks
Selecting a Response: Students given several choices and asked to select the right answer.	**Performing a Task:** Students asked to demonstrate understanding by performing a more complex task usually representative of more meaningful application.
Contrived: Tests offer these as a means of assessment to increase the number of times you can be asked to demonstrate proficiency in a short period of time.	**Real-Life:** Demonstrate proficiency by doing something.
Recall/Recognition: Determine whether students have acquired a body of knowledge. Can be a nice complement to authentic assessments. However, these tend to be much less revealing about what a student really knows/can do.	**Construction/Application:** Often ask students to analyze, synthesize, and apply what they have learned in a substantial manner, and students create new meaning in the process as well.
Teacher-Structured: What a student can and will demonstrate has been carefully structured by the person who developed the test. A student's attention will be focused on and limited to what is on the test.	**Student-Structured:** Allow for more student choice and construction in determining what is presented as evidence of proficiency. Even when students can't choose topic/format, there are usually multiple acceptable routes toward constructing a product or performance.
Indirect Evidence: We can only make inferences about what the students might know and might be able to do with that knowledge.	**Direct Evidence:** Offer more direct evidence of application and construction of knowledge.

Table 1. *Attributes of Traditional Assessment and Authentic Tasks* (Mueller, n.d.)

TYPES OF AUTHENTIC TASKS

According to Mueller (n.d.), authentic assessments include tasks such as performances, products, and constructed response items that typically require more direct application of knowledge and skills. These types of tasks are described below along with common examples of each.

CONSTRUCTED RESPONSE. In constructed response task activities, students construct an answer out of old and new knowledge. There is no one correct answer; students are constructing new knowledge that differs from that constructed by other students. There is some level of students' thinking that is revealed in these tasks. Mueller states that constructed responses can be product-like (examples: short essay, making predictions, explain your solution) or performance-like (examples: measure objects, reading fluently, participation, conferences).

PRODUCT. In response to a prompt, students construct a substantial, tangible product that reveals their understanding of certain concepts and skills. Typically more substantial in depth and length than constructed response tasks. These are broadly conceived and allow more time between giving the prompt and the students' response. Examples include essays, article reviews, research reports, models, musical compositions, lab reports, error analysis, and games.

PERFORMANCE. Students can construct a performance that reveals their understanding of certain concepts/skills and/or their ability to apply, analyze, synthesize, or evaluate those concepts and skills. Examples include conducting an experiment, musical audition, dramatic readings, skits, role-plays, book talks, panel discussions, and teaching/explaining.

Authentic assessment provides a direct measure, captures the constructive nature of learning, integrates teaching, learning, and assessment, and provides multiple paths to demonstration. To create an authentic assessment, the standard or learning expectation must first be identified. Then the teacher should carefully select an authentic task that is appropriate for the chosen learning expectation, as well as identifying the criteria for the task. Lastly, a rubric tailored to the specific task should be created (Mueller, n.d.).

COMPONENTS OF ASSESSMENT PROGRAM IN PUBLIC WALDORF CHARTER SCHOOLS

An assessment program that is developed for a Waldorf charter setting will include summative, benchmark, formative learning, and formative diagnostic assessments. Observation and reflection are key when developing an assessment program that will be in line with the Waldorf pedagogy. Therefore, the bulk of the assessments will be both authentic and formative.

SUMMATIVE ASSESSMENT

Summative assessments are going to be a reality in a Waldorf charter school. These schools are mandated to take part in the standardized assessments from the state. There is an added layer of concern with these standardized state tests, as most of the tests are delivered via an electronic platform. Students now must also possess the knowledge of how to use a computer and accurately keyboard in order to have a chance to be successful on these tests. One welcome change with the electronic versions of the state tests is that most have an element of being adaptive. The rigor of how a standard is being asked will increase or decrease with how a student is performing on the test. The livelihood of many public Waldorf charter schools depends on how a school performs on these standardized assessments, so it is crucial that schools perform well.

BENCHMARK ASSESSMENT

Benchmark assessments should be used for accountability to the state. The benchmark assessments allow schools to assess students on the learning outcomes that they have determined to be necessary for each grade. Benchmark assessments also give students a way of being assessed on standards at certain rigor levels and question types that match how students will be assessed on the summative state tests.

These assessments should be based on the standards that the school has agreed the learning outcomes for each grade will be. The Alliance for Waldorf Public Education (n.d.) has created standards for Waldorf charter schools. These provide a good starting place, for the core subjects that are assessed in the state standardized summative assessments. However, these standards do not thoroughly address the subject specialty classes, social-emotional learning, and the sensory/motor skills/movement content that is addressed in the school as part of its curriculum.

FORMATIVE ASSESSMENT

Formative assessment continues to be where most of the evaluation and assessing takes place in the school. However, due to accountability measures to the government, it is imperative that there be a way to document what is observed, and how instruction is arranged and changed to meet the needs of all students in the learning environment. The types of formative assessment should be a mixture of both traditional (diagnostic) and authentic (learning) assessment, with a majority being authentic tasks. Rubrics and portfolios can assist with documenting what teachers inherently observe and know to be true about each of the students in their classes, as well as providing a formative assessment that gives the teacher feedback that can be used as part of the reflection process for the teacher and student. These assessment types can be extended to include specialty classes, social-emotional learning, and sensory/motor skills/movement.

RUBRICS. As a result of the increasing level of accountability put onto public Waldorf charters, educational organizations must be able to provide evidence of student performance and learning. While observation is at the heart of Waldorf education, it must be recorded in a concrete manner to satisfy these increasing accountability demands.

Rubrics are a scoring scale that is used to "assess student performance along a task-specific set of criteria," (Mueller, n.d.). Authentic tasks or assessments are typically criterion-referenced measures. A student's ability on a task is determined by matching the student's performance against a set of criteria to ascertain the degree to which the student's performance meets the criteria for the task. A rubric is developed to measure student performance and contains the essential criteria for the task and appropriate levels of performance for each criterion.

Mueller postulates that rubrics are comprised of two components: criteria and levels of performance. A rubric must have at least two criteria and at least two levels of performance. The criteria are the characteristics of good performance on a task. The rubric contains a method for assigning a score or development level to each project criterion. The rubric descriptors are used to describe the expected outcome at each level of performance. Descriptors can help the teacher distinguish from the work of others for each criterion and allows the teacher to be more precise and consistent when evaluating student work. Each descriptor is tied to a point or development level for each criterion chosen and makes it possible to objectively score or place each student into a performance level. Evaluating what performance level a student is working at also allows a teacher to give better feedback to the student, as well as providing an opportunity for the teacher to reflect on the student and class performance with particular skills or aspects of their lesson.

PORTFOLIOS. Public Waldorf charter schools that implement portfolios as part of the school's assessment plan can document student learning and progression of students' long-term learning goals. Portfolios capture a student's learning journey with the capability of using multi-media to document. Portfolios also afford an opportunity for a student to showcase their work in specialty classes.

Portfolios are a collection of authentic tasks that capture meaningful application of knowledge and skills (Mueller, n.d.). Thoughtful portfolio assignments ask students to reflect on their work, to engage in self-assessment and goal-setting. Mueller (n.d.) states that "Research has found that students in classes that emphasize improvement, progress, effort, and the process of learning rather than grades and normative performance are more likely to use a variety of learning strategies and have a more positive attitude toward learning" (Portfolios section, para. 4).

When developing a portfolio assignment, the purpose of the portfolio must first be considered. Mueller states that there are three distinct purposes: to show growth, to showcase current abilities, and to evaluate cumulative achievement. The growth portfolio emphasizes the process of learning whereas the showcase portfolio emphasizes the product of learning. Portfolios can be used for more than one purpose. According to Mueller, the questions outlined in Table 2 should be examined and considered when creating the portfolios assignment/project.

Purpose	What is the purpose(s) of the portfolio?
Audience	For what audience(s) will the portfolio be created?
Content	What samples of student work will be included?
Process	What processes (e.g., selection of work to be included, reflection on work, conferencing) will be engaged in during the development of the portfolio?
Management	How will time and materials be managed in the development of the portfolio?
Communication	How and when will the portfolio be shared with pertinent audiences?
Evaluation	If the portfolio is to be used for evaluation, when and how should it be evaluated?

Table 2. *Considerations When Developing Portfolio Assignment*

CONCLUSION AND FUTURE STUDY

Waldorf education values observation and reflection as a means to assess student learning. The same is true in public Waldorf charter schools. Public Waldorf charter schools have the burden of administering standardized state assessments that are not aligned with the Waldorf pedagogy.

A well-rounded assessment program that is tailored to public Waldorf charter schools should continue to rely on observation and reflection to assess for learning. However, the observations and reflection process should be documented by using assessment tools such as rubrics and portfolios that have clearly defined criteria to demonstrate particular levels of learning or development. Having such systems in place that are authentic and formative assessments will allow educators to have a clearer picture of where each student is in their learning journey. These systems could potentially aid in the child study process as well.

An assessment program that incorporates both a hefty formative assessment component and benchmark assessments that resemble the summative state tests in structure, assessing the learning standards that are covered in each grade within a Waldorf charter school, is able to speak to the discrepancies between the formative and benchmarks assessments compared to the state summative results. The lower grades tend to have lower summative scores when compared to grade-level peers, but schools can document student learning and growth of learning standards with formative and benchmark data. The summative scores of Waldorf charter schools meet or exceed the scores of their grade-level peers by the time they graduate from middle school. Therefore, Waldorf charter schools are able to justify the arc of the Waldorf curriculum.

More study is needed in the area of developing developmentally appropriate rubrics for first through eighth grades in the charter setting. The rigor and depth of knowledge for academic content would have to increase throughout the grade spans. Rubrics that address social-emotional learning, specialty classes, and movement or spatial dynamics should also be explored. Rubrics and self-reflection processes should be developed to aid in streamlined portfolio projects that can be used schoolwide and are appropriate for differing grade levels.

The development of an assessment program that incorporates formative assessment at its core helps both students and teachers to become more reflective of their learning and to develop future learning goals. This process also will lead to better performance on summative assessments as both the student and teacher are active participants in the learning process. This process allows for students to be motivated and engaged in the learning process while giving teachers ample opportunity to observe and reflect on the students and their learning.

REFERENCES

Alliance for Public Waldorf Education (n.d.). Retrieved November 18, 2019, from http:// www.allianceforpublicwaldorfeducation.org/

Ireland, H. (2015). Assessment for Learning in Waldorf Classrooms: How Waldorf Teachers Measure Student Progress Toward Lifelong Learning Goals. *Research Bulletin, 20*(2), 43-46. Retrieved from https://www.waldorflibrary. org/

Lamb, G. (2015). Charter Schools in Relation to the Waldorf School Movement. *Research Bulletin, 20*(1), 44-57. Retrieved from https://www.waldorflibrary. org/

Mitchell, D., Gerwin, D., Schuberth, E., Mancini, M., & Hofrichter, H. (2008). Assessment without High-Stakes Testing: Protecting Childhood and the Purpose of School. *Research Bulletin, 13*(2), 21-30. Retrieved from https:// www.waldorflibrary.org/

Mueller, J. (n.d.). *Authentic Assessment Toolbox.* Retrieved from http://jfmueller. faculty.noctrl. edu/toolbox/index.htm

Rawson, M. (2015). Assessment: A Waldorf Perspective. *Research Bulletin, 20*(2), 30-42. Retrieved from https://www.waldorflibrary.org/

Sparks, S. (2015). Types of Assessments: A Head-to-Head Comparison. *Education Week, 35*(12), s3. Retrieved from https://www.edweek.org/ew/section/ multimedia/types-of-assessments-a-head-to-head-comparison.html

Thayer, T. (2017). *Ipsative Assessment.* Retrieved from http://entreassess. com/2017/03/14/ ipsative-assessment/

Zachos, P. (2004). Discovering the True Nature of Educational Assessment. *Research Bulletin, 9*(2), 7-12. Retrieved from https://www.waldorflibrary.org/

How Can Waldorf Educators Build Resilience in Children Today?

by Stephanie Lorenz

Abstract

How can Waldorf educators build resilience in children today? My question truly began as an answer. I sought to find the answer over and over that human relationships are key. The specific answer to my question is for the child to have a relationship with at least one significant adult. Evidence clearly indicates the relationship is fundamental and integral to building resilience and success in the lives of children. The essence of Waldorf education being thought of as a relationship-based education confirmed the answer I had been seeking all along. How do we as educators instill success and build resilience in the youth we are entrusted to educate?

How Can Waldorf Educators Build Resilience in Children Today?

Waldorf education is a nourishing, relationship-based education. I consider my work as a teacher is to shine a light on all students. I must see them for who they truly are; I encourage my students to believe in their best selves. I initially received the gift of stumbling upon Waldorf education for my own children. Next, I rejoined the workforce as a teacher in a public Waldorf charter school. These experiences have guided me to the answer of my question. As a teacher, building relationships with students is paramount to delivering content or even adhering to state-mandated curriculum standards. Teaching in a public Waldorf charter school has afforded me the ability to work with students in small groups. I am able to tailor curriculum designed to meet the needs of the individual student. It is necessary to navigate the personal relationship with the student. If I do not show I care, then, in turn, some students may feel they do not need to care, as well. The text I immersed myself in to research my question was Rudolf Steiner's transcribed lectures, *The Child's Changing Consciousness as the Basis of Pedagogical Practice* (1996).

> Consequently, a pedagogy that springs from a true knowledge of the human being has to be largely a matter of the teachers' own inner attitudes—a pedagogy destined to work on the teachers' own moral attitudes. A more drastic expression of this would be: The children in themselves are all right, but the adults are not! ...Instead of talking

about how we should treat children, we should strive toward a knowledge of how we, as teachers and educators, ought to conduct ourselves. In our work we need forces of the heart. Yet it is not good enough to simply declare that, instead of addressing ourselves to the intellect of our pupils we now must appeal to their hearts, in both principle and method. What we really need...is that we ourselves have our hearts in our pedagogy (p. 65).

The astute skill of observation teachers are required to cultivate enables each child to be visible and accessible. Rudolf Steiner emphasizes that the teacher first understand the human being in all aspects of development. This is not purely visual observation. The totality of one person is "...perception and judgment of how body, soul, and spirit are permeated by spirit in entirely different ways during each of the first three periods of life" (p. 24).

Teachers need to clearly understand the phases of development for each child. To have the full picture of human life from birth to death guides the teacher's comprehension, through recognizing the seven-year cycles from birth to adulthood. The work of the class teacher, also considered the traditional grades teacher, is to guide the children through the change of teeth into adolescence. The students are moving beyond the imitation phase into their feeling life. Steiner emphasizes the importance of the teacher as a role model. It is crucial at this stage of development. "Children at this particular stage in life who have not learned to look up with a natural sense of surrender to the authority of the adults who educated them, cannot grow into free human beings" (p. 54).

Waldorf schools typically adhere to a looping method. The class loops with the teacher from one grade to the next. The familial bond created when students have the same teacher for a series of years engenders trust. The Northeast and Islands Regional Educational Laboratory at Brown University report, *Looping: Supporting Student Learning Through Long-Term Relationships,* states "More formally, looping has been working in German Waldorf Schools since the early part of this century" (p. 12). The report lists the following social advantages: Looping permits students to get to know one another well, facilitating social construction of knowledge. Long-term relationships result in an emotional and intellectual climate that encourages thinking, risk-taking, and involvement. Looping encourages a stronger sense of community and family among parents, students, and teachers (p. 8).

Having a class travel together through the grades, especially during the second phase of childhood, fosters strength and unity. Steiner points out that during this phase the teacher's concern must be directed toward the students' evolving life of feeling. Steiner emphasizes the tender transitional stages of this period. He goes on further to state the evolution of the imitative phase which "...connects with listening for what comes from the natural authority of the teacher" (Steiner, p. 99).

The work of the teacher is to create a relationship built on trust, along with fostering the natural growth of a child in each stage of development. Looping with a group of children enables the teacher to provide predictable rhythms and the familiarity to work with each individual child's temperament and uniqueness. I spoke with a teacher who has looped, taken two separate classes from grades one to five. Her current fifth grade class of students had struggled to behave well for a guest teacher. Upon returning to the classroom after the guest teacher had left, the teacher asked the class to reflect on their actions. One student replied, "We can't treat you disrespectfully. You are like our mom. You have known me for most of my life" (J. Walthard, personal communication, Dec. 11, 2019).

Understanding the dynamic of human relationships is imperative. In his book, *The Soul of Discipline,* Kim John Payne speaks of three distinct roles parents and caregivers must be for children: the governor, who is comfortably and firmly in charge; the gardener, who is watching for emotional growth and engaging in careful listening; the guide, who is a sounding board and moral compass. These three roles match well with the seven-year cycles Rudolf Steiner indicates. The gardener role is aptly named for the looping grades teacher taking children from the change of teeth into early adolescence. The role of the Waldorf school is to nurture the child's natural abilities in a safe setting. In her book, *Between Form and Freedom,* Betty Staley speaks of this second phase of childhood.

> From seven to fourteen—the soul develops. Children leave the security of the family and venture into the larger world of neighborhood and school. They come to feel at home in the wider circle of their community. They relate to this new world with their feelings, which are expressed in extremes (Staley 1998, p. 5).

Looping with a group of children through this second phase of childhood is an ideal. Waldorf education strives for this experience.

> The teacher is not a person who teaches but a facilitator, who creates the right climate for learning. Once this climate has been created, young children "love" their teacher, and it is this, rather than academic knowledge which inspires them to learn. It all depends on the teacher's character, that is, on self-education (Wiechert 2015, p. 20).

The Waldorf teacher's responsibility is to foster the unfolding of the human being along with cultivating key features of relationship.

> Teachers must not simply decide what they are going to do, or which method is right or wrong. It is far more important for them to recognize what is inwardly stirring and moving in these children— in order to guide and develop them further (Steiner 1939, p. 67).

In the New York Times opinion editorial piece on Jan. 17, 2019, titled "Students Learn From People They Love," David Brooks mentions neuroscience research showing how student and teacher brain activity synchronizes. Brooks referenced the study, "Brain-to-Brain Synchrony and Learning Outcomes Vary by Student-Teacher Dynamics: Evidence from a Real-world Classroom Electroencephalography Study."

> Brain-to-brain synchrony between the teacher and students varied as a function of student engagement as well as teacher likeability: Students who reported greater social closeness to the teacher showed higher brain-to-brain synchrony with the teacher, but this was only the case for lectures—that is, when the teacher is an integral part of the content presentation.

Brooks supports this evidence by declaring what teachers really teach is themselves—their contagious passion for their subjects and their students. Therefore, Brooks claims, "...children learn from people they love, and that love in this context means willing the good of another, and offering active care for the whole person."

Waldorf teachers have been called to lead their students as upright, social, moral, just figures, worthy of imitation, emanating love, engendering trust, and speaking with truth.

> We need to help each other, and we are also helped when we develop trust in the working of the spiritual world. Something we all need today is courage—courage to develop meaningful relationships within our own lives, to respect our children's individuality, to stand by decisions when we feel alone and weak and to do so without knowing all the answers or even being able to ask all the questions (Staley, p. 263).

The Practice of Resilience, as defined by *Virtues Project International:*

> When trouble comes, I stay strong. I have the flexibility to bounce back. I have the faith to overcome. I find comfort in community. I trust hardship to cultivate my character. I fully engage in living.

The Merriam-Webster online dictionary classifies resilience as a noun. First definition: "The capability of a strained body to recover its size and shape after deformation caused especially by compressive stress." The second definition of resilience from Merriam-Webster is "an ability to recover from or adjust easily to misfortune or change." Resilient children are survivors. Evidence suggests resilience is often cultivated by relationship and experience.

The Center on the Developing Child at Harvard University states, "The single most common factor for children who develop resilience is at least one stable and committed relationship with a supportive parent, caregiver, or other adult." In addition, "...regular physical exercise, stress-reduction practices, and programs that actively build executive function and self-regulation skills can improve the abilities of children and adults to cope with, adapt to, and even prevent adversity in their lives." This evidence reflects the work of the Waldorf teacher and pedagogy.

Adverse Childhood Experiences (ACES) include child abuse and neglect. ACES (the acronym) originated in a 1995 study conducted by the Centers for Disease Control and the Kaiser Permanente health care organization in California (cdc.gov/violenceprevention).

> Child abuse and neglect are serious public health issues with far-reaching consequences for the youngest and most vulnerable members of society. Every child is better when they and their peers have safe, stable, nurturing relationships and environments.

ACES are dramatically improved in the life of a child by fostering resilience. In support of harnessing and developing strategies for resilience in children, Dr. Kenneth Ginsberg and the American Academy of Pediatrics authored the 2014 book, *A Parent's Guide to Building Resilience in Children and Teens: Giving Your Child Roots and Wings*. They identified seven "C's" to help children build resilience.

1. **Competence** can be developed by helping children focus on individual strengths and empowering children to make decisions.

2. **Confidence** can be built by focusing on the best in each child so that they can see that, as well. This includes clearly expressing the best qualities, such as fairness, integrity, persistence, and kindness.

3. **Connection** exists by developing close ties to family and community. It creates a solid sense of security that helps lead to strong values and prevents alternative destructive paths to love and attention, thus allowing the expression of all emotions, so that kids will feel

comfortable reaching out during difficult times. Fostering healthy relationships that will reinforce positive messages.

4. **Character** can be strengthened by demonstrating how behaviors affect others, helping children recognize themselves as caring people. Demonstrating the importance of community, and encouraging the development of spirituality.

5. **Contribution** is built in children by stressing the importance of serving others by modeling generosity.

6. **Coping** can be shown to children by modeling positive coping strategies on a consistent basis, guiding your child to develop positive and effective coping strategies.

7. **Control**, for children who realize they can control the outcomes of their decisions are more likely to realize that they have the ability to bounce back. Helping your child to understand that life's events are not purely random and that most things that happen are the result of another individual's choices and actions.

Dr. Ginsberg also states that children need to know that there is an adult in their life who believes in them and loves them unconditionally.

In excerpt of Peter Selg's 2010 book, *The Essence of Waldorf Education*, Selg highlights Rudolf Steiner's concept that the work of the teacher is actually nurturing the spiritual relationship, essentially cultivating past and future forces, "...in the process of becoming."

> The supporting gesture is one of helping, or we could say of healing. This meeting of the life intention of the individual with the current time, the current societal constitution, is difficult. Preparing for this meeting and trying through support and awareness to prevent its failure is the true task of education.

In conclusion, the relationship is key. A loving, principled guiding relationship with at least one significant adult in a child's lifetime creates a wellspring of resilience to adversity. Waldorf educational pedagogy supports the idea of the class teacher who loops with the same group of children during their critical phases of development. This experience enables children to gain the strength to build and foster success in their lives.

REFLECTION

The roles of the teacher, parent, and caregiver are extremely important.

The task is daunting, yet tremendously rewarding. My question has been consistently answered while having the pleasure of working at Golden Valley Charter School for the past ten years. I have witnessed first-hand some very incredible teachers take classes from first to eighth grade. The remarkable bond formed between students and a single teacher who held them from age seven to fourteen, is truly an extraordinary relationship. These students who have been a product of this educational experience offer much resilience and live lives confidently knowing they have been seen, well cared for, and loved. In my heart, I am beyond grateful to have a stake in public Waldorf education. As we move into the year 2020, so much of the content from Rudolf Steiner's lectures recorded in *The Child's Changing Consciousness as the Basis of Pedagogical Practice* are timeless inspirations of how to be a complete teacher. I look forward to continuing to research this question, as it has truly become my passion. How do we continually build resilience in children today?

REFERENCES

Brooks, D. (2019, Jan. 17). "Students Learn From People They Love." *The New York Times*. https://www.nytimes.com/2019/01/17/opinion/learning-emotion-education.html

Center on the Developing Child, Harvard University. (n.d.). *Key Concepts. Resilience.* https://developingchild.harvard.edu/science/key-concepts/resilience/

Ginsberg, K., & Jablow, M. (2014). *Building Resilience in Children and Teens: Giving Your Child Roots and Wings.* American Academy of Pediatrics.

LAB at Brown University. (n.d.). *Looping: Supporting Student Learning Through Long-Term Relationships.* https://www.brown.edu/academics/education-alliance/sites/brown.edu.academics.education-alliance/files/publications/looping.pdf

National Center for Injury Prevention and Control, Centers for Disease Control and Prevention (2019). Preventing Child Abuse & Neglect. www.cdc.gov/violenceprevention

Payne, K. J. (2015). *The Soul of Discipline.* Ballantine Books.

Selg, P. (2010). *The Essence of Waldorf Education.* Steiner Books.

Staley, B. (2009). *Between Form and Freedom.* Hawthorn Press.

Steiner, R. (1996). *The Child's Changing Consciousness as the Basis of Pedagogical Practice.* Anthroposophic Press.

The Virtues Project (n.d). https://virtuesproject.com

Wiechert, C. (2015). "Class Teachers in the Waldorf School. Efficient teaching in Waldorf Schools and a new class teacher profile for the 21st century." *Pedagogical Section at The Goetheanum Journal No.* 54, 19-25.

25. Listening to our Teachers, Part 2:
Stories from the Classroom

As part of a general outreach effort to alumni of our Center for Anthroposophy and Antioch Waldorf Teacher Education programs, we asked teachers to share stories of transformation, change, and classroom success. This was part of our general wish, as described in the preface to this book, to better support teachers and celebrate their success. One of our dear alums, Ana Coffey, reached out to the teachers as possible and put together a small collection of their stories. What follows is a sampling of what they shared.

A Star Shining Brightly
by Rebecca Lynn Hipps

My research topic for my teacher training program was on developing greater reverence for the children that we teach. I got that idea from a Steiner quote that I see all over the place, about receiving the children in reverence, and I wanted to explore what that really meant. As I started out, I noticed that a lot of the resources I was finding talked about helping children develop reverence, but there wasn't as much about actually receiving the children in reverence and having reverence for the spirits in front of us in the classroom.

At the same time I was teaching 1st grade and I had several challenging children in my class, but there was one in particular that displayed some behaviors that I had never experienced in my eight years of teaching. It mostly resembled oppositional defiant behavior: like a teacher would ask him to do something and he would have a smile on his face but very boldly refuse to do it. There were times when he would just try to run out of the room. At one point he even got physical with my assistant and tried to slap her. But on the flip side, he was an incredibly intuitive child. I don't know that I've ever met a child so perceptive; I felt like I would tell stories and he would catch onto symbolism so clearly, in a very advanced kind of way.

As part of my research, I specifically wanted to explore my challenges with this child. One of the resources that I read was *Working with Anxious,*

Nervous, and Depressed Children by Henning Koehler, and there was a meditation that the author recommended for anxious children or children
with some kind of severe disability or behavior challenge, and it was to
imagine them, in the evening before you sleep, as this struggling bird.

So I started to practice that meditative work as part of my research
of exploring how we can develop reverence, defining reverence as love
or devotion toward something or someone: how can I develop this, particularly when I have a child that I have a lot of conflict with? I noticed
it started to happen that just as I was telling a story, or we were doing
something in class, I would have some insight, in the moment, of one little
change to make specifically for that child; or I tried to create opportunities
when I would be talking to this child individually, and I tried to see him
in a positive light. As I meditated at night, I would try to picture him in his
best light and hold that image in some of our harder moments.

There was a real turning point that year. I was telling a story about the
star in an apple, and I had a little song called "I Am Like a Star Shining
Brightly." After I had told the story and we had sung the song, this little
boy was cleaning up some lunch. The other children had gone out to play
and he had stayed behind, and I could tell he wanted to talk to me. He
said "So, do you think we're all kind of like apples?" I said, "What do you
mean?" He said, "Do you think we all have a star inside of us like a light?"
I said, "Absolutely." So he and I came up with a little hand signal: when I
saw his light shining brightly, I would make this signal so he would know
that I saw him in his best light.

That totally changed the tune of the year for us. I think he just needed
to see that I was looking for the good in him. I think the real value in what
I learned with some of the meditative work in my research, being mindful of the child and trying to focus on the good, increased my capacity in
the moment to see that good and act with more patience and reverence
toward the child. So I felt like that had a huge impact on my relationship
with that child that year.

He definitely continued to have challenges, I don't mean to make it
seem like everything went perfectly from then on, but I learned a lot from
that experience and I think a quote from one of the teachers that I inter-
viewed is something that's really lasted with me. She said, "The challenge
is to have reverence for the battle that each child is facing. If you can view
each child in your class as a knight facing a really hard dragon, and have
reverence for the battle they have chosen to fight, that will transform your
work and the way you see the child."

I have never forgotten that, and I also think it applies to our work with the parents. I think sometimes it's really easy to develop conflicted or judgmental thoughts toward the parents of some of our hardest children, and if we put that into the context of that quote, remembering that not just each of the children we teach, but the parents as well, are battling something hard—if we choose to see that and have empathy for that, it can really transform the way we interact.

Approach With a Generous Heart
by Cynthia Way

I took my class in the 3rd grade, so I was coming in as a relative newcomer. I was a parent, I wasn't even a class teacher: I aspired to become a class teacher, and I guess I was the only one my school could find. I had done a little training with the 3rd grade teacher; it had been the plan that she would leave for an extended absence in 3rd grade, so we had done the summer training together, but she had to leave much sooner than anticipated and never came back.

On the very first day of school, this boy came up to me and said, "What credentials do you have for teaching us?" And immediately I thought, "Oh! Somebody's been talking to their child." I was immediately put on the defensive, because of course I'd taken a "preparation for 3rd grade" training, but no other kind of training yet. We got off on the wrong foot, and basically during the course of the 3rd grade year he would do little things to get my goat, and I kind of let him, because I didn't know exactly how to meet this boy.

I just thought he was being the jerkiest jerk. In recorder class he would take his recorder and move his fingers around without even blowing into it, and I didn't know how to get him to do what I wanted him to do. During painting he would always make a lot of noise or do something disruptive, so I would put him out of the classroom at a desk so he could see what was going on from the doorway. We were just sort of at each other all year long.

In the end, I wrote a report and said, "When John learns how to play the recorder then that's when I'll teach him," very up on my high horse. The mother of course was understandably a little upset at my tone, and wrote a letter to the school about how I should be fired. When I received that letter I was so taken aback. I was mortified and I thought, "Oh my God, I have to do something to change." Obviously I had created a big problem, and I hadn't even realized that *I* was creating the problem.

So in the summer between 3rd and 4th grade I did an awful lot of thinking about this child. I also attended the beginning of the teacher training in Wilton, and it became clear that I needed to do a lot of meditation and reflection on him. When I did, I saw a child who was acting very much like a small baby. I had also learned something about his family life: his father had died when he was born, and his mother had had a very difficult time with that, of course.

I realized in my meditation that every single thing he did was like what a baby would do to try and get attention. It was a revelation to me: he even kind of looked like a baby, he was big and round, very round. He would raise his hand and say, "Mrs. Way?" from the other side of the room, and I'd go over to him and say, "Yes?" and he'd say, "Oh, nothing." He would do that time after time, and it would get me very angry. But when we began 4th grade I started realizing, "Oh, I should probably not respond to him in this rebarbative way, I should understand him as a child who really needs and wants something. Maybe I can truly approach him with a generous heart instead of a rejecting one." It was an attitude that I started approaching him with, and I would try to be very present in the moment, not get angry, and instead try and find a way of having compassion for him.

Before he had caught on to what I was trying to do, I was at the time giving my class French lessons, which he despised! I would go out of the room and come back posing as a French cousin. He thought it was so childish. He hated the language and would not speak it. Regardless, during the course of that 4th grade year, something really substantial occurred with our relationship. First of all, he stopped all the behavior that was interfering with the progression of lessons and stopped goading me. By the end of 4th grade and continuing through the rest of the time at school, we ended up forming a close relationship. When we went into 5th grade, he began to love being a student. He began to ask me all kinds of questions and became so engrossed with what school was about and what we were doing in class. It was such a different orientation to school than he had shown previously.

Eventually he went to a very good high school. He invited me to his high school graduation and kept in touch and confided in me. I felt that it was a real turnaround for him, because he could have had a miserable time in school, and instead he had a really good one. He flourished instead of devoting all his energy to fighting back against something. The whole notion of child study and meditating on the child is what helped us through that. Specifically it turned me around, because I realized he couldn't change himself, he was a child. I had the control in the situation, so it was really up to me. It was so hard, but I'm so glad I did it. I think it made a huge difference.

Here's the funny thing. Starting in 5th and 6th grades, I gave them little bits of Latin and Greek and he really enjoyed that, because by then he was totally into what we were doing academically. When he went to high school he took Latin, Spanish, and on his own time with the German teacher who worked at our school he became a fluent German speaker. Then he started traveling around the world, and before he even went to college he had already been to several countries and mastered several languages. Now I think he probably speaks easily over twelve languages; he's been to Japan, Pakistan, Saudi Arabia. He's been all over the place, and I just think it's funny when I think back to those first experiences of a foreign language. Now he's living in Madrid and he still sends me postcards once in a while.

Beauty as a Pedagogical Resource
by Caitlin McCoy

It felt like I was giving birth. I never have—I don't have children. But it felt like there was an idea that suddenly had a home, an idea that suddenly involved a lot of people who were thinking the same thing.

From the start I felt there was something alive in Missoula. Missoula is surrounded by beauty—there are rivers and lakes and glaciers and amazing wildlife, so people are really invested in this area. Since it's quite remote and isolated in its own way, people are interested in creating something unique in Missoula. When I moved here four years ago, there had been three attempts to start a Waldorf school, going back 20 years. So I felt like I was walking into an idea that somebody had left behind and had done some of the invisible spiritual work to harness it here. I felt like I had inherited some form here, and it didn't need help to be actualized, it needed help to grow, somebody to really tend to it, so that was me!

I was very nervous at first, just having been a teacher, having a great training through Antioch, but there's the other side of leadership and simultaneous parent education which I think any school needs and benefits from. This was in a state where nobody knows what Waldorf is and nobody's been to a Waldorf school; the nearest one was three and a half hours away. I felt honored to unfold this, and I felt like it had the opportunity to bring people in a direction they had wanted to go for quite some time.

The beginning was having the confidence and trust of the community. They were trusting us in sending their children to a brand new school, and I was trusting them that we would have this relationship to make it work. I think that has been incredibly beneficial for us. We have amazing families, we have amazing teachers, and if they aren't trained they're going to training, and we're on track to start a great program in 2021. The first few months I didn't know if it was going to take off, like a baby, and then it was like a toddler wobbling, and I'm wondering is it going to fall over, and now we're at this kindergarten age where we're steady, we can think about choices before we make them; we have a lot of board support to help with fundraising and strategic planning.

So now the school is in this really beautiful place of golden childhood, it's growing and needs to be tended, but it's being led by the people that are expressing interest. There's minimal marketing and advertising; it's the creativity of the forming of the school that attracts people here.

(Ana: We all struggle with our "elevator speech" about Waldorf education. So how do you talk to people who have no frame of reference at all?)

I generally ask them what they know, and a great icebreaker I did at a parent meeting was asking, "What's the weirdest thing you've heard about a Waldorf school?" I hear things like, "Is it a cult? What's with the losing of the teeth?" And I'm like, "Is this a cult? I don't know! If it is, it's really beautiful!" I kind of go by what brought them here. When they come to visit, there's a sigh, there's something that speaks to them that is organic and authentic. Something as simple as beauty has been forgotten in education, the importance of beauty as a pedagogical resource. Right now you come in through the preschool, and Waldorf preschools are beautiful, not for the sake of being pretty and cute, but for the sake of that sigh that adults express. That's what we hope the children feel every time they come in. The space was created just for you, and everything in here was made for you to explore and understand the world around you, because the world is beautiful.

At first it was difficult for me to feel that parents come here just because the school is pretty, but I learned that the beauty is actually touching their souls in a way that words might not fit. They are connecting in a certain way. I think after they have taken in the physical, they move into the soul realm of the school, our rhythms and our artistic work, the singing and poetry and stories and crafting that we do in the preschool. What we do here, what makes us feel good here, is what we are trying to impress on the children's senses very gently so they can have beautiful memories.

It's simple things, like on Monday mornings we make soup, so when they walk in the classroom smells like onions and garlic and butter, and that is a lasting soul memory. On Thursdays we make bread, and that is a lasting soul memory because all of their little beings are engaged. And in the spirit realm, I talk about things that make us feel alive, things like our festivals, our parent evenings, our workshops, and things that make us more than the physical and more than personality; we're really building something with each other here that's dynamic and alive.

I think in other schools it's not always possible, and it's been forgotten that adults spending time together is important. We don't have to do very much, but just being together and having a conversation or crafting, that parent dynamic widely benefits the children's experience at their school. And after we've gone through the physical, soul, and spiritual life of the school, then we laugh that we're totally a cult, we all wear the same color on the same day and we wear aprons. But I think the majority of the parents wind up staying because every level of the Waldorf school becomes more interesting and more thought-provoking the more time you spend here.

All the preschoolers that are of age are moving to kindergarten, and all nine of the kindergarten children are re-enrolling next year. So there's really great traction. The parents are not only believing and trusting our vision, but they're actively contributing to it by being on the board or being on the festival committee. I think they are really enjoying being involved in their children's education at such a young age, and understanding that school has the potential to reach more than just the children. It can be a really wonderful family experience.

First, Take Care of the Basics
Anonymous

This child came to me in the middle of 5th grade. He had spent the first seven years of his life in China, and he had been in other more conventional-type schools in California for four years. He came to us when he was 11. He immediately found friends in the group. He is sort of a phlegmatic, a wonderful addition to any class, like most phlegmatics, and he fit in with the group so well socially. He was actually chronologically a year older: based on his birthday he should have gone into our 6th grade, but there was an error.

This was the first of many communication difficulties with the parents.

His birth year was different on his application, and it wasn't until we celebrated his birthday in March of 5th grade and I asked him how old he was that he told me he was 12. He was actually in this country with only his mother; his father still lived in China and would come very infrequently. I think over the next three and a half years that I had this student, I saw the dad twice. So this was a boy who didn't have a whole lot of contact with his father. He would spend time in China over the summer break; he had a beloved grandfather there, and would see his father also.

While socially this kid was succeeding very well and becoming part of the group and forming a warm bond with me, he struggled academically. He was quite a bit behind the group when he joined the class, and he remained so throughout middle school. In 6th grade he found it so challenging to create a main lesson book, because of course he didn't have all those years when I guided how a main lesson book is created, and also you get to middle school and you're letting them do more of their own work, so he really struggled with that. This lack became more and more apparent as the years went on. It reached its zenith in 8th grade. At the beginning of that year, in October, I found out that his mother had actually returned to China and he was living with different people. The way I found out was, he was literally falling asleep at his desk. This was kind of a gradual thing where the mother was really not able to parent, not able to provide a stable home; 7th grade was really rocky for him also.

In 8th grade he crashed and burned, to the point that the high school faculty was saying he could not continue into our high school. His academics had gone from bad to worse. His habit, I started to learn, was sending me emails about assignments at 12:30 in the morning; at midnight he was ordering food from Grubhub at the houses of various quasi-relatives he was staying with. Finally we had him stay with a family in the class, who was willing to take him for close to a month. This was planned with his mother, who said she was going to come back after the New Year, so this was a stopgap measure. It was very difficult for the family, whom I had known for eight years because their daughter was in the class: he was on devices all the time, he was ordering food at their house even though they were providing dinner, sleep was almost nonexistent, and he was just physically, emotionally, and academically a mess.

We had a meeting with his mom when she came back in the spring and we laid out what had to happen, because he really was interested in continuing at the Waldorf school. She acknowledged that were some difficulties, and we set some conditions of what had to happen. I had seen glimmers in the 7th grade creative writing block, familiarly known as Wish, Wonder and Surprise: this child was writing paragraphs that were incredibly deep and beautiful. So in the spring of 7th grade I began to recognize that there was something very hidden in this young adolescent, and it was just this glimmer of wow, what potential this child has. And then it kind of went down again, and, as I said, 8th grade was really bad. He would hand in a main lesson book missing 2/3 of the work of every other student, even the poorest in the class.

I took the 8th grade on their class trip in which there was a rite of passage. The students wrote a code of honor for themselves, and we had an overnight bit where they went out and were by themselves from 4 o'clock in the afternoon until 8 o'clock the next morning, and then we had a celebration of that. This child broke down in sobs during the celebration, and something broke open. He articulated how amazing his experience at the school had been, and how he wanted to continue. At the end of the trip we had an amazing graduation ceremony, and I had asked parents to write a letter to their child which I read to them right before the celebration, and of course he was the only child who did not have a letter—so several other students actually wrote letters to him.

After all these experiences, after me kind of seeing these glimpses, we just need this child to have sleep and proper meals and proper adult supervision, and he's going to be great in the high school. He's living with a host family this year. He got the best score in the class on the Anatomy block quiz. He is smiling all the time, he's awake, he's engaged, he's so, so happy. That's the transformation of this human being. And it really came from him. We give the experiences, but that kind of breaking open and saying "This is what I really want," that came from him. Having the idea that there was potential in this child, and we just needed to give him bodily health, allowed him to blossom.

I went back to teaching 1st grade, so now I just see him once a week. He always has the biggest smile for me, and I am so happy seeing him. And all the teachers are coming up to me and saying, "You won't believe what he did in this block, you won't believe how he's playing his cello!" …which was a nightmare for his orchestra teacher. He has transformed across the board in every way.

Pumpkin Pie to the Rescue
by Nicholas Andrea

There was a student who had been in the class since 1st grade, and I had picked up the class in 2nd grade. I had been their music teacher in 1st grade. She always struggled mightily in math; it just never made sense to her and she couldn't memorize any math facts. She would still have to use manipulatives even in 3rd and 4th grade, and she would often ask the same question day after day. For example, we'd be doing a mental math number journey, like pick a number between 1-10 and then multiply it by 5, and she would say, "What does that mean?" I'd say, "times 5," and this would go on every day for several weeks.

Her capacity to remember was really limited, which made it difficult for her to memorize math facts. Even when the other children had mastered their times tables by the end of 3rd grade she hadn't mastered any of them, except maybe the ones and the twos. I had a lot of concern about her, and because these fundamentals of math were not mastered, anything of a higher conceptual order was exceedingly difficult for her, like long division or long multiplication.

The first shift that happened was that we entered the world of fractions. Since fractions are so pictorial in the way we teach it in a Waldorf school, I began with making pumpkin pies, and she loved that, of course. She is also an artist by nature, so I often thought of her when crafting my lessons. Everything I did in bringing fractions was very much of this visual nature, and she started to gain a kind of a central understanding of what fractions were. She started to enjoy success with that, which perked up her confidence a little bit, but her math fundamentals were still very weak.

I asked our remedial teacher if she would do some Extra Lesson work with this child, and she agreed. This went on for several weeks, and by the end it was really kind of miraculous what happened. All of a sudden she was able to answer these mental math questions, sometimes quicker than other students, which really floored me. I think this combination of bringing a more pictorial approach and having her do remedial work unlocked something in her. She was now able to access the knowledge that she probably already had but that was just locked up in her will, where it was inaccessible to her. So she did very well, and she ended up finishing the year with her understanding being within the normal range of the class.

She's not at the top of the class, but I don't have any worries about her anymore. She's right there with us, and most importantly, she feels good about herself. Her self-esteem was kind of trashed for the first couple of years of grade school, and she really didn't like coming to school. She's melancholic by nature so it was really hard for her, and the remedial work helped boost her self-esteem more than anything, so she feels like she can participate with us now. We're about to go into 5th grade, and I'm really looking forward to working with her next year. Nothing short of miraculous!

Teaching Children, Not Just Content
by Rachel Veach

This past school year I completed an induction program through the public sector that was required by the state of Colorado, in order for me to move from an initial teaching license to a professional Colorado teaching license. As part of the program I needed to complete 45 hours of professional development during the school year, which could include development that happened as a part of faculty meetings.

When the induction program advisers reviewed the training I had received through our school faculty meetings, which included sessions such as Restorative Justice, LGBTQ Awareness, Trauma-Informed Schools, Mindfulness for Teachers, Diversity Awareness, and The Importance of Reducing Anxiety in Children, their response was very affirming: "Wow. You are being trained to teach *children*. Anyone can teach content, but we need more people who can teach children, and learning in these areas is what will help you do that!"

It was a wonderful reminder to me of why we have the focus on the development of the whole child that is such a tenet of Waldorf education. In addition, the whole experience of completing this induction program gave me an enormous appreciation for the school where I work, and the way I was trained and supported throughout the year to really *see* every one of my students and focus on their needs as humans, rather than just their academic needs.

A Collective Seeing
Anonymous

I'm a class sponsor, and I just went through the past year with the 10th grade, which can sometimes be a little rough, as a class and individually. There was one boy in particular who had been having a difficult time socially and behaviorally in class, and we were wondering how best to help him.

This year it seemed to escalate a little bit: he would leave class without telling the teacher, he would just disappear. There were lots of difficult things he was dealing with emotionally and socially, but he was not very good at articulating them. He was the type to be really stubborn too, so if you tried to ask him what was going on, or ask him to explain what he was feeling or what was happening, he would just dig in his heels. The more you tried to investigate or speak with him, he would dig in his heels further.

I heard him one day talking about a video game, and he asked me if I knew about it. I didn't, but I saw that was how he was connecting with people, so I decided that I was going to buy the game and play it, and that could be my inroad. So that's what I did. He really opened up to me: he would come and ask where I was in the game, what I thought about it, how I liked the music and the art style and the story. It became a thing we could connect over that didn't deal with school or social issues. I learned to recognize things that were going to trigger him, and how to help him self-regulate.

As the year progressed, he continued to have difficult behaviors and expressed some things that gave me pause and worry. Having worked as a teacher in a high school where a student committed suicide, red flags were going up. I had done a training about directly asking students if they were having thoughts about hurting themselves or others. Midway through the year, I pulled him aside at the end of the day and said, "This may seem shocking for me to ask you, but I need to know if you are having thoughts of harming others or yourself." And he said he was.

First I needed to tell him that what he was feeling was not unusual, that I didn't want him to feel badly, that I had had those thoughts in the past too. Then I called his parents and we got therapists involved, and it became this huge idea of how do we directly address him and support him. I put into place a Student Success Team where we gathered the counselor, parents, and anyone else who could help support him, and we went through a process of identifying his strengths, raising questions and concerns, and then using his strengths to address the challenges and concerns.

Using a person's strengths is a tool I picked up from a brilliant counselor at another school. I wanted to show him that although he may feel frustrated and angry, there were lots of things he was really good at, and he could start from there to address some of the things he was experiencing that were untenable and unnerving. He's brilliant with language, has a really wicked sense of humor, is able to see multiple layers of meanings in words and make them funny, and he's a great writer. This could be a big social gift for him because people connect with him through his ability to use humor. What he notices, what he sees, is unique. I don't see many students who have that level of perception of language. He is really fun, which is why I felt so responsible for helping him through this. I really connected with him.

As the year unfolded, we all noticed him and observed him as a high school faculty, and every now and then we'd check in collectively about how he was doing and what we saw. As the year progressed, there wasn't any one thing that really changed, but he seemed to come out of it. He was a little different, everyone noticed; he was more sure of himself and saw his place and what he had to offer. It was amazing.

His birthday is in May, and his mom had the idea of throwing a surprise party for him. It ended up that everybody in the class—which he was on the margins of—came to this party to surprise him, even people he didn't consider friends. Everyone came together recognizing that, without us addressing it explicitly, he was having a hard time and we needed to bring him in. So he ended the year in such a different place from how he started. It's one of those amazing things that you can't really pinpoint to one exact thing, but it was a collective seeing—all the work that you do as a Waldorf teacher, meditating on them and holding them spiritually, asking for help, and just noticing, opening your eyes and being receptive to what they're experiencing.

Our final two stories are a glimpse of Waldorf teachers' ingenuity in addressing the Covid-19 forced homeschooling situation.

Ideas for Family Education
by Nadiéjda Fabian

Hello Parents, Teachers, and Schools!

I hope you are doing well in these challenging times and that your children are not feeling too much of the anxieties that have been stirred up. I am a teacher and a writer, and I have been thinking a lot about how the current situation can impact the children. So I decided to write a story about a group of children who are also experiencing school closures, separation from their friends, and confinement in their homes. It's a story intended to accompany the children each day and help them to pass through this unusual period with joy, confidence, wonder, warmth with their family, openness to the world, and a connection to nature even if they must remain indoors.

I am also proposing, for those who are interested, some meaningful and wholesome activities inspired by Waldorf pedagogy and the Slow-Parenting and Forest School movements. They include:

- Academic learning based on the story, which creates a unity between what touches the children's hearts and what nourishes their heads.
- Artistic activities that help centering, balancing, expression, and development.
- Learning games to start the day together, etc.

The idea is to help create magical educational moments together as a family every day, regardless of the children's educational level. To help parents create the joy and enthusiasm for learning that can be experienced in the classroom but which can be difficult to reproduce at home because of the mix of ages where each child is working on different subjects and lessons. The lessons are aimed particularly at children aged 6 to 12 years old, however many of the activities can include younger and older children as well. I also include some advice for parents on how to organize themselves while juggling homeschooling and working at home, how to reassure anxious children, etc.

For all this and more, please visit my blog:
http://samelblog.com/homeschooling-during-quarantine/

Warmly,
Nadiéjda

Online Instruction
by Lisa Babinet

Thursday and Friday, I taught my eleven eighth-grade Algebra students by Zoom. They are in by audio only and they can see me, and I use my doc camera as a whiteboard. They are all muted by me and can raise their hands, and when I call on them, I unmute them. Also, I call on them in class. It seems to be working as well as can be expected.

Day 1 memory: At the end of the class, I unmuted everyone and one student started, "I look into the world…" and quite a few others joined in. Needless to say, it brought me to tears.

Day 2 memory: My 22-year-old son had just arrived back from college and was nearby as I was teaching. While he was watching me run the class by Zoom and mute and unmute the students, he started cracking up. Later he told me that he had a picture of how it would be in the regular classroom if the teacher could mute and unmute the students at will.

Appendix

"Giving Lectures and Presentations," from Rudolf Steiner

One should at least put some value on the organism of speech and the genius of language as well. One should not forget that valuing the organism of speech, the genius of language, is creative, in the sense of creating imagination. He who cannot occupy himself with language, listening inwardly, will not receive images, will not be the recipient of thoughts; he will remain clumsy in thinking, he will become one who is abstract in speaking, if not a pedant. Particularly, in experiencing the sounds, the imagery in speech-formation, in this itself lies something that entices the thoughts out of our souls that we need to carry before the listeners. In experiencing the word, something creative is implied in regard to the inner organization of the human being. This should never be forgotten. It is extremely important. In all cases, the feeling should pervade us how the word, the sequence of words, the word-formation, the sentence-construction, how these are related to our whole organism. Just as one can figure out a person from the physiognomy, one can even more readily—I don't mean from what he says but from the *how* of the speech—one can figure out the whole being from his manner of speech (Steiner, *The Art of Lecturing*, p. 95).

Ordinary tea, as I have repeatedly mentioned, is a very good diet for diplomats: diplomats have to be witty, which means having to chat at random about one thing after another, none of which must be pedantic, but instead has to exhibit the ease of switching from one sentence to another. This is why tea is indeed the drink of diplomats. Coffee, on the other hand, makes one logical (p. 97).

One more thing is required besides all the others I have already mentioned: responsibility! This implies that one should be aware that one does not have the right to set all of one's ill-mannered speech habits before an audience. One should learn to feel that for a public appearance one does require education of speech, a going-out of one's self, and plasticity in regard to speech. Responsibility toward speech! It is very comfortable to remain standing and to speak the way one normally does, and to swallow as much as one is used to swallow; to swallow, to squeeze, and to bend and break and pull at the words just the way it suits one. But one may not remain with this squeezing and pushing and pulling and cornering and similar speech mannerisms. Instead, one must try to come to the aid of one's speaking even in regard to the form. If one supports one's speaking in this manner, one is quite simply also led to the point where one addresses an audience with a certain respect. One approaches public speaking with a certain reserve and speaks to an audience with respect. And this is absolutely necessary. One can accomplish this if, on the one side, one perfects the soul aspect; and, on the other side, formulates the physical in the way I have demonstrated (p. 100).

What does it mean to address one's listeners with a question? Questions which are listened to actually work mainly on the listener's inhalation. The listener lives during his listening in a breathing-in, breathing-out, breathing-in, breathing-out. That is not only important for speaking, it is also most important for listening (p. 104).

[B]ecause of the fact that inhalation is engaged by a question being thrown out, the whole process of listening is internalized. What is said goes somewhat more deeply into the soul than if one listens merely to an assertion. When a person hears a straight assertion, his actual tendency is to engage neither his inhalation nor his exhalation. The assertion may sink in a little, but it doesn't actually even engage the sense organs much (p. 105).

Also belonging to the feeling-logic of the speech is the fact that one does not talk continually in the same tone of voice. To go on in the same tone, you know, puts the listener to sleep. Each heightening of the tone is actually a gentle nightmare; thus the listener is somewhat shaken by it. Every relative sinking of tone is really a gentle fainting, so that it is necessary for the listener to fight against it. Through modulating the tone of speech one gives occasion for the listener to participate, and that is extraordinarily important for the speaker (p. 106).

You should speak some sentences in such a way that what you have at the beginning is a verb, or some other part of speech which is not usually there. Where something unusual happens, the listener again pays attention, and what is most noteworthy is that he not only pays attention to the sentence concerned but also to the one that follows (p. 107).

These sorts of things, if they are rightly felt, are those artistic means which completely replace what a lecture does not need, namely, sheer logic. Logic is for thought, not for speaking; I mean for the form of speech, not for the way of expression (p. 109).

What *does* have a lasting effect in a speech is an image which grabs, that is, which stands at some distance from the meaning, so that the speaker who uses the image has become free from slavish dependence on the pure thought-sense.

Such things lead to the recognition of how far a speech can be enhanced through humor. A deeply serious speech can be elevated by a humor which, so to say, has barbs. It is just as I have said: if you wish to forcibly pour will into the listeners, they get angry. The right way to apply the will is for the speech itself to develop images which are, so to speak, inner realities (p. 109).

Very few know what a great difference exists between hearing, say, the sound of church bells or a symphony, and listening to human speech. With human speech, it is really the innermost part of the speaking that is heard. The rest is much more merely an accompanying phenomenon than is the case with the hearing of something inanimate. Thus, I have said all that I did about one's own listening so that the speaker will actually formulate his speech as he would criticize it if he were listening to it (p. 113).

"Social Intelligence"

Soft skills

LinkedIn also ranked "soft" skills—the interpersonal qualities employers want most in their staff. The list looked very similar to the 2019 rankings, with creativity holding onto the top spot.

However, emotional intelligence also made an appearance in this year's top five. This is the ability to perceive, evaluate, and respond to both your own emotions and those of others.

LinkedIn said this emphasized the "importance of how we respond to and interact with colleagues."

The top 5 most in-demand soft skills globally

1. Creativity
2. Persuasion
3. Collaboration
4. Adaptability
5. Emotional intelligence

Source: https://www.cnbc.com/2020/01/17/blockchain-is-the-most-in-demand-job-skill-in-2020-says-linkedin.html

"Adult Learning"

Additional content from Knowles, *The Adult Learner:*

The andragogical model is based on several assumptions that are different from those of the pedagogical model:

1. *The need to know.* Adults need to know why they need to learn something before undertaking to learn it. Tough (1979) found that when adults undertake to learn something on their own, they will invest considerable energy in probing into the benefits they will gain from learning it and the negative consequences of not learning it. Consequently, one of the new aphorisms in adult education is that the first task of the facilitator of learning is to help the learners become aware of the "need to know."

2. *The learners' self-concept.* Adults have a self-concept of being responsible for their own decisions, for their own lives. Once they have arrived at that self-concept, they develop a deep psychological need to be seen by others and treated by others as being capable of self-direction. They resent and resist situations in which they feel others are imposing their wills on them. This presents a serious problem in adult education: The minute adults walk into an activity labeled "education," "training," or something synonymous, they hark back to their conditioning in their previous school experience, put on their dunce hats of dependency, fold their arms, sit back, and say "teach me." This assumption of required dependency and the facilitator's subsequent treatment of adult students as children creates a conflict within them between their intellectual model—learner equals dependent—and the deeper, perhaps subconscious, physiological need to be self-directing. And the typical method of dealing with psychological conflict is to try to flee from the situation causing it, which probably accounts in part for the high dropout rate in much voluntary adult education.

3. The role of the learners' experiences. Adults come into an educational activity with both a greater volume and a different quality of experience from that of youths. By virtue of simply having lived longer, they have accumulated more experience than they had as youths. But they also have had a different kind of experience. This difference in quantity and quality of experience has several consequences for adult education.

It assures that in any group of adults there will be a wider range of individual differences than is the case with a group of youths. Any group of adults will be more heterogeneous in terms of background, learning style, motivation, needs, interests, and goals than is true of a group of youths. Hence, greater emphasis in adult education is placed on individualization of teaching and learning strategies.

It also means that for many kinds of learning, the richest resources for learning reside in the adult learners themselves. Hence, the emphasis in adult education is on experiential techniques--techniques that tap into the experience of the learners, such as group discussions, simulation exercises, problem-solving activities, case methods, and laboratory methods instead of transmittal techniques. Also, greater emphasis is placed on peer-helping activities.

But the fact of greater experience also has some potentially negative effects. As we accumulate experience, we tend to develop mental habits, biases, and presuppositions that tend to cause us to close our minds to new ideas, fresh perceptions, and alternative ways of thinking. Accordingly, adult educators try to discover ways to help adults examine their habits and biases and open their minds to new approaches.

4. *Readiness to learn.* Adults become ready to learn those things they need to know and be able to do in order to cope effectively with their real-life situations.

5. *Orientation to learning.* In contrast to children's and youths' subject-centered orientation to learning (at least in school), adults are life-centered (or task-centered or problem-centered) in their orientation to learning. Adults are motivated to learn to the extent that they perceive that learning will help them perform tasks or deal with problems that they confront in their life situations. Furthermore, they learn new knowledge, understandings, skills, values, and attitudes most effectively when they are presented in the context of application to real-life situations.

6. *Motivation.* Adults are responsive to some external motivators (better jobs, promotions, higher salaries, and the like), but the most potent motivators are internal pressures (the desire for increased job satisfaction, self-esteem, quality of life, and the like) (Knowles pp. 64-68).

Andragogy in Practice Model (from Knowles, Holton, and Swanson, 1998)
(Knowles, p. 149)

Grow's Stages in Learning Autonomy

Stage	Student	Teacher	Examples
Stage 1	Dependent	Authority, coach	Coaching with immediate feedback, drill. Informational lecture. Overcoming deficiencies and resistance
Stage 2	Interested	Motivator, guide	Inspiring lecture plus guided discussion. Goal-setting and learning strategies.
Stage 3	Involved	Facilitator	Discussion facilitated by a teacher who participates as equal. Seminar. Group projects.
Stage 4	Self-directed	Consultant, delegator	Internship, dissertation, individual work or self-directed study group

(Knowles, p. 187)

Kolb's Experiential Learning Model

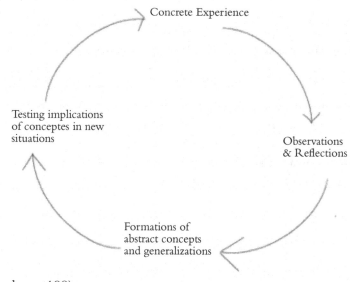

Concrete Experience

Observations & Reflections

Formations of abstract concepts and generalizations

Testing implications of conceptes in new situations

(Knowles, p. 198)

KOLB'S MODEL WITH SUGGESTED LEARNING STRATEGIES

Kolb's Stage	Example Learning/Teaching Strategy
Concrete Experience	Simulation, Case Study, Field Trip, Real Experience, Demonstrations
Observe and Reflect	Discussion, Small Groups, Buzz Groups, Designated Observers
Abstract Conceptualization	Sharing Content
Active Experimentation	Laboratory Experiences, On-the-Job Experience, Internships, Practice Session

(Knowles, p. 198)

"Empathy and Self-Compassion"

"Self-Compassion as a Predictor of Interleukin-6 Response to Acute Psychosocial Stress" by Juliana G.Breines, Myriam V. Thoma, Danielle Gianferante, Luke Hanlin, Xuejie Chen, and Nicolas Rohleder. *Brain, Behavior, and Immunity*, Volume 37, March 2014, pp. 109-114. https://doi.org/10.1016/j.bbi.2013.11.006

ABSTRACT

We examined the hypothesis that self-compassion is associated with lower levels of stress-induced inflammation. On two consecutive days, plasma concentrations of interleukin-6 (IL-6) were assessed at baseline and at 30 and 120 min following exposure to a standardized laboratory stressor in a sample of 41 healthy young adults. Participants who were higher in self-compassion exhibited significantly lower day 1 IL-6 responses, even when controlling for self-esteem, depressive symptoms, demographic factors, and distress. Self-compassion was not related to day 2 IL-6 response but was inversely related to day 2 baseline IL-6 levels, and to increase in baseline IL-6 from day 1 to day 2. These findings suggest that self-compassion may serve as a protective factor against stress-induced inflammation and inflammation-related disease.

The Future of Waldorf Education: Beyond 100
by Torin M. Finser

Adapted from a speech at the Center for Anthroposophy, New Hampshire, June 2019.

In 2019 we celebrate the 100th anniversary of Waldorf education. This evening I would like to look beyond 100, toward Waldorf education's future. But first, a look at the past. Taking the number 100, let us divide the past century into three periods. We will look at the number 33⅓, first from a more external point of view and then from an internal aspect.

If we add 33⅓ to 1919 we come to 1952. I would call the years from 1919 to 1952 Waldorf education's European period. Of course the Steiner School in Manhattan was founded in 1928 and schools opened elsewhere, but the first school was founded in Stuttgart, and Waldorf schools proliferated during that period throughout Europe, in Scandinavia, and the U.K., including reopenings after World War II.

During the next 33⅓ years, ending in 1985/86, there was an explosion of enthusiasm for Waldorf education in the Americas, particularly the U.S. This observation may be influenced by my having gone to a Waldorf school in the 1960s, doing Waldorf teacher training in the 1970s and starting my career in 1978: I experienced it firsthand. That was the time of the environmental movement, the anti-war movement, and the rejection of old forms of working. The embrace of alternatives was in full swing. And in those years there were very few critics of Waldorf education. The Association of Waldorf Schools of North America was established, and there was a lot of energy in the movement.

The final 33⅓-year period brings us to 2019. My experience as a traveler is that in this last period the explosive growth has been largely in Asia. I have been to Korea, India, Nepal, China, Australia, New Zealand, and Taiwan, and have had the pleasure of experiencing enthusiasm for Waldorf education and the rapid growth of schools.

One can wonder: Where will new growth occur in the future? When giving what I was told was the first-ever Waldorf talk in Amman, Jordan last winter, I had a sense that something is dawning in the Middle East. The question I am left with is—how we can best learn from each other across continents, cultures, and languages? With our present-day communication tools, are we adapting fast enough, and can we form more of an international Waldorf learning community?

Now, everything external has an internal component. The inner aspect of 33⅓ years can be viewed from a variety of angles, from biography to

Christology. I cannot do justice to either tonight, but summarizing these approaches, one can say that death and resurrection are central themes. We are talking not just about physical death, but the death forces that come with materialism, calcification, divisions, growing polarization, and other aspects of our society today. And by resurrection we mean rebirth, renewal, and finding new beginnings.

In 2019, on the "3 times 33⅓" anniversary of Waldorf education, these competing life/death forces are tripled, stronger than ever. Waldorf education is at a tipping point. Will it die, or renew itself?

Tremendous spiritual forces are at work right now in our movement. There is a kind of battle going on between life and death. Before looking at renewing impulses for the future, I'd like to share some of the symptoms of the death forces at work today in the Waldorf movement, at least in the United States.

Several schools have recently closed. Four in the Eastern region are questioning whether they can continue beyond next year. Others are in various forms of crisis: in one, things are apparently so bad that teachers and board members are resigning and parents are leaving in droves. Then there are the struggles in New York State and elsewhere around vaccinations. One larger, well-established Waldorf school in New York had to cut $1 million from its budget over the summer.

These are all symptoms of death forces. A living organism needs community, healthy relationships, and a place for an experience of the sacred, something rare today. If these qualities are sundered, divided, then we extend an invitation for death forces to enter. But an aspect of death that I find much more troubling is what I call the "slow drip": the phenomena of regular budget deficits that can lead to stagnating salaries, cutbacks in programs, last-minute combining of classes, then more deficits and cutting back more programs, until you become so vulnerable as a school that you feel it's all hanging by a thread. Consequently teachers and school families live with an ongoing debilitating uncertainty.

I feel the Waldorf movement is yearning for a renewal, but there's a wrestling match going on right now and whatever we do in the next few years will be decisive. In fact, Rudolf Steiner said that at 100 years, a movement or institution either dies or needs re-founding on a new basis.

So I would like to posit seven aspects, pathways, opportunities, ways to bring new life and strength into the Waldorf movement over the next years.

1. The first has to do with core principles as pillars. Core principles, those unalterable facts upon which Waldorf pedagogy rests, are like the pillars of the temple of Poseidon in Greece, which I recently visited. The Aegean Sea was beautiful and shimmering; the blowing wind, the play of the light, everything was in motion. And yet those pillars have withstood the test of time and are literally rock solid.

I would like to suggest that each school actively take up conversations around "What are the core principles that are essential to our work?" AWSNA has published some core principles that form a good starting point, but each school needs to begin in-depth conversations among faculty, staff, board members, and parents. There are many differences among key groups within our schools that have rested under the surface for too long. We need to face them, even risking that some people may head for the exits. Internal divisions around core principles and values need to be confronted and dealt with. One board member in an AWSNA member school suggested that the school needed to become "Waldorf-aligned." We need to know, and then affirm, who we are. It is not only a matter of integrity, but now an urgent necessity.

Society today has become more fragmented and polarized than ever. The Waldorf movement cannot afford to become another symptom of a relativist culture. If we are to be respected and taken seriously, we need to be responsible to the spirit and knowledge that stand as a basis of the pedagogy. As Peter Selg writes in The Agriculture Course, "At the current stage of human evolution, the world of the spirit wants humanity to do particular things in the various domains of life, and thus it is up to us to pursue the impulses that come to us from the world of the spirit in a clear and true way. Even if this gives offense initially, in the long term it will be the only healing thing."

If we do the hard work around core principles, then out of the strength that comes with unity we can summon the courage to let everything else go. Our rich traditions have served us well, nourishing us in festivals, rites of passage, and much more. But just like the wind and waves surrounding the temple of Poseidon, we need to bring things into movement to provide a refreshing impulse. And for that we need to risk some empty spaces.

Rudolf Steiner said some interesting things about creating out of nothingness. It's not a very popular notion to talk about. But I do feel that in our situation, with this amazing curriculum and all the resources available to us thanks to anthroposophy, there is a tendency to carry around a lot of stuff and feel that if you simply accumulate enough material, you'll be a good teacher.

I feel the following words of Rudolf Steiner are particularly relevant for our theme of Beyond 100. Steiner said we need "a world from which the workings of the old causes will have disappeared, a world from which a new light will ray out into the future. The world is not subject to perpetual metamorphosis into different forms (which is our common habit), but the old is perfected and becomes the vehicle of the new. Then, even this will be thrown off, will disappear into nothingness, so that out of this nothingness something new may arise. This is the great, the mighty idea of progress…the continuous arising of the new." ("Evolution, Involution and Creation out of Nothingness," Berlin, June 17,1909.

My first point is simply: Can we establish the pillars, then let everything else move into this place of nothingness and start to re-create? We cannot just throw everything out. Without the pillars we would lose contact with the archetypes and spiritual essence behind our work. There are certain core principles without which we would not have Waldorf education: a developmentally appropriate curriculum, the freedom of the teacher, working with an image of the whole human being as presented in anthroposophy. There are many. AWSNA has seven; I have been working with 15, including Waldorf for social justice. I've been asked to publish them, but am resisting that request because this is the work each of us needs to do with our colleagues, parents, and board. The point is not to get something done and then put it in a file so we can say "Done that." The whole idea is to do the work together as a school! The conversations that happen when you talk about core principles in themselves bring new life forces into existence. We are talking about rebirthing Waldorf education.

Along the way, we must be willing to test assumptions and explore together. Take, for example, the important core principle of "Waldorf education as an art." Are we still on board with that? All of our teaching strives to be artistic, but it's not just the paintings on the wall. It involves science education and more. Everything you do in a Waldorf school you do artistically. If you ask people who know little about Waldorf, they'll say, "Oh yeah, they do a lot of art in their schools." But how does this core principle interact with the next one?

2. Waldorf education for social justice. Here, I would like to relate how one core principle—Waldorf education as an art—can be seen through the lens of social justice. In their Evolving Consciousness course, my students recently worked with a selection from *Unequal Childhoods* by Annette Lareau, a thorough study of class, race, language, and family life. Through this research we are introduced to several families, including the McAllisters:

The McAllister family lives in a part of the project consisting of rows of two- and three-story brick units. The brown, block-like units on their side contain five two-story apartments. Because the apartments have only one small window per room, they are dark on the inside. Sometimes residents keep lights on during the day....The refrigerator is broken. Ms McAllister has complained to the manager, but although she has been promised a new one, it doesn't arrive during the three weeks we are visiting. Ms McAllister makes do by storing some food next door in their friend Latifa's refrigerator and some in coolers packed with ice.... There is one bathroom. Three televisions are in the house.... most of the time at least one set is on.... Although the McAllisters once had a phone, for much of Harold's fourth-grade year they haven't had one due to budget constraints. Ms McAllister receives messages from the school at her sister's house.... (p. 135)

By comparing the family life of Harold McAllister with that of Alexander Williams (in a white, middle-class home) and others, Lareau describes how the *emerging sense of entitlement* contrasts with an *emerging sense of constraint,* right down to one's language skills in dealing with teachers, doctors, and other professionals. Alexander's free time is highly organized with after-school activities, while Harold has time for free play; Alexander has learned to negotiate with elders, even argue, while Harold is respectful. Both children learn the skills necessary to negotiate life in their spaces. However, in the larger world, Alexander's skills are more valued than Harold's.

My main point is this: When Waldorf schools are perceived as pro-art and anti-TV, we are invitational to some and exclusionary to others. A sense for social justice can help us become more attuned to this. For some, art can seem a luxury that assumes access. It is no longer enough just to celebrate how much art we do in our schools. We need to show how the arts can help all children, not just the privileged few.

So, with every core principle, I recommend that we attach the phrase "so that." Do we teach the arts so that we have beautiful pictures on the wall? Or do we teach the arts so that... and then the real conversations can begin! So that we develop emotional intelligence? So that we help children with judgment formation? So that we help children decide between right and wrong, good and evil? So that we help children make choices? And we need to demonstrate how the artistic process involves all these elements of character education. These are the conversations we need to have! Why are we doing what we are doing? And how do our language and our understandings influence who sits at the table?

3. Next, I would like to propose that we engage in active work with our alumni. We recently had five of our children home for the high-school graduation of the sixth. All have now graduated from Waldorf schools. We had amazing conversations; they have so many astute insights. They have met hundreds of people, have formed networks of colleagues in their professions in technology, business, public health, investment advising, security services. The Waldorf movement now has thousands upon thousands of alumni, working in all professions, connecting and learning. I feel we've just begun to tap the alumni resources available to all.

My father is 87. He's looking forward to being in this room next June for his 70th High Mowing School reunion. Imagine a school like High Mowing celebrating a reunion with people 87 years old! The resources are immense, and I don't just mean financial resources, although all these points are somewhat interconnected. It's mostly the connecting with others who can help us take the next steps in this renewal process of Waldorf education. For that, however, we need to go beyond alumni reunions as nostalgia to active questioning, listening, and learning to support Waldorf Beyond 100.

One of our sons, for example, said, "You know, the way you talk about Waldorf isn't working for us. You need to talk about Waldorf as entrepreneurship. That's what it has meant for me. It's all about entrepreneurship. The things that have happened in a Waldorf school have helped me become a good businessperson."

AWSNA is building an alumni platform for all the member schools. Our Center for Anthroposophy in New Hampshire has received grant funding and will launch an alumni association for our CfA and Antioch alumni, not just according to the traditional format, but looking at new ways of doing it, and engaging alumni in conversations around its creation. We are beginning with two events during the Renewal courses, and we will then follow up regionally and online. We also have a survey underway (info@centerforanthroposophy.org) and are collecting stories of teacher success (acoffey@waldorfmoraine.org).

4: Accessibility. Education in this country began with private schools: William and Mary, Harvard, Yale. This was long before Horace Mann started the first public school in Massachusetts and went on to become President of Antioch College. Long before public education, we had a tradition of private education. As I see it now, we have a fault line between private (or independent) schools and public education, which has a long history in our country. Public education has emphasized accessibility, and truly every child deserves an education. Private education has emphasized choice in admissions and freedom in teaching. Private education (including homeschooling) has also historically served marginalized populations (e.g., Native American, African-American) as ways to maintain cultural integrity and provide an alternative to traditional, state-sponsored schooling. And private education has also been a way to circumvent public education when community members did not agree with judicial edicts such as integration. Both models have pros and cons. But we are caught in this divide. Teachers are pulled in different directions and we are competing against each other, at least financially, in recruitment and retention. More important is the question: what is our vision of how independent and public Waldorf schools can support each other? What is our vision of the totality of the movement?

Many worthy independent schools are seriously challenged today. A high level of freedom to teach without testing or state mandates comes at a price. It comes with a heritage of private education in this country and a tuition model that is a burden for so many parents. So we need to find ways to network with key individuals who can help us turn the tide.

I am reminded of a story Jörgen Smit told me. For many years he went to public school conferences in Norway, where he met a gentleman from the public sector and they became good friends. The man asked if he could come and visit the Waldorf school in Oslo. After a week of observing classes and talking to teachers, he said, "You're doing everything and more that the state schools are doing. You should get the same level of funding." They had a conversation about freedom in education and how to support the Waldorf schools by providing, say, 80 percent aid (without mandates) instead of the usual 100 percent provided to state schools. Jörgen's friend went on to become a Minister of Education, and all of Norway's Waldorf schools began to receive government support with minimal restrictions. Rather than simply falling into the old fault lines of history, I believe it is possible to address both accessibility and freedom in this age of the Consciousness Soul. But we need to work together to do so!

In Norway, and in countless other situations, it all starts with a human connection. We need a thousand Jörgen Smits! The traditional open house events at which we hope people will discover us will no longer work. We have to reach out, take an interest in others, and network. That is the foundation of establishing accessibility.

5. Which then leads to money and social finance. We have inherited the private school tuition model, and we have old attitudes toward money and finance. I'm surprised how often in a Waldorf school where the faculty is so proactive and advanced in the pedagogy, the very same people carry a lot of old concepts around money. And board members often provide needed expertise but also bring old concepts of money, such as that tuition can "buy" an education. We need a complete revolution in how we work with money in our schools.

As a 10-year-old, I mowed lawns for neighbors. Some people paid me a dollar for a small lawn, others $5. From an early age we learn that you work to earn money. Now we need to turn that around in our schools and work with our parents to develop the notion that money frees us to work. This sounds like the same thing, but it's very different. A few years ago the Center for Anthroposophy made a change. We used to pay staff and faculty at the end of the month, and we started paying people on the first of the month, before the work. Money can free us to work, but especially in education, it does not pay us for the work.

I remember getting my first paycheck in Great Barrington at the end of my first month of teaching. I was shocked to find it in my mailbox one afternoon. I was having so much fun with my class, and then this check came along and suddenly there was something jarring about it. I didn't equate what was going on in my classroom with the check.

Then there is the old notion of "You get what you pay for." How many times have you heard that? You went out and bought cheap shoes and they fell apart? You got what you paid for! This works with commodities such as shoes. But can we be flexible enough in our thinking to change that into something such as "paying forward"? Lisa Mahar tells a wonderful story of going to a workshop for which no tuition was charged, but participants were required to attend a short session on finances. So partway through the workshop, leadership presented the workshop budget: this is how much it costs for the instructors, utilities, food, and so on. They then explained: "The reason you're all here for free is because the last people who took this workshop were so appreciative, they made donations so we didn't have to charge you." After some questions and conversation the workshop leaders said, "Here's the donation box. If you think this workshop is valuable and should happen again, make donations for the next group." So the attitude of the leadership was that if the work is valued, it will be supported. And if the participants had declined to support it, that would have told the leaders to move on and do something new, to innovate: also a good outcome.

To change how we work with finances, we need to work more intensively with parents, for so many see education as a commodity. I've heard several instances just in the last few weeks of parents asking for a refund. So, if I go to the store and I buy a pair of sneakers and a few days later they fall apart, I have no problem going back to the store and asking for a refund. Shoes are a commodity. But education is not.

However, for the sake of argument, let's take the opposite position that education is after all just another commodity, another business. If you take that point of view and follow it through to its logical consequences, a business has assets that can either depreciate (thus a refund or tax write off) or appreciate over time. So if you have a child in your class who ends up being the next Jeff Bezos in thirty years, your school should receive a large portion of his net worth, currently $165.6 billion dollars, the appreciated asset you helped create.

The old attitudes in our schools regarding money are holding us back. We need regional workshops on money and social finance, perhaps led by RSF Social Finance. We need to radically change our business model if Waldorf is to flourish beyond 100.

6. We need leadership development. This is crucial to the future of our schools. As many of you know, we do Waldorf administration and leadership workshops at Antioch University New England. Let me describe one scenario. A Waldorf school asks a senior colleague to step up to a leadership role because s/he is respected and loved, and the teacher agrees out of devotion to the future of the school. The teacher agrees to take up that task, even though s/he may not have the necessary skill sets in human resources, conflict management, communication, facilitation, all those things. But that person, a true reluctant leader, agrees to give it a try.

Meanwhile, board members might be saying, "Those teachers take weeks to make decisions, and every time there's a conflict it gets worse. They don't know anything about marketing or how to manage the website, and our retention rates are slipping. We need to hire some experts. We're going to bring in a marketing specialist followed by an admissions director." Usually these new employees do indeed have the needed expertise, but often they do not share the values and anthroposophical insights that the teachers carry. So when you put this well-meaning pedagogical leader in with these outside experts, it's like asking your oral surgeon and your car mechanic to collaborate! From an organizational point of view, this is what often happens in our schools. It is a systemic problem, which I see far too often.

Just as there are ways to straighten out finances or solve a pedagogical problem in the classroom, there are tools available for us to deal with
reluctant leaders, lack of role clarity, and cultural differences. But we are
not using them! Eurythmy in the workplace, role playing, presentations of
recent research in leadership development, case studies, social color exercises, and group discussion are some of the techniques available to help
prepare our school leaders to work together on fundamental aspects of
leadership. So much can be done when you bring the pedagogical and
administrative leaders together in five-day institutes. (For more information, contact lthomas@antioch.edu.). But in order to do so, our schools
need to see the need, and support their leaders.

**7. Circling back to an earlier theme, we need to reclaim our
original social mandate as Waldorf schools.** In the lectures Rudolf
Steiner gave in August 1919 in Education as a Social Problem, he not only
describes the threefolding impulse, but also the current social challenges of
his time, such as egoism and materialism. These lectures came on the heels
of a concerted effort at the end of World War I to introduce new ideas
on addressing social issues. When they did not succeed, Steiner turned his
reform efforts in the direction of Waldorf schools as a beacon for social
change. And his requirements, such as equal education for boys and girls,
were all social in nature. Indeed, during preparations for the 1923-24
Christmas Foundation Conference, Rudolf Steiner said that every spiritual
movement that truly advances mankind must be there for all of humanity.

Today we need to attend to the social needs of our time. We need to
address the opioid crisis, racism, affordable housing, environmental degradation, and income inequality, to name a few. Waldorf schools cannot
solve these issues, but we need to engage in conversation with community
members, engage with local groups addressing these issues, and demonstrate how deeply we care. Helping others may be the best way for us to
help our schools.

So if we look Beyond 100, I suggest a new focus on Waldorf education for social justice. What would that mean? There's a lot we're doing in
the curriculum that deals with social justice; many schools give generous
scholarships, and public Waldorf schools are usually open to all. But from
the outside, Waldorf often looks like an expensive refuge for the lucky few.

For things to change in our schools, we each need to be able to change
from within. Meditative work and efforts to change attitudes and old
ways of thinking are needed before we are sustainable. One of the most
fundamental change agents is taking an interest in others. And when we

recognize others, we need to celebrate their success. Recently, I had the pleasure of once again meeting the founders of the House of Peace in Ipswich, Massachusetts, where they inherit troubled situations from around the world, with children and families from Syria, Venezuela, Afghanistan and other countries. Carrie Schuchardt spoke beautifully about how interest leads to empathy, which then leads to a new experience of the Sophia. The Sophia lives in anthroposophy. What can happen when one begins to reach out and really experience the other? Rudolf Steiner says in the "St. Francis Lectures" that this interest in the other actually builds a new universality and a kind of moral strength to go forward.

In conclusion, I would like to point out the symbiotic relationship among some of my key points tonight. If we look at Waldorf Beyond 100 we can begin to highlight some of the key themes that deserve our attention moving forward: working with our alumni as never before, changing our attitudes and practices concerning money, collaborating to enhance both educational freedom and increased accessibility, clarifying core principles, and reclaiming our social mandate. The good news is that any effort around any of these impulses will yield exponential results, reinforcing each other and building positive momentum. So if we're able to work with our alumni more intensely, they will help us with the social justice piece. And the social justice piece will influence accessibility. And the accessibility will influence resources and funding.

All these things can work together, but we're going to have to summon the courage: a new courage to serve the Waldorf movement.

I would like to end on a note that emphasizes the transitory state we are in today. This is a time when we need to look at nothingness, a place where all the old ways may be, indeed are, falling away. We need beginners' eyes, and we need to walk new pathways. This will require a certain vulnerability in not knowing in order to know.

As Antonio Machado puts it (quoted in *Meditation as Contemplative Inquiry*, by Arthur Zajonc):

> Wanderer, the road is your footsteps. Nothing else.
> Wanderer, there is no path. You lay down a path in walking.
> Walking you lay down a path, and when you turn around you see the road you'll never walk on again.
> Wanderer, there is no path. Only tracks on the ocean foam.

Contributing Writers

Developing the Art of Imagination: Why Creative Speech Formation is an Essential Part of Teacher Training: *Debra Z. Spitulnik's* love for the art of Creative Speech and the richness of Waldorf Education stem from her training as a speech artist and her years of class teaching. She is the Creative Speech teacher for the Washington Waldorf School, the Center for Anthroposophy, and the Antioch University New England Teacher Training program.

Practicing Between and Beyond: Tri-une Thinking and the Training of High School Teachers: *Douglas Gerwin, Ph.D.* is the Executive Director of the Center for Anthroposophy, a member of the Leadership Council of the Association of Waldorf Schools of North America, and an adjunct faculty member at Antioch University New England. He divides his time between adult education and teaching adolescents, as well as mentoring Waldorf schools across North America.

Characteristics of Teacher Educators: *Florian Osswald* is the Head of the Pedagogical Section at the Goetheanum and a longtime high-school teacher and educational consultant.

Personal Hygiene for Teachers: *Jennifer Hudziec* (she/her), BS, LMT, stewards a healing practice in New Hampshire that weaves together contemporary shamanism, polarity energy medicine, massage therapy and ancestral lineage repair work. She may be reached at jenhudziec. com.

The Effects of Silence on Teacher Well-Being: *Chelsea Nealy* wrote this as a student at Antioch New England University. She is the seventh-grade class teacher at Golden Valley Orchard School, a public Waldorf charter school in California.

Foreign Language teaching for Social Justice in Waldorf Schools: *Thea Bieling* wrote this as a student at Antioch New England University. She teaches Spanish in grades 1–8 at Golden Valley Orchard School. She attended California's first Waldorf charter school, Yuba River, and has taught Spanish, dance, games, and circus arts at Waldorf charter schools for the past nine years.

The Essential Components of an Assessment Program in Grades 1–8 in a Public Waldorf Charter School Setting: *Jennifer Hoover* wrote this as a student at Antioch New England University. She is the Assessment Coordinator, middle school math teacher, computer and keyboarding instructor, and Faculty Chair at Golden Valley Orchard School.

How Can Waldorf Educators Build Resilience In Children Today? *Stephanie Lorenz* wrote this as a student at Antioch New England University. She is the Assessment Coordinator at Golden Valley River School in California and teaches math, science, and technology. She has worked at Golden Valley for over ten years and is a parent of a Golden Valley middle schooler and alumna.

Bibliography

Albrecht, Karl. *Social Intelligence*. San Francisco, CA, Jossey-Bass Publishers, 2005.

Argyris, Chris. *Knowledge for Action*. San Francisco, CA, Jossey-Bass Publishers, 1993.

Breines, J. G. and Chen, S. "Self-Compassion Increases Self-Improvement Motivation." https://doi.org/10.1177/0146167212445599 (May 29, 2012)

Buffett, Warren. "Warren Buffett's Simple Career Advice Will Transform How You Approach Your Job." https://www.cnbc.com/2019/01/18/warren-buffetts-career-advice-could-change-how-you-approach-your-job.html

Duistermaat, Henneke "How to Write with Power and Authority, Even if You Feel Like a Nobody," https://copyblogger.com/write-with-power/ (Jul. 12, 2016)

——. "How to Write So Vividly that Readers Fall in Love with Your Ideas" retrieved from https://copyblogger.com/visual-language/ (Aug. 15, 2016)

Finser, Torin M. *Guided Self-Study: Rudolf Steiner's Path of Spiritual Development*. Great Barrington, MA, SteinerBooks, 2015

——. *Organizational Integrity*, Great Barrington, MA, SteinerBooks, 2007.

——. *School Renewal, a Spiritual Journey for Change*, Great Barrington, MA, Anthroposophic Press, 2001.

——. *Silence Is Complicity*. Great Barrington, MA, Anthroposophic Press, 2007.

Freire, Paulo. *Pedagogy of the Oppressed*. Tr. by Myra Bergman Ramos, New York, Continuum Publishing Company, 1990.

Hahn, Herbert. Recollection (Jan. 11, 1967). *Towards the Deepening of Waldorf Education*, Fellowship of Waldorf Schools, Forest Row, UK, 1977 (p. 25).

Jacob, S. "The Power of Three," *The New York Times*, Jan. 5, 2014.

Jarman, Ron & Masters, Brien. *Child and Man* Journal, UK.

Knowles, Malcolm S. (with Holton & Swanson). *The Adult Learner*, Burlington, MA, Elsevier Publishers, 2005.

Illich, Ivan. *Deschooling Society*, New York, Harper and Row, 1970.

Kozol, Jonathan. *Illiterate America*. Anchor Press/Doubleday & Company, 2011.

Mackay, Paul. *The Anthroposophical Society as a Michael Community*. Temple Lodge Publishing, 2013.

Meier, J.D. *Getting Results the Agile Way*. Innovation Playhouse, Bellevue, WA, 2010.

Neff, K.D., Rude, S.S., Kirkpatrick, K.L., "An Examination of Self-Compassion in Relation to Positive Psychological Functioning and Personality Traits." *Journal of Research in Personality* (Vol 41, Issue 4, August 2007, pp. 908-916) and https://doi.org/10.1016/j.jrp.2006.08.002

Osswald, Florian, et al., eds. *Journal of the Pedagogical Section at the Goetheanum*, March 2020.

Patzlaff, Rainer. "Language—the Child's Elixir of Life," 2019 lecture, *Modern Research and the Depth of Dimensions of the Spoken Word*; Stuttgart, Verlag Freies Geistesleben, ISBN 978-3-7725-2858-3.

Pomerantsev, Peter. "The New Propaganda: Fighting the Bot Farms and Troll Armies," *The Guardian Weekly*, Aug. 2, 2019, p. 41.

Poppelbaum, Hermann. *Memory and its Cultivation*, London, New Knowledge Books, 1960.

Santoro, Doris A. *Demoralized: Why Teachers Leave the Profession They Love and How They Can Stay*. Cambridge, MA, Harvard Education Press, 2018.

Sinar, E., Wellins, R.S., Paese, M.J. "What's the Number 1 Leadership Skill for Overall Success?" https://www.ddiworld.com/global-offices/united-states/press-room/what-is-the-1-leadership-skill-for-overall-success (Feb. 23, 2016)

Smit, Jörgen. *The Steps Toward Knowledge Which The Seeker For The Spirit Must Take*. Tr. & ed. by David Mitchell, Fair Oaks, CA, AWSNA Publications Committee, 1991.

Spitulnik, Debra Z. *Speech as an Educational and Healing Tool for the Future*, Master Thesis, Antioch University New England, 1995.

Spock, Marjorie, *Group Moral Artistry II, The Art of Goethean Conversation*, Spring Valley, NY, St. George Publications, 1983.

Steiner, Rudolf. *The Art of Lecturing*. Spring Valley, NY. Mercury Press, 1984.

——. *Balance in Teaching*. Great Barrington, MA, Anthroposophic Press/SteinerBooks, 2007.

——. *Education as a Social Problem*. Spring Valley, NY, Anthroposophic Press, 1969.

——. *The Foundations of Human Experience*. Hudson, NY, Anthroposophic Press, 1969.

——. *The Foundation Stone*. London. Rudolf Steiner Press, 1979.

——. *The Four Seasons and the Archangels*. London, Rudolf Steiner Press, 1984.

——. *The Genius of Language*. Hudson, NY, Anthroposophic Press, 1995.

——. *Human Values in Education*. Great Barrington, MA, SteinerBooks/Anthroposophic Press, 2004.

——. *Rudolf Steiner in the Waldorf School*. Hudson, NY, Anthroposophic Press, 1996.

——. *Practical Advice to Teachers*. Great Barrington, MA, Anthroposophic Press, 2000.

——. *The Roots of Education*. Hudson, NY, Anthroposophic Press, 1998.

——. *Speech and Drama*. Spring Valley, NY, Anthroposophic Press, 1986.

——. *The Spiritual Guidance of the Individual and Humanity*. Great Barrington, MA, SteinerBooks/Anthroposophic Press, 1992.

——. *The Stages of Higher Knowledge*. SteinerBooks, 2009

——. *Verses and Meditations*. London, Rudolf Steiner Press, 1970.

Tautz, Johannes. *The Founding of the First Waldorf School in Stuttgart*. J. Pewtherer, D. Gerwin, eds., Ghent, NY, AWSNA Publications.

Van Houten, Coenraad. *Practising Destiny*. Translated by J. Collis. London, Temple Lodge Publishing, 2007.

Made in USA - Kendallville, IN
1223223_9781943582488
01.08.2021 1500